CRADLING
the
PAST

A BIOGRAPHY OF MARGARET SHAW

Madelaine Wong and Margaret Shaw

Published by:
Nose Hill Publishing
3757 Douglas Ridge Way S.E., Calgary, AB T2Z 3C3

Distributed by:
Nose Hill Publishing
3757 Douglas Ridge Way S.E., Calgary, AB T2Z 3C3

Library and Archives Canada Cataloguing in Publication Data

Wong, Madelaine, 1959-
Cradling the past: a biography of Margaret Shaw / Madelaine Wong and Margaret Shaw.

Includes bibliographical references.
ISBN 978-0-9811099-0-9

1. Shaw, Margaret, 1921- 2. Alberta — Biography.
3. Parents of autistic children — Canada — Biography.
I. Shaw, Margaret, 1921- II. Title.
FC3675.1.S46S46 2009   971.23'02092   C2009-904081-6

Cover design by Rik Zak.

Book production by Northwest Printing,
Calgary, Alberta, Canada.

Printed in Canada.

For my family, sisters and brothers.

For James, Karen, Michael, Emily and Thomas.

A special thanks to Laural Grimes,
my one woman cheering squad, for her advice.

*M*y mother is a story teller. Her life was full of amazing and sometimes distressing experiences, but for many people of her generation, the experiences were not uncommon. As a child of the Great Depression, she endured extreme poverty. She then saw the world at war, and witnessed throughout her life fantastic technological changes. She raised a large family, suffered severe physical and emotional pain, but somehow got through it all with a smile on her face and a hope for the future. However, she did not emerge from her experiences unscathed. The hurt left her scarred with an overly-sensitive nature and nervous disposition. The results were serious bouts of depression from which her whole family suffered.

She has "the gift of the gab" and speaks and writes with eloquence and with emotion. She is self-effacing, sometimes describing herself in unflattering terms, but she always wants to see the good in other people. She is a shy extrovert, sensitive, imaginative and full of love. While some quietly observe and silently contemplate, she contemplates life aloud. While some suppress and stifle painful memories, she articulates hers. She is always eager to communicate her feelings and experiences, even the commonplace, and is eager for others to express their's. She says, "Tell me your news," and then listens to a litany of ordinary events with her full interest, enjoying the everyday stories, delighting in the achievements of her children and grandchildren.

As a tribute to my mother, I gathered her stories, both written and oral, and recorded them together with my own stories and memories. I contributed to her stories and she to mine, and together we offer them to her children and grandchildren, so that the stories may never be lost.

This is the story of one woman, but is also the story of a generation of people, those who survived tremendous hardship, and did their part to make Alberta and Canada what it is today.

Chapter One

Small Town Reunion

$\mathscr{S}$he waved through the knee-high grass to look for anything familiar. She raised her hand to her forehead to shade her eyes from the hot July sun, which threatened to burn any pale and exposed skin, and scanned the prairie horizon. There were not many landmarks remaining, only a few bushes and rotted fence posts and indentations in the ground where houses once stood. Years before, the houses had been lifted from their foundations and dragged to various farms to be used as granaries or as cheap lumber. Nearly all evidence of human existence in this place was gone. Even the roads had disappeared. All was overgrown with grass.

Eventually, she found the site where her childhood home once stood. She could picture the dreadful little house with peeling paint and cracked windows that was draughty in the winter months, a poor shelter that leaked precious heat from the coal-burning, pot-bellied stove. Long after it was abandoned, it was dragged away by a farmer who filled it with grain instead of people. He left nothing behind but a slight depression where the cellar had been, and two forlorn bushes that once completely surrounded the house. The ugly perennials dug themselves into the gumbo soil and were indifferent to the lack of rain and whining wind. The hedge was as tough and stubborn as the people who abandoned it long ago.

Margaret spent much of her young life in this small prairie town and on a farm nearby, but it was not a carefree time. They were years of half-living, loving and hating her childhood. It was a time of grinding poverty, anxious parents, fear and helplessness. Her home was filled with love, laughter, songs and story telling, but it was a home in which she was forced to grow up too fast. Knowing what heavy responsibilities adults faced, she had not wanted to grow up, but neither did she want to remain a helpless child.

She looked up at the clear blue sky that sat like an upturned bowl over the farmland that surrounded her. The peaceful, dry prairie spread out before her just as she remembered. The countryside in all directions was uninterrupted by hills, trees or tall buildings. She smiled as she looked out at the endless horizon. The swaying fields of wheat, barley and oats brought her a sense of peace, but the memory of those difficult days also brought a sense of dismay. She snapped a picture with the camera that hung around her neck and then made her way back to the green Ford Pinto that she had left parked by the side of the gravel road that led into the centre of town.

Her hometown of Munson, Alberta, was celebrating its one-hundredth birthday. It had once been home to many hundreds of souls but by 1980, it had shrunk to less than one hundred individuals. Despite the near demise of the town, her mayor, a woman of tenacious purpose, had gathered the townsfolk and farmers from the across the countryside to welcome back all who had ever lived there.

Margaret was fifty-nine years old in 1980. She just had her hair dyed and curled that morning in anticipation of the big event and was glad it wasn't raining. She self-consciously patted down her soft curls to make sure they were still in place, pulled her blouse down over her chubby middle and wished again that she could have lost a few pounds before coming to the reunion. Burrs clung to her socks and the legs of her pale blue polyester pants-suit as she trekked through the spindly, thorny vegetation. Carefully, she stepped over the rough terrain, so as not to trip in any gopher holes hidden by the long grass. After all, she was not as sure footed as she used to be. "All I need is to fall and break my ankle out here without another soul in sight," she thought. Grasshoppers leaped and scattered ahead of her with every step. Their chirping songs filled the summer air. She stopped every so often to admire the delicate wild flowers, the Wild Rose, Lady's Slippers, Brown-eyed Susans and Geraniums that poked up amid the grass and choking weeds. She admired their ability to grow in such difficult conditions.

Margaret drove back to where the reunion activities were to take place, in the centre of what remained of the town. Only two of the original buildings still stood, the hotel and the schoolhouse, but neither was now used for its original purpose. Gone were the livery stables, the pool hall, the general store, the post office, the undertaker's, the barbershop and the churches. All of the empty lots were taken over by weeds and grass.

The only houses in the town were a few mobile homes and trailers and three new homes built by the mayor and her two sons.

Former residents descended on the remains of the town in surprising numbers. They came from the United States, Eastern Canada, British Columbia and all over Alberta, including Calgary, where Margaret lived. Local farmers cut trails where the streets used to be. They scattered gravel to keep feet from sticking in the gumbo soil. They erected a "Welcome" banner and a large tent to serve as shelter for the meals.

At the afternoon barbeque, the former residents munched on roasted pork and hamburgers and peered into each other's faces in hopes of recognition. They studied nametags for some clue. Is there any resemblance to the slim, lithe bodies of youth and these stout women and balding men who were once schoolmates? Could that crippled man in the wheelchair really be the schoolyard bully? Is that haggard man leaning on his wife's arm the town's "Don Juan" of long ago? The wild girl, the one with the "reputation" for loose morals was unable to attend. She lay in a hospital bed, stricken with a stroke. Margaret's memories flooded back along with old antagonisms, attitudes, hurts, joys and sorrows that were for a time forgotten, frozen in a time capsule. Those memories resurfaced at the reunion.

*W*hen Munson first gained town status in 1880, there were thousands of acres of untamed grasslands dotted with homesteads. The railroad brought many settlers and homesteaders who worked the land. The pioneers faced winters that were bitterly cold, and hot, dry summers that brought mosquitoes, grasshoppers and flies that tormented the settlers who tried to make a living from the land.

At the turn of the twentieth century, when Margaret's parents arrived in Western Canada, it was still mostly frontier, but what had brought them to this forsaken bit of prairie? Why did they choose Munson to raise their family? Every family has its story. This family's story will begin with Margaret's mother Daisy, across the Atlantic Ocean, in the country of Ireland.

Daisy Butler

*D*aisy stood in the doorway of her home and watched her father, William Butler, roll up his pant legs after a day's work and pull his bicycle out on to the street. He was a jeweller and a bicycle repairman and he ran the business out of his home. He smiled at his daughter and kissed her cheek. His long moustache tickled her face making her giggle. "There's my wee girl. Be good for your mum." He then casually bumped his bicycle along the rough streets of Limerick, swerving around rain filled potholes, pedestrians and horse-and-buggy traffic as best he could. His was headed for the pub, where he would pass the evening with old friends, drink a few pints, laugh and sing songs.

> *Did you, ever go to into an Irishman's shanty*
> *Where money was scarce and the whiskey was plenty?*
> *A three-legged stool and a table to match*
> *And the geese were put under the table to hatch?*

He came home from the pub giddy and slightly inebriated and gave his children smoky hugs and kisses that smelled of ale. There were seven children in all, George, Daisy, Evelyn, Kathleen, Bill, Ormand and Vera, not to mention two sets of twins who were miscarried. William was then greeted at the door by his stern wife who was not fond of all his merrymaking, and was again chastised for spending their hard earned money on the drink.

Daisy's proper Christian name was Margaret and most likely the nickname had come from her dad. Daisy thought of her father with fondness, and remembered his lovable, easy disposition. On the other hand, her mother, Bridget Madden, was a neglectful, loveless and sometimes abusive woman. Daisy did not remember ever being hugged or kissed by her mother. Bridey, as she was known to most people, worked as a midwife. She was often away from her home, attending to expectant mothers and their babies, and she often left Daisy and her other children alone at home to fend for themselves.

Young Daisy was frequently abandoned in her high chair for hours at a time, to keep her out of trouble until her mother's return. A foot defect, together with neglect, had left her unable to walk until she was four years old. At age eight, in the year 1897, Daisy was sent to Mercy Orphanage to attend boarding school. She had some learning disabilities, but did the best she could and completed her schooling at age fifteen, with a grade eight education. She returned to live with her parents and soon after, the family left Limerick and took up residence in Listowel, County Kerry, where she grew to adulthood.

Bridey announced one day, "We're putting you on a ship Daisy. Do you want to go to Canada or the United States? Your uncles are both willing to take you on and help you get a start." Bridey's brothers had done well in the new land. There was Harry in Calgary, Canada, and Joe in Chicago, U.S.A.

The Maddens: Harry, Lizzy, Joe, Bridey (mother to Daisy) with their parents (names unknown).

Daisy was taken aback by the announcement. She knew little about either country but eventually replied, "I think I would like to go to Canada." Her parents gave her five pounds English sterling, which was the minimum amount of money required for an immigrant entering Canada, and she packed a trunk with a few possessions. Daisy Butler then said good-bye to her family who had gathered on the docks to see her off, and she left Ireland, on route to Liverpool, England. There she boarded the ship bound for Montreal, Canada.

She lay awake on the cot in the small cabin on board the ship. The gentle rocking of the ship was not enough to lull her into sleep that first night. She thought sadly of her parents and her brothers and sisters, "Will I ever see them again? What kind of place am I going to? What will become of me?"

The days on board she preferred not to stay in her stuffy cabin. She was outside looking out over the seemingly endless ocean when she was approached by a sailor. Naturally, a pretty young woman traveling alone is bound to draw the attention of young men. He was interesting and friendly. He told her wonderful stories about all the places he'd been. Daisy was fascinated. She had never before been off the island and was quite ignorant of the world. Much to her dismay though, the sailor became overly friendly and tried to steal a kiss. Daisy was much bothered and indignant and told him off in no uncertain terms.

Days later, she watched the approaching shore of Canada from on board the ship that had carried her from her home two weeks previously. It was June of the year 1909. Her black, waist long hair was tied in braids with thick ribbons like a young girl, though she was twenty years old. Indeed, she could have been mistaken for a child being slightly built and standing only five feet tall. Her innocence was evident in her wide blue eyes as she peered over the railing. There were many immigrants on board that ship, but most were traveling with their families, not alone, like Daisy. She felt rather ill, but it wasn't seasickness. She had long since gained her sea legs. She had walked confidently on deck while other passengers were still being advised by the sailors to "suck a lemon" to quell their queasiness. Her butterflies were the result of the uncertainty of what was facing her in the new land.

The ship docked at Pier 21 in Halifax and Daisy was then put on another ship that wound its way through the St. Lawrence Seaway on route to Montreal. It was still a wild looking land, even though much of the thick forest had long since been hacked away to be used as lumber for buildings or fuel for homes or steam vessels.

Daisy spent the first full day in Canada going through the immigration process. When that was completed, she gathered her trunk and other meagre possessions, and found a horse drawn taxi. She was driven through the streets of Montreal on route to the train station. Sitting on the cart beside the driver she drank in the sights of the city and was amazed at what she saw in the strange new country. Back in the Old Country, she had heard talk of people who had brown skin and wore strange clothes and spoke different languages, but nobody like that lived in Ireland. She stared in disbelief at Native Indian women with babies strapped to their backs, at Chinese laundry men as they hung their customers' wet clothing on lines between buildings, and she gawked, open-mouthed, at the first black man she had ever seen.

She bought a ticket and boarded the train that was to take her to meet her Uncle Harry. She was to stay with Uncle Harry and his wife Lizzy and their children until she could find employment. The train from Montreal to Calgary took many days. She had no idea that Canada was such an enormous country. There were miles and miles of forest, wetlands and grasslands interrupted by small towns with unusual names such as Winnipeg, Moose Jaw and Swift Current. Daisy gazed out the window and wondered when she would ever arrive at her destination. Her bottom was sore from days on the train's wooden seat. Her neck and back ached from trying to catch some shut-eye on the rocking, bumping, noisy locomotive.

It was early July when Daisy finally arrived in Calgary, Alberta. The province, she learned, was named by John Campbell, the Marquis of Lorne, and a former Governor General of Canada. He named the province after his wife, Princess Louise Caroline Alberta, the fourth daughter of Queen Victoria. "Such a regal name for such a dreary looking land," thought Daisy. Calgary had grown considerably in the decade 1900 to 1910. During that decade the population climbed from 4000 to 40,000. The city was built beside a river but was almost completely devoid of trees and everything looked as if it needed a good drink of water. To the west, in the distance, she could see the outline of the Rocky Mountains jutting like giant sharp teeth into the horizon. Already she missed the green, lush, rolling hills of Ireland.

She began her life in Canada by working as a nanny for her Uncle Harry's daughter, Lily. Daisy worked hard for her cousin, keeping house and caring for her three children. She was unhappy though. Lily and her husband treated her more like a servant than family, so Daisy was determined to find different employment. Besides, they were not, in Daisy's opinion, very upstanding people. Lily's husband, Mac, was a liquor retailer for the Riverside Hotel and the King Edward Hotel in Calgary. Mac had fled to Calgary from Ottawa to escape a bad reputation he had made for himself there, in his association with thugs and hooligans, and it was rumoured, an attempt made on his life.

Mac continued in his bad ways and associated with equally unsavoury types in Calgary. During the Prohibition years, 1916 to 1923, he continued to supply liquor to the hotels, as a bootlegger, and he found it to be considerably more profitable than selling liquor legally. The Liquor Act outlawed the sale of intoxicating beverages except if they were to be used for scientific, sacred or medicinal purposes. Not surprisingly, alcohol quickly became a frequently prescribed cure for many ailments. Establishments were allowed to sell "temperance beer" which contained only 2½% alcohol, but there were many "under the table" sales going on. The law was difficult to enforce as a lot of money could be made from hauling wagonloads or truckloads of liquor from other provinces into Alberta. Prohibition ended when the United Farmers of Alberta Government took over the sale of liquor.

Many settlers and businessmen from Eastern Canada used the Riverside Hotel as a meeting place.

Uncle Harry (brother to Bridey)

It was while attending a dinner at the Riverside Hotel that Daisy met her future husband, Bill MacCallum. She was very impressed by Bill after their first meeting. She thought he was polite and well spoken, and very handsome, with bright, intelligent blue eyes. He was a small man, standing only five feet five inches tall, and was slightly built. Except for some fine, feathery hair, he was completely bald. He was clearly a Scot with a name like MacCallum, though his accent was Canadian. She left the hotel to return home with her Uncle Harry, but she never forgot about Bill. It would be years before they met again.

Bill was born in Grey County, Ontario and grew up in Berlin, (later called Kitchener), Ontario. Later, he spent some years in Ottawa. He was dissatisfied with his life there and decided to follow the call, "Go west, young man." He worked his way across Canada as a cook in lumber camps before arriving in Alberta where he bought himself a homestead and set to work, but being slightly built, he found the work difficult. He was probably more suited to an office job than heavy farm labour.

In time, Daisy gladly left her cousin's home and took a job at the Hudson's Bay Company in the city's downtown. She was living at the Sacred Heart Convent, located in Calgary's city centre, so it was a quick and easy walk to work everyday. Sometimes a priest named Father Albert Lacombe would say Mass at St. Mary's Cathedral. It was a church that he helped to build. He was already an old man when they met, but Daisy loved to hear him talk. She admired him greatly for the work he had done with the Native Indians.

Father Lacombe evangelized the Cree and Blackfoot and also worked to bring peace between the two tribes. Former Prime Minister John A. McDonald had once called on him to convince the Plains Indians not to join in the North West Rebellion of 1885, and Father Lacombe complied.

The good Father recognized that the native population was afflicted with many problems. The decimation of the bison left many of them starving and the introduction of small pox caused the death of many. The use of alcohol among the natives further contributed to their problems. Father Lacombe was a man who cared deeply about the poor and the needy so he wrote to Prime Minister John A. McDonald, stating that the Canadian Government, "…is itself not free of blame." He was rightly called, "…a peacemaker with a great sense of justice."[1]

[1] www.pioneersalberta.org/lacombe.albert

In 1909 he organized a hospice to be built for the care of elderly people in the town of Midnapore, near the city of Calgary. It was named Lacombe Home and he resided there until his death in 1916 at the age of 89. Daisy was touched that though he chose to have his body buried in a crypt in St. Albert, Alberta, his heart was buried in Midnapore, next to Lacombe Home and the Sisters of Providence Convent. The "man with a heart" truly left his heart in Calgary. "Someday," she thought, "I will go to Midnapore and visit the spot where his heart is buried, and maybe I'll have a look at Lacombe Home. Who knows, maybe when I'm old I will live there." She smiled to herself at that absurd thought. No woman in her twenties can ever imagine herself growing old.

After ten years in Calgary, Daisy felt she was in need of a change and decided to join her brother Ormand who had immigrated to Chicago, U.S.A. She thought she might find better employment there. She was already thirty, long past the age when most women marry, and so she had resigned herself to life as a spinster, but Daisy changed her plans about moving away from Canada after a visit to her cousin Lottie Gallagher. Lottie lived on a farm near the village of Munson.

"Why don't you write a letter to Bill MacCallum? He lives not too far from here, near the town of Michichi. He's such a nice man," Lottie said.

"MacCallum is a Scottish name. He can't be Catholic," said Daisy. As a devout Catholic, Daisy would never consider a "mixed marriage."

"Oh indeed he is, though his father was a Presbyterian," Lottie assured her.

"Well, in that case I will write to him and invite him to visit. I think it's about time I got married," said Daisy.

Bill walked twenty-three miles to meet Daisy at Gallagher's farm the very day he received the letter. Daisy saw him as a good, kind-hearted man, and they married three weeks later, in July of 1919, at St. Anthony's Church in Drumheller. Daisy was thirty years old and Bill was forty-two.

After the wedding, Daisy sat beside Bill on the horse-drawn wagon as he proudly drove past green wheat fields. "I planted all this in the spring. It sure looks like a bumper crop. The house is just over there. It's not big, but it's home." He then showed her the barn where he kept the two dairy cows, the horses, a few pigs and the chickens. It was a fine little farm.

Daisy entered her new home by the back door and surveyed her surroundings. The walls were made of wooden boards nailed together. Small rays of sunlight shone through the cracks. "That will need insulation before winter," Daisy said to Bill, indicating the walls. Bill nodded in agreement. Of course he had filled all the cracks with sod the previous summer, but it would all need to be replaced. A black pot-bellied stove sat in one corner. On it was resting a copper cooking pot. A pot of coal sat near the stove. A roughly cut wooden table with two chairs sat near a sparkling clean but curtainless window. Nails were hammered into the walls of the kitchen and held various cooking utensils. Also in the kitchen were some cupboards that held a few dishes and some canned goods.

Daisy MacCallum (nee Butler)

Bill MacCallum

Daisy's brother Ormand

Daisy's sister Evelyn

Bridey and Daisy's sister Vera

The room adjacent the kitchen was the living room. The only furniture in this room was a small sofa, its fabric bleached by the sun that beamed in through another set of curtainless windows. "I'll need to get busy and sew some new curtains," said Daisy.

A set of stairs led to two bedrooms upstairs, one of which contained a single bed. Bill said, "I will build a bed in the other bedroom if need be, if God is so good as to bless us with a baby."

Bill carried in Daisy's trunk and her sewing machine that she had purchased from the wages she earned at the Hudson's Bay Company. It was shaped like a small table, but when the top was flipped over it revealed the sewing machine. A foot peddle at the bottom made the needle go up and down.

A honeymoon was out of the question when there was so much work to be done so the couple went straight to work attending to the many required tasks. They worked hard together on the farm. The fine, silty soil in that part of the prairie formed unusually sticky mud when wet. It was excellent for growing crops because it retained the moisture in the ground. They sold the wheat for a good price and together with the milk and eggs they produced, they made a small profit. The money was tucked away in anticipation of the birth of their first child.

Naturally, there were some troubles with wild animals on occasion. Coyotes, skunks, weasels and badgers would sometimes kill the chickens. Bill brought home a puppy from town one day and trained it to run off the wild animals and alert Bill and Daisy when threat was imminent. The couple produced their own milk, butter, eggs, meat and vegetables. Sometimes they would go into town for flour, rolled oats, tea and sugar, but if the family ran out of something, they simply went without. Bill dug a cellar below the house to keep things cold, but food didn't always keep well. They would also eat rabbit or wild duck when the opportunity presented itself.

Bill was very much in love with his new wife. He couldn't carry a tune, but loved to sing songs to her from the old country.

> *Black is the colour of my true love's hair.*
> *Her lips are like some roses fair.*
> *She's the sweetest smile and the gentlest hands.*
> *I love the ground whereon she stands.*

Two years after the marriage, in May, 1921, Daisy gave birth to a girl and they named her Margaret. Daisy and Bill were very proud of their little girl, especially when both had nearly given up on the idea of ever having a family. They looked lovingly at her little face, and remarked how much she resembled her father, except for her black hair, which clearly came from her mother. They marvelled at her tiny hands and feet and loved to take turns holding her. One day Daisy dressed her firstborn in a frilly bonnet and dress and sent her with her father to show off to the folks of Michichi. The farm wasn't far from town so off Bill went pushing his infant daughter in the pram. On his return, Daisy eagerly asked Bill, "What did the people think of my little Margaret?" She naturally assumed that everyone would agree that the baby was beautiful.

He replied, "I don't know, I went down all the back alleys with her."

Daisy's face fell, and she was about to berate him for his odd behaviour, but one look at his reddened cheeks and she understood. Bill was embarrassed at being a first-time father at the age of forty-four. He was not to be a first-time father for long. One year later, in 1922, the couple had a son, George.

Daisy loved to go to the silent picture shows. Sometimes the family would walk into town to watch a movie at the school house. The map of Canada was turned to the wall and movies were projected on the back of the map. The people from town and the farms gathered around and for five cents they could watch Charlie Chaplin, Rudolph Valentino or Lillian Gish have wonderful adventures. Daisy had a wonderful sense of humour and the Charlie Chaplin shows hit just the right cord with her. She also loved any shows with dancing. They reminded her of her childhood when she was a champion Irish dancer.

Even little Margaret loved the movies. When she was two-years-old she tugged on her mother's dress and asked, "Walk a show yubbies Mama?"

Daisy laughed, "Okay Margaret, we will put your rubbers on and walk to the show."

For a time, the little family lived happily on the farm. Daisy's eyes lit up when as she watched her two youngsters play. When Margaret was three, she enjoyed playing with the dolls her mom had made out of yarn while George made a circular track around the kitchen table on his little wagon, with one small leg tucked under him. The wheels made a whirring sound as he pumped with the other leg on his rounds. The occasional

Margaret, age 6 months.

bump of the wagon on the legs of the table would send the supper dishes clattering and Bill's nerves jangling, "Watch now lover," he would say, "don't go breaking your mom's nice dishes."

There was much work to be done on the farm. In the morning, the children would follow their dad out to the barn to watch him milk the cows. Clean streams of milk flowed into the pail while the barn cats gathered, hoping for a bit of spilled milk for their breakfast. Daisy had many chores to do in the house in addition to cooking and cleaning. She churned the fresh cream into butter. She made her own bread. She drew the water from the well for cooking and bathing and to wash the clothes. She sewed or knitted clothes for her family, and washed them with the soap she had made herself. Daisy found it was much cheaper to make her own soap from wood ashes, animal fat and lye, than to purchase it. She scrubbed each item of clothing one at a time on the scrubbing board and

Bill, Daisy, Margaret and George on the stone boat.

then squeezed the water out with the ringer. She then carried the damp laundry outside to hang on the line.

Bill spent his days tending to the animals and the crops and at the end of the day when they children heard the clip, clop of horses' hooves they knew that he had returned from the fields. George and Margaret ran outside to greet him. The horses, Babe and Nell, were pulling the stone boat. It was a flat contraption, looking rather like a rectangular table top; used to move bales of hay when the ground was too soft for a wheeled vehicle. He picked the children up one at a time and put them on the stone boat, then Bill slapped the horses' reins and the children squealed with delight as they were given a bumpy ride across the prairie.

As Bill unhitched the horses Margaret would gallop across the yard imitating the horses, skipping and lifting her feet high behind her and then neigh and whinny like the horses. George followed suit and galloped beside her in a game of make-believe.

One day, when Margaret was about three years old, her dad had returned to the house for his afternoon meal, while she sat at the back door of the house and watched as a cow wandered into the backyard. While it munched the fresh, green grass, she approached the cow. "Nice cow, you give us lots of milk from your throat. We need milk to grow, and thank you Mrs. Cow."

Her parents, who had been listening from the kitchen, laughed at the little soliloquy to the cow. Margaret was shy and sensitive by nature, and was embarrassed by the attention, and ran quickly away.

Bernie and Cecilia

In 1924, Daisy was expecting again, and to everyone's surprise, gave birth to a set of twin girls, Bernie and Cecilia. Following their birth, there was now, no doubt, mountains of diapers to wash by hand. Their proud father looked at his growing family, and as usual, he broke into song.

There was a man by the name of Timber,
He got married to a woman named Woods.
They were spliced by a funny little parson,
He was a joiner – did a lot of good.
Now Woods and his wife were as happy as can be,
Just like a box of tricks.
When after a while as you can see,
They were blessed with a bundle of sticks.
Oh, whack fall the diddle and the dim dum day,
For in the bed there was little room to lay.
Woods on the sofa and now he said,
O – oh, o – oh, o – oh, OH…
There are too many splinters in the bed!

Four-year-old Margaret entered the little kitchen of her home on the farm and opened the door to the pantry. There was no refrigerator because nobody had refrigerators in 1925, though some of the more well to do people had iceboxes. She sometimes watched the horse-drawn wagons come by to deliver great blocks of ice to her neighbours, and then she would ask the driver for a small piece of ice. It was lovely to suck on, on a hot day. She would let the ice melt in her hands, and then wipe her cold, wet hands over her face to cool her. In the pantry, Margaret was happy to find a box of fresh, tart apples. She gladly bit into one. Its sweet juicy goodness ran down her chin. She crunched and slurped until she had eaten it to the core.

When evening approached and the little house grew dark, Daisy lit the coal oil lamps that hung from the ceiling. Some people in the area had gas lamps that were a little more efficient than the coal oil, and they gave a better light, but as usual the MacCallums had to make do. Daisy's footsteps echoed across the wooden floor as she gathered flour, sugar, lard and apples. She prepared the ingredients for her pie. Together with the chicken and potatoes, the family had quite a feast. During Margaret's

Daisy with Margaret, Bernie, Cecilia and George.

early years, the family made do with just the bare necessities but there was nearly always enough to eat.

"Mom, can we get a pretty flowery carpet like our neighbours?"

"No Margaret, we can't afford a carpet, now go and get me some water."

Margaret went outside to the well with her bucket. She reached up and turned the handle. A cool autumn breeze ruffled Margaret's thick, black hair and she shivered. She thought of her lucky friend who had a pump right in her kitchen, and didn't have to go outside to get water. She carried the bucket unsteadily with both hands and delivered the water to her mother. She then ran to use the outhouse before it got too dark. The flies buzzed angrily around her as she sat, but this didn't faze her. She had never heard of indoor toilets. She wiped herself with a page from the Eaton's catalogue and hurried back to the house.

In the kitchen, the family had gathered. This is where the family spent most of their time, talking about the events of the day. Most people in those days regarded their living rooms as off limits for most of the time. The room was kept in the dark so the sun wouldn't fade the upholstery. Casual company ate in the kitchen and only on special occasions would the dining room be used. This of course wasn't an issue for the MacCallums. They didn't have a dining room. On the main level of the house there was a kitchen and a living room. There were two bedrooms upstairs, one for the children and the other for the parents and the babies. Daisy picked up the coalscuttle, which was a metal bucket set beside the stove, and dropped some coal into the stove. She put her hand in the oven to see if it was warm enough for the pie, and then she put it in to bake. While it baked, she went outside to gather her laundry from the clothesline. In the winter, she hung the clothes in the kitchen, because that's where the heat was. The wet clothes would drip into the cracks of the floorboards, where it would freeze, causing the floor to be slippery. Winter was still another two months away however, and there was still much work to be done to prepare for the cold days ahead.

With the help of his neighbours, Bill was able to bring in his crops, so there was food in the house, for now. He stretched out gratefully on his bed. His back was aching from the day's labour. He loved his family dearly but he worried how long he would be able to carry on doing a young man's work at his age.

Autumn brought about severe changes in the weather. A chilly north wind rattled the shutters of the windows on the little house. Nippy breezes blew in through the cracks of the poorly insulated walls. The children lay cuddled under their blankets in the morning and could see their breath rise from their mouths in little puffs. The edges of the blankets were crunchy hard with frost from their breath. "Look George, I'm smoking," said Margaret. She imitated the actresses they saw at the movies and held an imaginary cigarette between her fingers. She drew in a breath and elegantly blew out the "smoke" and fluttered her eyelashes. George giggled at his sister's antics and pretended to smoke also.

Their dad got a fire started downstairs but it was unlikely that any of the heat would reach the bedrooms upstairs. "Get up you lot, we're going to Munson to shop," Bill said cheerfully.

It was time to load up on supplies for the winter, so they entered Fastman's General Store. The shelves were lined with canned goods and various packages. There were barrels on the floor full of flour, oats, sugar and other goods. The children eagerly ran to look at the round glass containers full of candy. Bill gladly gave each child a nickel and each received a bag full of candy. Meanwhile, the adults shopped for supplies.

They later made a stop at the post office. They were happy to receive a letter from Daisy's brother Ormand. He had sent a money order for $15.00 as a present for the twins. Any extra money was most welcome. Daisy and Bill felt blessed to have such generous relatives and bought some one cent postage stamps so they could write a note of thanks.

Their father promised them a trip to the town of Drumheller the following week. What a treat that would be! They would go to the pharmacy and to the fabrics store to buy some material so Daisy could make some clothes for the children. "Maybe someday, we will go to Calgary. That would really be something for you to see." said Bill.

When the day of the big trip finally arrived, the family rode in the horse drawn wagon to Munson and then on to Drumheller. The little children watched the prairie rolling by. There were miles and miles of open spaces, as far as the eye could see. They saw farmers hard at work bringing in the last of the crops and saw herds of cattle in the fields. Occasionally they spotted nervous deer grazing, always watchful for coyotes or farmers with guns.

It was mid-morning when they arrived. The twins were snuggled into the pram and were jostled and bumped about on the uneven wooden sidewalks and unpaved roads. Margaret and George each took one of their father's hands and gawked, wide-eyed at all the sights this town had to offer. They tramped from store to store to make their small purchases.

They entered a store that was run by Mr. Chong, a man Bill had met some years before. He greeted the family warmly. "Hello Mr. MacCallum. I'm so glad to see you again." He shook Bill's hand and smiled at Daisy and each of the children as he was introduced.

"So, Mr. Chong, has your wife arrived from China?" Bill asked.

Mr. Chong's smile vanished. He was not a recent immigrant, but was born in Canada. His father arrived in British Columbia in 1882. The Government of Canada had declared that a railroad should be built from Canada's east to west coasts. The Canadian Pacific Railway was in need of cheap labour and willing workers. Between 1881 and 1885, over 15,000 Chinese, mostly men, arrived in Canada to work on the construction of the railroad. After its completion their services were no longer required, and so the Government of Canada passed the first anti-Chinese bill, imposing a head tax of $50.00 on new Chinese immigrants.

The elder Mr. Chong was eventually able to raise enough funds to bring his wife to Canada in 1890, and they produced three children. The eldest boy was born in 1891. He made his way to Alberta and set up shop in Drumheller. In 1921, he wrote to his parents and asked them to arrange a marriage for him. They in turn, wrote to people in their home province in China and found him a suitable match. Unfortunately, by 1921, the head tax on new Chinese immigrants had increased to $500.00. He had worked hard and saved his money in an effort to pay the head tax for his wife-to-be, but in 1923, the Canadian Immigration Act was passed, excluding all but a few Chinese from entering Canada. The Immigration Act was not repealed until 1947, and so like many other Chinese men of his day living in Canada, he would never marry and never have children.

He lowered his eyes and shook his head. "No, Mr. MacCallum, it didn't work out. I am not lucky like you. Take care."

Chapter Three

Times Are Hard

n the mid 1920's, the surface of the earth became dried and cracked, and farmers across Western Canada watched their crops wither and die. The people prayed for rain and looked hopefully to the sky, but year after year their hopes for a good crop were dashed. Bill MacCallum's farm was no exception. He watched helplessly as the unrelenting summer heat and winters that brought very little snow destroyed his homesteading dreams.

The economy of the Province of Alberta was quite dependent on the export of wheat, so without the income that wheat provided, people all over the province suffered. Thus, the Great Depression seemed to hit Western Canada sooner than other parts of the world. The drought persisted year after year and Bill's health continued to decline. The arthritis in his back got worse. Everyday he worked hard to coax a few scraggly plants to grow, and each evening he went home wracked with pain. With time, the pain became so intolerable that he decided in 1925 that he could no longer run the farm. He reluctantly sold the farm and moved his family to the west end of the town of Drumheller where, for a time, his fortunes improved when he got a job as a bricklayer. The work was hard on his body but he persisted for the sake of his family. This would be the first in a series of temporary jobs for Bill, and only the beginning of the troubles that lay ahead.

After the bricklaying job ended he worked at a grocery store delivering fruit and vegetables. The children took turns sitting beside their dad in the wagon behind two big dray horses. The horses' sturdy haunches pulled the heavy wagon laden with groceries all over town. The children watched their dad carry sacks of new potatoes, carrots and turnips to customers' doors. There were also crates of leafy lettuce, sweet strawberries and apples with an aroma so sweet and heady the children thought they were in heaven.

George

It was Bill's habit to come home every Saturday night from the grocery store with an ice-cream cone for each of the children. One evening Margaret was so sleepy that she didn't want to wake up for her treat. Her dad, with a huge grin on his face, put the cone against her mouth so that she would have a sweet surprise when she awoke. She woke up a little later with her face smeared with ice-cream. She was so startled and cross that she marched straight into the kitchen and deposited the treat in the garbage. She lived to regret that little temper tantrum for years after. The Great Depression struck, it seemed, very suddenly afterwards, and there were no ice-cream cones or any other treats for a long time.

Bill lost his job at the grocery store and was unemployed again. Try as he might, he could not find another job. Though the coalmines were still in operation, they preferred young, strong men, to a small, arthritic man closing in on fifty years old.

He was by no means the only one who could not find work. Many unemployed and homeless men, or bums, as they were called, rode the rails across Canada in search of employment. Canada did not have a welfare system in place at that time and so the men were dependent on the goodness and generosity of others simply to stay alive. They would wander from house to house in search of a handout. From inside their home the MacCallums heard some men singing for their supper.

Halleluiah I'm a bum. Halleluiah bum again.
Halleluiah give us a hand out to revive us again.
Oh I don't like work, and work don't like me.
And that is the reason that I'm so hungry.
Halleluiah I'm a bum. Halleluiah bum again.
Halleluiah give us a handout to revive us again.

Though they had little to eat themselves, Daisy and Bill shared the little food they had with the hungry men who ate quickly and ravenously. Between mouthfuls one of the men asked, "Is there any work to be found hereabouts?"

"I've been out of work for awhile myself but you might try at the mines," Bill suggested.

"Yep, times are hard. Thank you folks very kindly for the meal."

In the next few years, there would be many knocks on the door, with desperate men begging for food, and Daisy and Bill rarely refused them.

As time went on, Bill continued to be in and out of work. It was not unusual in those difficult days to have little or no groceries in the house. Daisy looked sadly at the food she had set out on the kitchen table. It troubled her greatly that all she had to feed her family was a can of tomatoes and some lettuce from the garden. Her husband and children entered the kitchen and they too looked sadly at the table. "Let the children eat," said Bill. "I had lots to eat when I was young." So Daisy and Bill watched the children consume the last bites of food in the house, even though their own stomachs growled and ached.

In the evenings, Margaret sat on the stairway that led upstairs to the bedrooms and listened to her parents talk and worry about how they were going to feed the children. Little Margaret bowed her head in prayer, "Please God, send my parents some money."

Daisy tried not to let the situation get her down. Even when the outlook was grim she encouraged her husband as much as possible. "God will provide," she said, again and again, or she would recite an old Irish verse, "Lord bless us and save us, said Mrs. Joe Davis. They're bound to persuade us that herrin's is fish." The meaning of the verse is lost, but for Daisy perhaps it meant that life can be difficult and complicated, but you will be far worse off if you let it get you down. Do the best you can and above all, trust in the Lord.

It was hard though, not to become discouraged, on those long summer days when the sun beat down relentlessly on the parched landscape and the sky held no promise of rain. The wind blew and blew, turning the precious topsoil to dust and whirling it up in great dust devils to be carried away. The farm folk would search the sky for rain-bearing clouds and sing a little tune.

> *Oh it ain't gonna rain no more, no more,*
> *It ain't gonna rain no more.*
> *How in the heck can I wash my neck,*
> *If it ain't gonna rain no more?*

The hungry children cried, "Mommy, I'm hungry," while Daisy swept the dusty wooden floor.

Farmers at work.

"Maybe today Bill will find a job and come home with a few potatoes and a bit of bacon," she thought hopefully. She had no food to give her children. She opened the back door to deposit the dirt outside and wandered into the backyard to try to clear her head. The earth was hard and cracked by the merciless sun. There wasn't much grass to speak of. The grasshoppers had chewed most of it down to the ground. The shabby yard smelled of tar from discarded old drums, their sticky black surfaces crawled with flies in the heat of summer. The flies and the grasshoppers seemed to be the only creatures that flourished during the drought. They plagued the people day and night.

The hot gust of wind fluttered Daisy's worn-out dress and more dirt was blown into the house through the open door. She looked to the cloudless sky and wondered if the wind would ever stop wailing. The sound was a fitting accompaniment to the sorrow that rent the little house on those hot summer days.

Daisy carried on bravely for years caring for all her children but could never engage Bill in any talk of their lost dreams. It tore at his heart that he couldn't provide for his family. A man feels it's his duty to put food on the table and he needs to know that his family is safe and well fed. Though it was not his fault, he felt he had failed. It was years before he could speak of it.

The year was 1925. Outside it was overcast, but the clouds would not release any rain on the scorched earth. They only teased the people with false hope. Daisy was thin and tired and looked older than thirty-six years as she sat rocking her sick baby. The baby girl was feverish and crying fitfully while her anguished father looked on helplessly, his eyes filled with dread. The baby's twin sister Bernie was sleeping in a crib in a corner of the kitchen. A pail of soiled diapers were in another corner of the room beside a metal tub and washboard, just a token of the work to be done when the present crisis passed. Bill's feet made a scraping sound as they traced an erratic path across the bare board floor of the kitchen.

The two small children, George and Margaret, came down the stairs and peeked uncertainly into the room. The girl broke the mood momentarily by asking, "Daddy did you buy some candy for us?"

Her gaunt, shabbily dressed father turned on the child with sudden anger. "Candy? You want candy and your little sister is so sick. I've no money for candy not even for groceries or milk or medicine!"

The little girl looked hurt and startled by this sudden and unexpected outburst, especially from her dad who had always been so kind and loving to his children. Daisy spoke up then, "She's just a child, Bill."

She handed the sick baby to her husband. Then she put her arms around both of the older children and held them close. "Your daddy doesn't mean to be cross. Cecilia is so sick and we don't know what to do. Pray that he will get work so that we can buy some food and medicine for her. Now go outside and play. The doctor will be here soon."

The doctor entered about a half hour later carrying his bag. He had a gruff manner but he had tended his patients in Drumheller for several years without regard for his own needs. For the doctor it had been a trying time. There had been an outbreak of dysentery among children, and many cases of mumps and over twenty deaths from spinal meningitis in the last month. He suspected the latter in this case of Cecilia and was steeling himself for what he had to say to the family.

He entered the house through the kitchen door, took the baby in his arms and carried her over to the counter. After examining her he faced the frightened parents.

"I'm sorry to have to tell you this, Daisy and Bill, but your baby has meningitis and her chances for recovery are small. You should buy some sweetened condensed milk for her. She may be able to keep down if you get some. They sell it at the drugstore."

"Where are we going to get the money for milk?" the baby's father asked. He wasn't talking to anyone in particular but started walking out the door.

"Wait," his wife called. "You look after the children and I'll find out if I can get credit for two cans and pay for it when you get a job."

"He'll never let you charge milk or anything else. There is no work for anyone now and all the storekeepers are being pretty stiff about giving credit, unless you own something they can take. Collateral, they call it." He looked around the room. "We sure don't have anything they would want." He slumped into a kitchen chair. "I shouldn't have waited until I was in my forties to get married. It's even harder to get a job when you're older and there are a hundred younger men waiting for the same chance." He held his head in his hands and struggled for self-control.

The doctor was used to tragedy of all kinds and this incident was nothing new. He put his hand on Daisy's shoulder and smiled encouragingly. "Try to get the milk; the druggist might soften a bit if you tell him your baby is so sick."

"I'll try," Daisy answered and she put on her sweater to leave. It wasn't long before she returned, but there was no package in her hand.

"You didn't get any milk," said Bill. "Did he say anything at all?"

Daisy looked up at her husband and shook her head. "He put the two cans of condensed milk on the counter but when I asked him if he could wait a little time for his money because you are out of work he took them back. I explained that this kind of milk might help Cecilia, and she is so sick. He just said that if I didn't have any money he wouldn't let me have the milk."

All night, Bill and Daisy took turns watching over the baby, but it was apparent that she was only getting worse. In the morning the doctor was summoned again. By this time the child was screaming with pain. She arched her spine and her face was red from fever. Her parents laid her on the softest pillow in the house. It's the only comfort they could give.

"She won't live," said the doctor. "It is a matter of hours now."

The older children were called to be with their dying sister. They were too young to understand death but they were quiet through most of her last moments. The little girl didn't ask for candy anymore. Her three-year-old brother sat on the floor and hammered at a couple of nails in a board. He pretended he was a carpenter. The twin sister of the sick baby sat on a blanket and played with a rattle.

Time seemed to hang suspended until a small cry from the mother focused everyone's attention. "Oh! She's almost gone Bill. Look there is a light on her face. She must be seeing God. God is so good to let me see her with that glow on her face." Daisy held her baby tenderly and kissed her forehead. The infant took one final breath, and was still. "She's in Heaven now Bill," Daisy whispered.

There was muffled sobbing in the room. The boy and girl walked out rather dazed into the yard. Sometime later Margaret returned to the house alone. She stood at the kitchen table and watched as her mother washed the baby's body and put Johnson's baby powder all over it. The body was limp and the little girl didn't understand. Then Daisy dressed the body in a white baby dress and laid her in a basket.

Bill began scrubbing the cupboards furiously. He kept his back to his wife. Daisy approached him gently. "Why do you bother with the cupboards now?" she asked. "Come and sit down for a while."

Bill couldn't answer because he was crying for his loss. The tears streamed down his cheeks and he wouldn't look at his dead baby. The only time Margaret saw her father cry was when Cecilia died. To her, the world seemed a hard and unforgiving place.

Daisy covered the basket with a small blanket so Bill could take the baby to the undertakers. "The doctor says that I must have neglected Cecilia, but that isn't true is it Bill? I guess he just felt bad that he couldn't save her."

"We did our best Daisy. Nobody can fault us."

That night when Daisy was saying her prayers she said, "Please God, let me see Cecilia just one more time before she's buried," and the glowing little face of the baby appeared before her.

Bill had to borrow a suit from a friend for the funeral, because he only owned one pair of trousers and one shirt. The funeral was a sad, but not uncommon event in the town. She was buried in the town graveyard like the many others, both young and old, who did not survive the lean years.

A week passed and the druggist stopped when he saw Daisy on the street.

"How is your baby, Mrs. MacCallum," he asked.

"She's dead," was the quiet reply. Those words summed up the despair of the times and the horror of poverty.

Daisy and Bill were devastated for many years afterwards. It was years before Bill could even speak the name Cecilia.

Some weeks later, a lanky teenage boy watched four year old Margaret play in the scrubby grass of her front yard. It was a bright, sunny morning, with dew still sparkling on the grass. He watched the door and windows of the small house, vigilant for an adult. He spied the child's mother, when she appeared every so often to peek out the window at her daughter. Eventually, the boy heard the creak of the clothesline in the backyard and knew that the woman would be occupied for at least a few minutes. He made his move. "Hey, come with me, we'll go for walk," he said to the small girl. He took her by the hand and led her down the street. Margaret looked curiously, but without fear at the big boy. She knew his name was Ben and he lived just down the street. She glanced back at her house, wondering if she should say good-bye to her mother.

"Where are we going?" she asked innocently.

"To town."

They walked the main streets of the town, into shops, back alleys and eventually to the edge of the Red Deer River.

"My legs are tired," Margaret complained, so they sat on the river bank for a while. The boy talked very little. "Where are we going?" she asked again." I'm getting hungry."

"Come this way." He led her further along the bank and towards a farmer's potato field. They sat in the field and the boy dug with his hands in the soft dirt until he unearthed a few small potatoes. He rubbed off the dirt and offered it to the small girl. She bit into the hard, cold potato, all the while watching his face, curious about why he had brought her here. The sun was now high in the sky. The boy stood up suddenly. "Take off your knickers," he ordered the little girl.

Margaret was terrified now. "My mother wouldn't like it if I did that." She stood up and backed away a few steps, preparing to run. She didn't know where she would run. She didn't know the way home.

He watched her for a few seconds, as if debating what to do. He then wandered over to a field surrounded by a barbed wire fence, where some cows were grazing. "Watch this," he said, and he picked up a stone from the ground and hurled it at a cow, hitting it hard on the rump. The startled cow ran a few paces forward and looked back with a dull expression at the two humans behind the fence. The boy laughed and continued throwing stones until the small herd moved across the field, out of harm's way.

He then led the girl back into town past a group of houses much like her own. She looked for her own house and for her mom, but saw nothing familiar. It never occurred to her to call out to any of those strangers for help, and no one took any notice of the pair. Margaret was so tired she could barely set one foot in front of the other.

"I have to go home now," she said.

The sun was beginning to set, and Margaret finally recognized her house. Ben took Margaret's hand in a tight grasp and glared threateningly at her. "You don't tell anyone about this, you hear? Or I'll come back and beat the snot out of you." The boy then let go of her hand and disappeared around the corner.

Margaret wearily opened the door and was greeted by her distraught parents. "Where were you? What happened? We had the police looking for you."

She hesitated, remembering the ominous warning, and then broke into tears and explained as best she could the strange occurrences of the day, and then she was given some supper and sent to bed.

In the fall of the following year, in 1926, Daisy went into labour. Bill tore out of the house and down the street in a frantic search for the doctor. By the time he arrived home with the doctor, Daisy was already in heavy labour.

"Bill, take the children and get out of the house, and stay out until after this baby is born," ordered the doctor.

Bill quickly hustled out four year old George, two year old Bernie and five year old Margaret to the back yard where a chilly autumn wind blew.

The children shivered. "It's cold out daddy, why do we have to stay outside?" asked George.

"Your mommy is having a baby. We have to stay out of the way."

Bill ran back into the house and was in a frenzy to gather pieces of cloth to stitch together a tent to keep the children warm. Margaret was puzzled by her dad's haste and nervousness but watched the tent get made in jig time. It was raised in the middle by a stick and the father and children climbed inside to tell stories while they awaited the birth of the baby.

Hours later, the doctor called Bill and the children to come inside to see the new baby. Everyone trouped into the bedroom and there he was, a chubby, round faced boy wrapped snugly in a blanket. The children clamoured onto the bed for a closer look.

"We will call him Billy," announced Daisy. She was exhausted but very pleased with her baby and pleasantly surprised at the quick birth of such a big boy.

Bill smiled proudly at his family as they chattered excitedly and begged for turns to hold the baby. He counted four children again. It was a happy home. Bill was employed, for now, and could afford to feed his children. He sank onto the sofa and picked up the Eaton's catalogue and began flipping through the pages. He would get busy and order some new clothes and shoes for his family.

Bill would find work where ever he could. No job was beneath him, but there were many desperate days where he could do nothing but sit back and watch his children go hungry.

It was in the summer of 1928 when Bill lost his job again and by September the poor family was three months arrears in rent. They were forced to live on what they could grow in their tiny garden. Bill was readying himself for another day of job searching, when suddenly; there came a loud knock on the door.

"Mr. MacCallum! Do you have the rent you owe me?" yelled the landlord.

Bill opened the door with his wife standing behind him. Four half starved children timidly watched the exchange between the adults. "No, I don't have your rent yet. I'm very sorry. I'm going into town again today to look for work. I promise I will pay you back everything I owe."

"Damn right you will, now get out of my house!"

Standing behind the landlord were three large, stern looking men. Bill and Daisy took their children's hands and walked obediently outside. They watched in shock and horror as the three men entered the house and emptied it of everything, and scattered the items on the front yard. The bailiff then arrived with his notebook, and counted every stick of furniture, every pot, dish, fork and spoon, worn blanket, and every piece of clothing the family owned. The family watched in dismay and disbelief as all was about to be sold at auction.

"Please," begged Bill, "Don't take everything. How will we live? Where will we go?" His lips trembled as he tried to maintain control.

Tears streamed down Daisy's face. She reached out and clutched the landlord's sleeve, and pleaded with him. "Don't take the children's coats. They will need those in the winter."

He shook her off and turned his hard blue eyes to meet hers. He was unmoved. There was no pity, no compassion in his face. He had seen it all before. This was just another poor, deprived family. Their problems were no concern to him. He was not responsible for the drought. He had to make a living like everyone else, besides, hadn't he already been generous? Didn't he let them stay in his house for three months rent free? The pile of junk on the front yard was not worth much. He would never really get back what he was owed. He stood with arms crossed and watched the proceedings.

Margaret was seven years old. She was too young to be subjected to such trauma but just old enough to comprehend what was happening to her family. She felt deeply ashamed to see her parents' cracked dishes, dented furniture and even her own worn-out underpants thrown onto the grass of the front lawn for all the neighbours to see. That poor assortment of items represented everything her family owned. She noted the distress in her parents' faces and the wide-eyed, confused looks on her brothers and sister, who did not understand but knew that something was desperately wrong. Bernie hid behind her father while Billy clung to his mother's leg. George stood apart, hands at his sides, looking lost and bewildered.

Margaret dropped to her knees in the scraggly grass, clasped her hands together and looked to Heaven and prayed as she had so many times before, "Please God, send my parents some money."

Farmers and the town's people gathered and waited for the sale. Margaret looked at the faces of her neighbours, at the children she played with at school, as they examined her family's personal belongings. None would make eye contact with her.

The bailiff called out, "Let the bidding begin at $5.00 for this 1918 Singer sewing machine."

Before anyone could raise his hand, the crowd turned when they heard the pounding of horses' hooves approaching the house at high speed. A bow-legged cowboy by the name of Jake had arrived in his horse drawn wagon. He pulled hard on the reigns, bringing his team to a sudden stop and sending a cloud of dust into the air. He hollered, "Stop the sale! Just hold up there. They'll be no auction today!" He jumped from his wagon and walked over to the bailiff. He snatched away his notebook and turned to face the crowd. "Now don't you folks feel ashamed of yourselves? Would you throw this poor family out on the street with nothing?" He pointed

Daisy, Bernie, Margaret, Billy and George

to the family huddled together. "Would you let these children starve to death in front of you or die of the cold next winter?" The people shuffled in their places and they dropped their gazes to the ground. "Now let's all give them a hand up instead." He then walked among the small crowd with cowboy hat in hand. He begged and borrowed money here and there from neighbours and presented the money to the landlord. "That oughta be enough now."

George and Billy

With the money he was able to pay back the rent and buy back all the family's possessions. He and Bill then loaded everything into the back of Jake's wagon and the family started off in search of another home.

Margaret looked back at the dispersing crowd and at her very relieved parents and offered a small prayer of thanks.

The MacCallums left Drumheller and returned to the town of Munson in hopes of better luck, but jobs were no easier to find in Munson. Bill was able to find temporary work here and there, but nothing long term. Employers still preferred younger, stronger men.

To help with the income the family took in boarders, young men who worked in the mines around Munson. The small house was more cramped than ever but this monthly contribution helped the family buy some of the necessities of life. On Sundays the MacCallum children listened to the "funnies," or comics, read to them by the boarder they had. How grown up Margaret felt as she told George one Sunday, "Don't tell Richard that Dad already read us the funnies." She imagined that the boarder would be greatly disappointed not to be able to do that task himself.

The children were offered rare treats, when the family could afford it, like money for candy or a movie. One day, George and Margaret were allowed to go to a movie by themselves. About half way though, Margaret thought it was over and went home. Imagine her consternation when George arrived home later, having seen the whole movie. "Not fair!" she yelled, being a firm believer in a fair division of everything.

$\mathcal{M}$argaret was shy and gentle, but was also an easily frustrated, quick-tempered girl, and sometimes her mother, who was little, but tough and wiry, would spank her for her outbursts. Her mother expected a lot of her and she tended to get the blame whenever something happened. "You're the oldest Margaret, you should know better."

Her dad though, never hit his children. He would only shake his head and scold them, "By gum, you outfit better behave yourselves."

There were times when Margaret's quick temper was useful. She had a little friend named Johnnie who was a bully. He would pummel another child at the slightest provocation. They played together peacefully for a week or two, much to the amazement of their parents. Margaret was the only child who ever got along with Johnnie. Then one day his true nature surfaced and he began punching her.

"Stop that! You get away from me you devil!" she screamed, and ran away. He chased her until she spied a brick lying on the ground. She picked it up and hurled it at him. It hit him on the chest so he stopped his attack and went home. Their friendship ended abruptly and he never bothered her again.

$\mathcal{O}$ne Saturday, Margaret and her family went to Fastman's General Store, located in the center of Munson. It was a place to shop but was also a meeting place for the town's folk. The people stopped by regularly to socialize and exchange stories.

She said to the children with her, "What would you save if the store was on fire?" Fires were not unusual occurrences in those days, because most buildings were made of wood and heated by coal or wood burning stoves. All the children named what they would save.

"I would grab all of the candy!" said one.

"I would take all of the food and give it to my mom," said another.

By a horrible coincidence, the very next day, on Sunday morning, the store burned down. The children remembered what they had said when they were standing by the candy counter. They didn't save anything of course, and the poor man lost his store.

$\mathcal{T}$he first time Margaret heard a radio she was seven years old. The parish priest was given one by one of the more well to do people in the town. He used to set it up on the fence that surrounded the church so all the people in the town could come and listen. The town folk would sit on the grass and listen to news of far away places, and then everyone would get up and dance when the music played. It was wonderful, good fun.

Previous to obtaining their own radio, her family's chief source of entertainment was talking. In the evenings, Bill told tales of blizzards, prairie grass fires, trips to the Badlands by horse and sleigh to dig coal from the hills near Drumheller. Many winter evenings were spent recounting these simple adventures, while Bill paused only long enough to put more coal in the kitchen stove, and shake the clinkers, or coal residue, down into the ash pan.

The MacCallums had many visitors to their home, including a number of bachelors, whom Bill and Daisy would take under their wing to provide friendship and a decent meal. Hank would visit on Sundays sometimes. He lived in a one-room shack and farmed in a semi-profitable way. He owned a Model A Ford and to the delight of the family, would take them for a drive after dinner. Over time, however, he became tired of his lonely sedate life and turned to the beer parlours of Drumheller. He developed a love of alcohol and a love for the ladies of the night and quit visiting the MacCallums. They never heard from him again and the lovely rides in the country ceased.

Daisy, Bernie, George, Bill, Billy, Margaret

Percy was a bachelor farmer who lived in the Drumheller Valley. He was meticulous in his housekeeping and generally kept to himself. He decided one day that he needed a wife and so sent for one from Europe. She was, in his opinion, a "poor woman" and he didn't mean in the economic sense, so he sent her away. Margaret was reminded of domestic animals that are regularly purchased by farmers that turn out to be inferior quality for the money spent. Without an iota of regret, he discarded her and returned to his solitary lifestyle.

Not everyone in the town was as hard working and dedicated to their families as Bill. Gordie was a happy-go-lucky drunk. He was a sociable man, and was well liked by his friends despite his rough life style and the terrible neglect of his large family.

His wife, she's something else.
He picked her up in a mining town some years ago.
Poor thing is stupid in the head, but just as well,
She don't complain about him and his ways.
On the east side of the wood frame hotel,
Gordie lets the wheels of the truck bump against the curb,
Then eases his burly frame outside the cab.
He gives the door a thump because it sticks.
The hood is crumpled back and partly broken off,
But what the hell, the damn truck still runs!
It gets him to his job and back to here,
The beer parlour, and when that closes up,
It gets him home again to sleep it off,
In a grimy bed beside his wife.
Marrying him was one step up for her,
From prostitution to married state,
Complete with ten or so starving kids,
A matter of no concern to him, although at times
He will admit that some of them are cute,
Especially the youngest one, a girl.
If he has time between his job and beer
He has been know to hold her on his knee,
And call her "Sweetie-pie" and "Daddy's girl".

His other kids smile when he does that.
Well anyway, he's back here standing by his truck,
Sour smells greet him from the noisy cave
Where beer is slopping by the bucketful,
Makes his mouth water, and he turns impatiently
As some guy makes a wisecrack at his truck,
"Say Gordie, when are you getting that thing fixed?
You old bastard you don't give a damn, do you?"
Gordie laughs good-naturedly but not to be outdone,
"Laugh all you want that truck's got guts."
"I'll say it has, and they're showing too!"
With loud laughing they slap backs,
And enter the side door to join their friends
At ring-stained tables in the crowded bar.
The noise is deafening and the air smoke-filled,
Best of all the beer is cheap.
And the women in this place are available,
And more than willing.

Chapter Four

The Great Depression

The drought brought wide spread poverty to Southern Alberta in the late 1920's, but to make the situation worse, the stock market crash of October, 1929, brought down the economy of the United States. Its collapse quickly affected Canada because their economies were so closely tied. Canada was very reliant on trade with the United States and countries across Europe and Asia, with much of its Gross National Income deriving from exports. In Western Canada, the people saw the price of wheat drop to record low levels, so that farmers could not cover their production costs or pay farm taxes. They accumulated debts and many lost their farms to foreclosure. What followed were wage cuts in every sector of the economy and many people were put out of work. Hundreds of thousands if not millions of people struggled to meet their daily needs.

Everyone did not suffer in the same way during the Great Depression. Wages dropped as did prices, so as a result, the standard of living of some property owners and employers actually increased. On the other hand, farmers suffered terribly as prices for their goods decreased. Those who were already earning low wages earned even less, and the unemployed suffered most of all.[2]

Canada was so severely affected by the Great Depression of the 1930s that ultimately, one in five Canadians became dependent on government relief. The four western provinces, Manitoba, Saskatchewan, Alberta and British Columbia, in particular, were very badly affected. In 1931, thirty-three percent of the Canadian population was engaged in agriculture. By 1933, thirty percent of the Canadian labour force was unemployed. The farmers were plagued by crop failures and the lowest price for wheat in recorded history and ultimately sixty-six percent of the rural population was forced into relief.[3]

[2] www.yesnet.yk.ca/schools/projects/canadianhistory/depression
[3] www.yesnet.yk.ca/schools/projects/canadianhistory/depression

Canada did not have an adequate system to dispense welfare to those without jobs, and though it was a national problem, the federal government insisted that unemployment was a provincial and local problem and for many years, refused to provide work or relief. Prime Minister William MacKenzie King would only provide moderate relief to the population because he thought the financial difficulties of the depression would soon pass. The result was fiscal collapse and bankruptcy for the four western provinces. The people paid the price with their lives. Scurvy, dietary deficiency, diseases and even death by starvation were common in the latter half of the 1920's and the 1930's.[4]

Richard Bennett, a Conservative, won the federal election in 1930 on the promise to restore prosperity to the country. He provided relief programs but these contributed to the federal deficit and the government had to cut back on spending. The result was a deepening of the depression as government employees were put out of work and his promised projects were cancelled. His military-supervised relief camps for young men also made him unpopular, and he lost the election in 1935 to Mackenzie King's Liberals.

The Premier of the province, John Brownlee of the United Farmers of Alberta, served from 1925 to 1934. In a brilliant and far-sighted move his government was able to secure mineral rights from the federal government in 1930. This move would prove to be extremely beneficial to the province in subsequent decades. Alberta was to become a very prosperous province, but for the present time, the UFA did not do well in dealing with the difficulties of the Great Depression, and in 1935, the Social Credit party came into power led by William Aberhart.

Ultimately though, the federal government did assume some state responsibility for the economy and social welfare. In 1934, Bennett's government created legislation to establish the Bank of Canada, and in 1935, the Canadian Wheat Board, to market and establish a minimum floor price for wheat. In 1940, the federal government introduced National Unemployment Insurance.

Some families were torn apart when faced with such difficult circumstances, but Margaret's family's faith in God was the glue that held them together. Her parents' strong Catholic faith was evident in all they

---

[4] www.yesnet.yk.ca/schools/projects/canadianhistory/depression

did, and especially in how they raised their family. They were a very religious family, with prayers in the morning and evening and before and after meals and they always attended Mass on Sunday. They were taught to be virtuous in all matters of behaviour. Imagine Daisy's horror when a neighbour lady asked for assistance in covering up a lurid affair with a local policeman. "Meesus Ma-Call-um, my po-lees-man will come to see me. Rap on the door if you see my husband come."

With no money for a doctor or medicine, Daisy often feared that her family would become ill. She constantly worried for her children. "Button your coat, so you don't catch a chill," she said. If they got sick she might apply a mustard plaster, or caster oil or an enema, to try to keep the complaints to a minimum. Once Daisy had seized upon a remedy for what was ailing her brood, they got the remedy, come what may. If nothing else, they would receive a good hot cup of tea.

*L*ife for a child in the early days of the Great Depression was probably not perceived as bad as it was by those living through it, because of lack of understanding of the situation. Because everyone was poor in the 1930's, it was years before the MacCallums realized just how really poor they were. There was no money for anything resembling luxury and often not even for necessities. This was regarded as normal and everyone believed it was likely to remain so for foreseeable years.

Few children, or adults, for that matter, had spending money. One afternoon, Margaret and her little friend Grace were walking along the wooden sidewalk. With their footsteps they heard coins rattle, and looking down they saw a nickel and a dime. Grace was much better off than Margaret, but she made a grab for the dime, then she saw the nickel rattle away, so she left the dime on the sidewalk and went after the nickel. Margaret decided to help herself to the dime despite Grace's loud objections. "I don't care," Margaret said, "You wanted the nickel, so now you have it, and I have the dime."

> *The old wooden sidewalk made tracks by our house in the village,*
> *And all the other peoples' houses on our street,*
> *Until it reached the main road going east and west,*
> *Then it stretched its arms at right angles to its body*
> *And pointed west to the big houses, to Millionaires Row,*

And east, to the Post Office and other businesses of the town.
The Post Office was the favourite destination,
For our family at least,
A letter might contain a cheque from relatives.
They saved us from financial scrapes sometimes.
Our small town wooden sidewalk laid flat on its face,
It creaked and groaned and heaved when people walked on it,
Making rusty nails pop up, which no one ever pounded down again,
And so the boards talked back to us when we walked along its length.
"Hurry you silly children," it said, "You're late for school again.
Watch that heave in my humpy spine or you'll trip for sure,
And tell your mother that it's all my fault."
When we were small we used to crawl on hands and knees
Along the length of those old splintered boards,
To see what lay beneath the spaces,
Maybe a glinting coin.
Sometimes these treasure hunts resulted in a fight,
The winner darting to the store for a candy.
Later when we grew older and too proud,
To walk heads down in case we'd miss a dime,
We'd find the sidewalk lead us past the barbershop,
Boys hung around there and took turns shooting pool,
And whistling at the girls.
The barber chewed tobacco and admired girls,
While spewing thin brown juice, across the sidewalk.
At our town's reunion I looked,
For remnants of that simple trail,
That tried its best to keep our feet from mud and snow,
I saw the weeds poke up through its dead grey remains.
The prairie grass is king again.

The family had to do without many of the necessities of life, which included new clothes and shoes. Margaret was sent to school day after day in shoes that were too small. Her toes were curled and cramped, and this likely led to her ongoing foot problems and toe deformities. Many families faced similar problems. A Mennonite family from a farm about three miles south of town sent their children Erna, Mary and Jacob to school in their bare feet in spring and fall while the weather was nice, to save their shoes, big clods of shoes, but precious to that poor family. Another family searched the garbage dumps for anything useful, including orange peels, which they would grind up and add to their food for flavour and nutrition.

One of the local farmers, a vibrant man in his late twenties had a very fine herd of fat cattle prior to the drought and depression. He had taken out a large loan to buy the animals and the land, and he and his wife looked forward to a long life together raising cattle and a family on the farm. Then the drought began. He was forced to sell off some of the animals and he borrowed even more money to buy hay for the remaining herd. As the drought dragged on, he found it more and more difficult to feed his cattle. It wasn't long before the poor man took ill and died, leaving his young wife a widow and in charge of a herd of starving cattle.

The widow lay in her bed night after night and listened to the bawling of the hungry herd. In a fit of desperation she rose from her bed one evening, took her husband's rifle and entered the barn. She looked pityingly at the animals that once represented the dream shared by her and her husband. The beasts stood side by side in the barn, their ribs and hip bones protruding, heads hanging. Some stepped towards her, hoping for a bit of feed. Instead she raised the gun and one by one shot every last animal in the barn, until at last it was quiet. She then sat on the floor of the barn amid the dirt, feces and blood, and turned the gun toward herself. All night she sat and contemplated taking her own life. When daybreak broke and sunlight streamed through the cracks in the boards of the barn, she raised herself up and emerged, and carried on living as best she could.

There were many stories of suffering during that time. Many people lost their farms and their homes. Malnutrition and lack of medicine contributed to the death of many. Few, it seems lived through those decades and emerged unscathed.

> *Rolling farmlands and winding creek beds,*
> *Holding shapeless platters of muddy water.*
> *Some filthy banks of snow remain,*
> *Protected from the sun.*
> *Last year's weeds and grey-brown grass,*
> *Give hilly fields a tired look.*
> *Dead plants not yet buried,*
> *Dull prelude to the spring.*

In 1929, Margaret was eight years old and the family moved again, this time to a rented farm west of Munson. Bill became the caretaker of the farm. It was actually a serfdom of sorts. The landlord allowed the family to stay on the land and work the farm, for a price. For the privilege of working the land they paid the rent by handing over a portion of the crops.

The children had a two and a half mile walk to school. In winter it was hard except when they were able to hitch a ride with some of the neighbouring farmers such as the Windles or the Adams. George would often forge ahead through the snow to make a path for his siblings. In spring and early summer the walk was more pleasant and the children were able to take their time walking to school. They picked wild onions, rose hips and sweet stems of new wheat or oats to eat on the way.

In winter, the rented farmhouse was as draughty and cold as were all the other houses in which they lived. Insulation was virtually non-existent and the houses were heated with coal and wood stoves. Fires were kept roaring in the pot-bellied heaters but water froze in the pails and basins during the night. The family was seldom warm in the winter and poor Bill had a difficult time buying enough coal to keep them warm.

Of course in the winter came Christmas, and the family loved Christmas most of all. Daisy and Bill made a big fuss about the holiday, with a tree, and as many presents as they could afford, homemade or otherwise.

The day before Christmas 1930 was beautiful. Snow, white and soft, melting a little, gave a pristine beauty to the landscape, but Bill was discouraged. Even the weather, which had turned sunny, failed to ease the grim set of his mouth. He was worried about tomorrow, Christmas Day, and not a cent to buy toys for the children or for groceries. The knot in his stomach tightened every time he thought of his four children and their happy, expectant faces. Up to now, there had always been something for them at Christmas. He'd made several trips to town in the sleigh in the past few weeks to try to collect forty dollars owed to him, but to no avail. His friend John did not have the money to pay him back. There was no more time left now, and he was feeling pretty desperate, left to scuff the softening snow with his worn rubber overshoes, and worry.

The 1930's were years of blighted hopes and ambitions, full of feelings of fear and helplessness. Funny that he should come to this, a man with his pride and spirit. He was independent, hardworking, honest and hating every minute on this unproductive, neglected farm. It was neglected because there was no money in the thirties for anything, and unproductive because there had been no rain to speak of, for years. It was not his farm. He only lived there with his family. The owner allowed them to stay because it was better not to leave a farm deserted. There was, for instance, a man who made the rounds of the country in his wagon, picking up whatever he could find if the buildings were unoccupied. So Bill was really nothing but a caretaker there anyway, for an owner who was surly and begrudging of the situation.

Back in Ontario, Bill had turned down a partnership with his brother in a wholesale tobacco business, to come out West and make a living on a homestead. What a cruel joke. He failed at his homestead and lost his farm. He had no money behind him and bouts of arthritis had sapped him of his strength.

Bill surveyed the farm where he stood. The snow, which came last night, had laid a glistening mantle over the broken farm implements and spare bits of machinery. The ancient threshing machine lay like a hulking ghost under its cover, and the hayrack and haymow and horse-drawn plough lay outlined in white like blanched skeletons. Their pure and still postures seemed to mock his past attempts at successful farming.

He glanced down on his calloused hands, knotted with work that brought little monetary reward, and little spiritual reward for that matter. Constant worry about feeding his family had dried up his reserve of spiritual strength and left him a little bitter. If only there was a Santa Claus who rode through the crystal air with gifts for all the poor children of the world, and a glitter of hope for their parents. Hope was the virtue that carried a man to survive year by year. This year, he had little.

The air had lost its bite and told that the Chinook winds were on the way. A high whinny came to him from the barn, reminding him of his duty to feed the two horses. The cow needed to be milked also, and as he entered the rickety old barn she swung her head around to look at him reproachfully from huge bovine eyes. Everything reproached him today, nibbling more and more at his pride, reminding him of his foolishness in leaving the East, of trying to turn his city ways into the ways of a farmer. Nothing fitted his ideas of a good life out here, not the shambling leaky-roofed farmhouse in which he sheltered his young family, not the cruel, long winters endured with little in the way of protection, and most of all, not his empty pockets on the day before Christmas.

He returned to the house with his pail of milk and scraped his snow caked shoes on the metal scraper at the back door. Daisy was making baking powder biscuits again, and she looked up to give him one of her sweet, optimistic smiles. Like the children, she was excited about Christmas, but the knowledge that there was no money on the day before did not quell her faith that something good would happen.

Bill tried to avoid the excited questions that immediately engulfed him from the two younger children, Bernie and Billy, as soon as he returned the kitchen. Their enthusiasm for Christmas made them dance around him like excited puppies. The two older ones, George and Margaret, could read the message on the strained faces of their parents. They also overheard whispered consultations at night when they were supposed to be asleep. Their quiet resignation clutched at Bill. The hard times spared no one and he realized his children had to mature fast if they were going to survive.

"These days we can't afford house plants," he would scold, if they complained of the cold. "By gee, you'd better make do. It's a hard world and you just better learn to get along."

Daisy often admonished him for his lack of faith, but kindly, and not accusingly. "It's no use to worry anymore. God is good and something will happen. We'll go to Midnight Mass tonight. That's the most important part anyway. The children will see the manger scene and hear the Christmas Carols. We'll still have Christmas."

It was curious how her simple faith could both calm him and infuriate him. She was like a child in some ways, but he was secretly glad that she didn't reinforce his feelings of despair.

He was in an irritable mood, and now he had to get ready for church. He had no good clothes to wear, but for Christmas he would dress up as best he could by wearing his cuff links and collar stud. Today, however, he could not find them. "By gee, my mother had order, everything in order. Before I had you outfit I never had to look for anything. Con sarn it! Will you outfit get a move on and help me find my cufflinks and collar stud?!"

He looked at the Christmas tree that the children had so much fun decorating. What will they think in the morning when there is nothing under its branches?

Around five o'clock in the afternoon it was starting to get dark, so he lit the coal-oil lantern and made his way again to the old barn. He must harness the horses and get the sleigh ready for a ride to town. It usually took about two hours of steady plodding in the snow for the two horses to pull the sleigh over the country roads.

Daisy had a pleasant singing voice and the children, nestled in blankets with hot bricks to keep their feet warm, joined her in Carol singing. Bill, in spite of himself, felt the anxiety lifting as the singing worked a sort of magic in him. The sky was star filled. The air was calm and crisp. The horses' hooves clip clopped, like an accompaniment of drums to the lifting voices. "Silent night, Holy night, all is calm, all is bright…" Did he discern a promise in the voices of his wife and children, an undertone of love and encouragement from sources he couldn't see? Whatever it was, it was truly beautiful, and the past weeks of fretting faded and left him unburdened for the first time.

He slapped the reins on the broad backs of the horses and made a clicking sound with his tongue, so that the horses broke out into a trot. The children squealed with joy at their father's change in mood and the faster pace of the horses. They stood up in the sleigh and shouted their delight as they came near the town.

The mail had been slow that year. The postmaster in town kept the doors open even at this hour on Christmas Eve, for the farm folk who didn't get into town often.

"Might as well see if the relatives down East sent us some letters this year." He stepped out of the sleigh and made his way indoors. "Anything for me today, P.J.?" In answer, P.J. Tarr pushed four parcels over the counter and several letters. His hands trembling, Bill gathered up the mail and awkward under the load, carried them to the sleigh. There were three cheques from his relatives and two from Daisy's relatives. In all, the total came to over a hundred dollars — a fortune. The parcels would be opened Christmas morning.

No gift of the Magi was welcomed with more gratitude. Bill had to assure the children that he wasn't crying. It was just the crisp night air that made his eyes water.

Bill glanced down at the children huddled together in the sleigh as they made the last short trip from the post office to the church. Whatever had inspired their relatives to send gifts at just the right time? He fervently hoped that someday they would know the tremendous favour they had done him, he who needed so badly a return to faith. Long after the gifts were gone and the money used up, he would know that love is never lost. He just needed to know where to look for it.

*B*ill and Daisy persisted for two years to try to make a living from the unproductive farm. The work was hard and the rewards were small so they decided to try their luck back in the town of Munson, where Bill could work odd jobs for the town's people.

Margaret heard the whistle blow three long shrill sounds. In fact it could be heard all over the village. "Tweet, tweet, tweet", the whistle said, "Come to lunch Martin."

It was the summer of 1931. Martin was eight years old and Margaret was ten. She didn't much like Martin. He bullied her little sister Bernie. His mother dressed him in blue overalls and called him Pet. He was an only child. Martin's father was an undertaker and the kids in town teased him about that and the whistle and the overalls. "Tweet, tweet, tweet," insisted the whistle. Then his mother's voice, "Where are you Pet? Your lunch is ready."

Martin's mother used the whistle to call her son for different reasons and the number of tweets told him the exact reason each time. One long whistle meant he had to practice the piano. Two meant that he must come back and play in his back yard. Three whistles meant that lunch was ready; four tweets meant dinner and five sharp ones meant bedtime. There were other whistles whose meaning was known to Martin only, and how he hated it all.

Martin hated the whistle, his big loose overalls, the way his mother called him "Pet" and also his haircut. His mother believed in saving money every way she could. That was the reason that she had the barber cut his hair close to his head with clippers, so it would not need cutting often. It stood up in stiff bristles and the other kids liked to rub their hands up and down the back of his head to make him say, "Ouch." He also hated the heavy boots laced above his ankles. He wore them because his mother said they were more serviceable than running shoes or low shoes.

One day when he had to stop playing because the whistle blew again, he decided to do something about it. There was an old shed near the livery stable. He pretended to be heading home so that the other boys would not follow him. They were calling after him, "Is your lunch ready Pet? Are you going home to practice piano Pet?" Their taunting made him more determined than ever to teach everyone a lesson. He was filled with hate for his mother, the kids, his clothes, everything.

The grass was tall near the fence so he crouched down for a few minutes until there was no on in sight. The whistle was still telling him to come home but he paid no attention to it. By creeping steadily between the fence and the ditch he made his way to the old shed.

It was cool and damp behind the boards piled up against the wall in the shed. He pulled himself up into a small curve behind them and drew his feet in so that they could not be seen from the door. He could hear the whistle faintly and his mother calling, "Martin, come home to dinner."

"Let her find me," he said to himself, "Just let anyone find me." He looked down at the toes of his heavy boots and thought of the number of kids he had kicked with them. "Served them right for teasing me." He was big for his age and some of the kids were afraid of him, especially the girls.

Martin wasn't sure how long he lay hidden behind the boards. The whistle was quiet now but voices were calling him, his mother, and the neighbours. He felt shivers run through him. It felt good to fool them and he made up his mind that he would stay there forever.

Then it got dark in the shed as the sun went down. He could hear the sounds of feet running and men calling each other. Someone pulled the rope on the village fire bell. "Ding dong, ding dong, ding dong," it tolled.

"I wonder why they are ringing the bell?" he thought. "Maybe they're calling the farmers to look for me." He began to feel important and wondered if he would be a hero when he finally showed himself. A small pain started in his stomach and then he remembered that he had not eaten for a long time. The voices outside seemed to be coming nearer.

"Do you think the kid could be hiding in here?"

A lantern sent shadows dancing around the shed. He shivered inside his overalls as the men tramped around. Then someone saw his foot pressed against the boards and he was pulled out feet first from his hiding place.

"What are you doing hiding in here?" someone asked, "Everyone in town has been looking for you. You scared your parents half to death "

Martin thought that he had better answer these men quickly. "The other kids were chasing me," he said half sobbing, "They were going to hit me."

"Who was going to hit you?" his father asked coming forward. "No one will hurt you son. Tell me who it was."

Martin thought quickly. "George and Jim," he said. "They were going to beat me up." There was no use telling his strict father the real reason. His father would believe the story about George and Jim anyway and would speak to the boys' fathers. Maybe the kids would be afraid to tease him then. You could scare kids but you couldn't change parents much. He would have to find another way to get rid of the whistle, the overalls and the name, "Pet." He quietly followed his father home.

> *Small towns are,*
> *Unsophisticated in the planning of the streets,*
> *Two rows of stores or shops that face each other,*
> *And houses scattered here and there.*
> *People stepping in and out of doorways,*
> *Nobody in a hurry really, and no traffic jams.*
> *Farmers stop to visit with each other even though*
> *They see each other several times a week.*
> *Old people eye a stranger as a child would,*
> *Without embarrassment; they ask you why*
> *You have ice caked on the fenders of your car,*
> *When there is no snow left in town.*
> *They don't ask your name, they're just curious*
> *About the weather that you passed through,*
> *South of here.*

Chapter Five

School Days

$\mathcal{D}$aisy decided to start George and Margaret together in grade one when Margaret was seven years old and George was six. Daisy thought Drumheller was a very rough town so she didn't send Margaret to school at age six because she was afraid that Margaret wouldn't be able to defend herself. The little girl was indeed in need of some protection even on the first day of school. While waiting outside the school for the teacher to call them indoors, her trusting nature and innocence allowed her to mistake friendly overtures from two mischievous little boys, who disguised an intention to slip a large dusty moth inside the back of her dress. George chased the rascals away while Margaret wiped away her tears and wondered what other sorts of horrors awaited her at school.

The teacher called the children inside and took row call. There were thirty or so children in the grade one class. The teacher began by removing the strap from her desk drawer. She took some time explaining its purpose and on what grounds it would be employed. Margaret trembled in fear as she sat in her desk, watching the teacher's hands caress the strap. Margaret was determined that she would never have the strap used on her.

"You will now stand beside your desks, hands at your sides, for the singing of 'Oh Canada' and then we will recite the 'Lord's Prayer.'" She then checked the children's hands and nails for cleanliness, sending those who did not pass inspection to the water barrel outside to wash themselves.

They were a shabby bunch of kids who attended the school in Drumheller in the 1920's. Many children came to school barefoot in the spring and fall to save on the cost of shoes. The bottoms of their feet were black with dirt and tough as horses' hooves. Most wore their clothes until the material was worn thin. Daisy and the other mothers darned socks and patched and repaired as well as they could. Nothing was thrown away or wasted.

Over the next few weeks of school, the teacher grouped the children by ability. The brightest children sat in the first row, the average children in the middle, and the slowest children in the last rows. George was a very bright and hardworking student. He was put in the highest group and in fact in the desk for the smartest student, in the first row. By Christmas, he was moved into grade two. Margaret remained in grade one in the middle row. She was deeply embarrassed by this, but at the same time she felt very proud of her little brother.

Penmanship, or calligraphy, was a highly valued skill, and even in grade one students were taught cursive writing, not printing. Perfect form was encouraged, which was difficult considering they had to use a fountain pen, which was dipped into ink. Any child careless enough to splatter, smudge or spill was given a sound scolding by the teacher. Children did their writing exercises from the left side of the scribbler right over to the right side of the second page. Memorization of facts was considered the most important part of schooling and most learning was done by rote. The children could look forward to prizes for best spelling, vocabulary or arithmetic scores. They might receive a crisp apple or perhaps a new pencil.

The children had little playground equipment; no bats or balls, no hockey sticks or pucks, so during recess they became involved in games such as hop scotch, kick the can, fox and goose or fox and hares. Margaret gleefully ran outside. She wanted to be the first on the playground to claim the swing which she loved most of all. She had just swung her small, scrawny frame onto the seat when she was pushed from behind. "Get off!" demanded an angry voice.

It was one of the big boys in third grade. Margaret meekly dismounted to relinquish her seat, but before he could take the seat he was pushed so hard from behind he fell sprawling on the ground. It was Nettie. Though she was only in grade two, she weighed eighty pounds and was big enough to intimidate anyone on the playground.

"We'll take turns," she announced to Margaret.

Margaret smiled shyly and climbed up onto the seat again. Nettie pushed the swing high into the air. Margaret squealed with delight as she pointed her toes towards the sky and tried to touch the clouds. After several minutes the swing slowed and it was Nettie's turn. Nettie's wide bottom filled the seat of the swing until it was flowing over. Margaret put her small hands on Nettie's broad back and pushed with all the strength her slim forty-five pound body could muster. Margaret detected a strong, sour odour rising from Nettie. The smell welled up around her like a cloud but Margaret dared not say anything about it. She didn't want to offend her newly found ally. She held her breath and pushed again and eventually got the swing moving.

*T*heir move to the much smaller town of Munson meant that the MacCallum children would be educated in a one room school house. In the winter the ink wells would freeze overnight in the schoolhouse so in the morning they had to place the wells on the wood-burning stove to thaw them out. On the playground there were snowball fights and snow fort building.

At home, in the winter, it was difficult to do homework when the sun went down so early. They strained to read under the dim light of a coal-oil lamp. When their eyes got too tired they liked to step outside to view the millions of stars, or watch flickering columns of multi-coloured lights dance across the sky when the Northern Lights put on a show.

I remember where I walked along the dirt path to school,
Laughing and scuffing my shoes.
The grass that bordered the path was fragrant
In the late spring and summer.
By fall it was spiked dry and brittle.
The path curved here and there.
Daydreaming feet had marked the course before,
And other feet that followed wore it down.
The winter snows filled in the groove,
Making it grey black and slippery.
The warmth of spring turned the snow to slush
And the path to mud.
This caked on our shoes and socks
On the way to school.

*T*o further Margaret's education, it was decided that she was to be sent to a school-convent in Calgary as a boarder. Her parents could not afford the tuition, but the Ursuline Convent did take a certain number of charity cases and Margaret was one.

The shiny linoleum was unbelievably clean and slick, so much so that footing was uncertain. Everything gleamed including the walls, halls, tables

Margaret (far left) and her classmates in Munson.

and chairs. All gave the impression of purity; nothing dirty or unworthy would be allowed within these walls. The Reverend Mother grasped the child and gave her the traditional kiss on both cheeks; welcoming her arrival against the stiff celluloid bib of her habit. "So this is our new boarder. Welcome to your new home dear. I am Mother St. Phillip."

Margaret smiled weakly and glanced at her surroundings but quickly dropped her eyes to the floor as the nun's piercing blue eyes met hers; not hostile but not friendly either. No twelve-year-old was to be a match for this seasoned veteran of a strict religious order, which took its job of training its girls most seriously.

"We will gather in the parlour. Come this way."

Margaret took a step forward and slipped slightly on the highly polished floor. She reached out a hand to steady herself against the wall.

"We don't put our hands on the walls," the nun cautioned, "young ladies who soil the premises must clean up after themselves."

"I'm sorry." Shame always came easily to Margaret. She looked down the long hallway as slippery as a skating rink, and considered how she might negotiate its length without touching any walls or falling on her buttocks. For one horrified moment she thought she might wet herself. She hated her childhood awkwardness.

They sat in a semi-circle in the parlour; the nervous young priest, two nuns, Margaret's Irish mother, looking like an immigrant newly arrived off the boat in her shabby clothes, and Margaret, in her thin cotton dress.

The young girl perched uncertainly on the edge of the tapestry seat. After much praise was heaped on the priest for his great charity in delivering this latest boarder to their doors; the plan progressed for Margaret's board, and exactly how she would be kept.

As the adults discussed the arrangements, Margaret contemplated the floor. Its highly waxed beauty contrasted sharply with the not-too-clean floorboards of her family home. She was in an alien world and wondered how she would fit in to a place where not a speck of dust was to be found, nor any item left out of place. Her inadequate clothing contrasted with the prim curtains and tables laid with starched cloth and delicate doilies. She glanced about at the gleaming windows and sacred pictures that hung on spotless walls.

Tea arrived with cakes and dainty cups. Margaret's spirits brightened and she licked her lips in anticipation, until she counted the number of cups and plates and it became apparent that only the adults were to be included in the feast. She tried to look unconcerned although her thin body craved the sweet, delicious cupcakes and cookies. Her pride would not let her betray her craving. She felt her mother's eyes upon her and with concerted effort she drew her body straight and held her hands on her lap.

Daisy felt her daughter's agony and asked, "How about you, Margaret, wouldn't you like something to eat." Her eyes were full of love and pity.

Margaret held her head high. "No thank-you mom, I'm not hungry."

Reverend Mother sent a paralyzing glance in her direction as if she had uttered a profanity. Margaret glanced beseechingly at her mother and became increasingly nervous. The priest appeared oblivious to any of the embarrassment and munched his cakes with disconcerting pleasure, and basked in the praise of the sisters who apparently couldn't get over the extent of his goodness and generosity. If she had dared, Margaret would have told him that she did not wish to be the object of pity, and that she would gladly walk the eighty miles back home if it meant she would not have to stay here, so far away from home, amid such formidable creatures as these sisters. But she didn't dare. At this point in her life and in this place, she was not allowed a will of her own. She said good-bye to her weeping mother and allowed herself to be led away.

Soon after, she heard loud cries and protests coming from the hall. There was another young girl who had no wish to be part of the convent boarder scene. She wailed in wild abandon and flung herself down on the stairs. "I hate this place and no one can make me stay," she shrieked. She held on to her mother's arm and wouldn't let her go.

From her vantage point, Margaret noticed the fine clothes the family wore. "She must be someone whose parents can afford to pay, and she acts like a spoiled brat."

The nuns tried in vain to calm the girl, and her parents, after many bribes and threats, finally took her back to the car. They had not succeeded in passing on their rebellious daughter on to the long-suffering nuns. Margaret couldn't tell if she saw relief or tight-lipped anger on the face of Mother St. Phillip. She was obviously not used to this sort of behaviour from children. Margaret hurried down the hall so that she would not be scolded for gawking at the little drama.

The dormitory was another source of speechless amazement. Dirt and disorder, the twin devils, had never existed here, in this godly place. Shrouds of gleaming, starched cotton separated single beds. Basins and water jugs, toothbrush holders and facecloths were all in perfect military order. Margaret couldn't take her eyes off her own toothbrush and toothpaste, a luxury she never dreamed she would own. Until now, a wet rag with soap had sufficed to clean her teeth. She felt rich and pampered.

"This is where you'll sleep," instructed the Mistress of Dormitories. Each nun had her own domain, which she ruled with firmness, a smattering of kindness, but with little humour. Nothing was ever considered trite in the care and discipline of the raw material of womanhood. The "Rules" prevailed and dictated. It was no wonder Margaret was scolded by Mother Mary Agnes days later when a bar of soap was found sitting in a small pool of water in the soap dish. The soap was covered with sticky, obscene, dripping goo. The scandal!

"Shame on you, careless child!" the nun reprimanded.

She soon learned that her former careless ways would not be tolerated. Beds were to be made according to a specific formula with tight corners and no wrinkles or unsightly bulges. Perfect manners were required at the table and during classes. Above all, obedience was the law.

*A*bout a month after arrival at the convent, Margaret became acquainted with a most distressing sensation that began in her throat and made her eyes water. It then overcame her chest and caused her breath to come unevenly. What followed was a choked cry, which she held for as long as she could. When she could hold it no longer it came out as long sighs, cries and sniffles. Nothing was fun anymore and the sight of other children playing sent her to far corners of the playground to be alone. One day, someone said, "She's homesick," and finally she had a name for her frightening condition. In her mind she denied that she missed her parents and her sister and brothers.

While watching a group of people pass on the sidewalk one day in front of the school, she thought she saw a familiar face. The woman was walking toward the convent. Margaret jumped up and ran smiling towards the woman. When she was about ten feet away she discovered to her horror that it wasn't her mother. Ashamed, she stopped running and tried to appear nonchalant, and prayed that she had not been observed.

"You thought she was your mother, didn't you?" a girl called out, and the whole world it seemed, started to laugh at her. She was so full of shame that she wanted to disappear. She ran to the back of the school and hid for a while. Tears would not come. She did not feel strong enough to endure this place. Her self-confidence was low and diminishing daily. She felt weak, friendless and unprotected. Worst of all she couldn't go home until Christmas when through the charity of the nuns, they would pay the train fare. She had to go back and face the sneering faces of her classmates after they witnessed her distress. It was another two weeks until the dreaded plague passed and she could smile again.

The girl in the bed next to Margaret's was Kathleen. She was often ill and a favourite of Mother St. Peter. Many times Kathleen would lie languishing in her bed breathless and pale. That nun would hold her hand and they would chat like the dearest of friends. Margaret envied Kathleen for her fragility and the attention she received. She also envied Kathleen's obvious prosperity, her new shoes and pretty ribbons in her hair.

Margaret had heard Kathleen and the other girls talking about the crystal sets they owned. Margaret was afraid to display her ignorance, so didn't inquire what a crystal set was, but she supposed it had something to do with radios. Margaret felt her poverty in every pore of her being. She was the object of charity, and charity not too lovingly given. She hated to be thought of as a second-class citizen. It was well-known in the convent whose parents had paid the tuition and who were the charity cases. Those with the most money were held in high esteem while the poor students felt degraded. She spent a lot of time thinking about her situation at the convent. "Maybe," she thought, "I can do some ironing for my board and room, and then they will treat me better."

Margaret often felt that she was being picked on by the nuns. "Why do I have to remake my bed? It's just as good as everyone else's."

Mother Mary Agnes rasped at her in a shrieky, high-pitched voice, "You had better do as you are told young lady or you will be thrown out on your head! You bold lump!"

"Oh how they love that description," Margaret mused, "someday I'll be rich. I'll have heaps of money, and I'll come here and fling it in front of the door and then they'll be sorry."

Kathleen and Margaret became friends though. Kathleen was like the "city mouse". She was the advisor, the big sister and critic. She was an Irish girl, Calgarian born. She would suffer Margaret's small-town ineptitude with tired tolerance. She rolled her eyes and said, "Now Margaret, you must hold the fork in your left hand and your knife in the right. The prongs must be pointed downward." She pushed her blond ringlets back and sighed, enduring Margaret's presence with lady-like martyrdom. Margaret was like the "country mouse", thrown into the alien world of city culture without the tools for survival. She looked to Kathleen to be her mentor and guide.

When Margaret returned to the convent the following fall for grade eight, Kathleen was not there. She had succumbed to her illness and died that summer. Margaret felt truly sorry for the times she had coveted Kathleen's possessions.

Another of Margaret's boarding school friends was Betty. Betty yearned to please the nuns, but she was not a scholar, and so failed to earn their admiration. It was generally assumed by the teachers that a failure to learn was one's own fault. Betty worked terribly hard. She was convinced that if she wrote each word in her spelling list over and over, thirty or forty times, she would finally succeed in getting it right. She seemed unaware of Mother St. Peter's contempt for her and would not join the other students in discussions of the unfairness of it all. Margaret could not understand why Betty did not resent the unhappy nun like everyone else and how she could be so accepting of other's faults. Betty was determined to see the good in every person. She was optimistic to a fault.

Mother St. Peter bestowed her endearments on a select few students. The rest were banished with cold contempt into the exterior darkness, like small planets lost in cold space. She used her power as an educator to criticize, humiliate and degrade. Her criticisms dug deep into the hearts of some of the more sensitive students, such as Margaret, until they were filled with feelings of worthlessness. Some, like Betty, were oblivious, and others became stronger and simply learned not to care about Mother St. Peter. Some of the students whispered that the reason she had entered the convent was because a man jilted her.

When Mother St. Peter was not about, convent life was good. Most of the nuns were kind but impersonal. It would have been considered highly improper to show love or caring for their charges. All the nuns were called Mother, but it was a misnomer. None of them were permitted to act like a mother. It was simply a title of respect for the religious office. It permitted no closeness, only widened the gap between adult and child. In Margaret it had the effect of instilling a deep sense of inferiority and unworthiness.

Anything verging on brushing against the almighty rules was unthinkable. It was believed by some that in order to make children conform, to obey and to believe, it was important to break their spirits as one might break a horse. The authoritarian method of teaching was yet to be replaced by one in which children were taught self-discipline and self-control. Self-control was not an issue for Margaret, at least not during her first few months at the convent. She was a shy and obedient child before she entered the doors of the convent.

Saturdays at the convent provided a relief for the students, in more ways than one. Every Saturday morning was laxative time for everyone, whether it was required or not. It was another implacable rule. Nature could not be counted on to keep convent girls well evacuated — no oversight of man or nature was permitted. Strict discipline was required to ensure their straight pathway in life and ultimately into Heaven, and all shortcomings of the natural order must be rectified. A clean body contributed to a clean mind, it was said. It was a potent laxative, without a doubt, and the girls were in fierce competition for the four toilets in the convent and the two outhouses. These were the only facilities available to take care of eighteen girls in states of fluctuating emerging all day Saturday. Winter presented a greater challenge when the outdoor facilities froze naked backsides to the wood of the toilet seat, but they were the only recourse to the losers in the race for indoor plumbing.

The students were allowed to bathe once a week and wash their hair every two weeks. Every Saturday morning was lecture time on personal hygiene and deportment. The voice of Mother Mary Agnes cut through the antiseptic air of the dormitory, summoning them all in a group to hear again the rules and regulations of scrubbing their bodies, "Cleanliness is like unto Godliness," she squeaked.

Margaret could control her behaviour and even to some extent her emotions. There were, however, two things she could not control, her body odour and the size of her breasts. Margaret dreaded the personal hygiene sessions because she knew Mother's accusing eyes would land on her for being the most offensive of all the girls for body odour. Underarm deodorant was unheard of. Her sweat soaked into the heavy blue serge uniforms they were required to wear and cultivated there until it wafted from her adolescent body. To make matters worse, the uniform was second-hand, so she had the former owner's contribution of sweat combined with her own. Despite her attempts at scrubbing herself and the underarms of the uniform, the putrid smell clung. The fastidious sisters were repelled by the stench. Margaret was lectured and admonished on the subject as if she had done it to annoy them.

One Saturday morning Margaret sat on her bed hidden behind her curtain praying that she wouldn't be missed or discovered, in hopes that she would not be humiliated again.

"Come out from behind your curtains Miss," Mother ordered shrilly, "you are the worst one of all in this department. Get out here and take your medicine."

Margaret crept out to join her classmates while all eyes turned on her unsanitary self. Her hands were clasped in front of her stomach, showing her patched elbows. She felt again that she was being unfairly singled out because she was a charity case.

Months later however, she was delivered from her smelly uniform due to a ravenous appetite and the excellent and unaccustomed quantity of food. She had never eaten so well. Her weight went from eighty-seven pounds to one hundred and seventeen pounds in only a few months. Her black hair gleamed and thickened and her cheeks glowed like roses. She burst the boundaries of her nasty second-hand uniform and was given a brand new uniform and a set of underarm dress shields, elegantly called "sweat pads". These could be washed out by hand every night and thus, Margaret became slightly more respectable.

Margaret burst the boundaries of her old uniform and she burst the boundaries of her training bra, and a number of other bras in very quick succession. She was an early bloomer, with great large blossoms. At just thirteen years of age she had a very womanly figure, compared to the other girls whose breasts had just begun to ripen. She did her best to conceal herself, though that was next to impossible. She became the subject of whispered remarks among her classmates, "Do you think they're real? I think she stuffs her bra."

One day, while dusting a little office, she overheard two of the nuns remarking on her development, "She has such big breasts. What are we going to do? She will need more brassieres, and she should have a girdle I suppose."

In a state of rage and humiliation, she dropped her dust rag on the floor. She stomped to their office door and knocked. The startled faces of Mother Louise and Mother St. Peter greeted her.

Half sobbing with shame and fear she stammered, "I'm sorry you are having so much trouble with me. I can't help it if my breasts are getting big and I never did want your charity. Anyway, why do you always leave money on the window of the office where I have to dust? Are you hoping I will take it and then you'll have a reason to kick me out? I'm going home right now if I have to walk all the way!"

Before she could go, Mother Louise took her gently by the hand. "We'll get the necessary garments for you. Meanwhile, you pull yourself together and get ready for supper."

"My parents will pay for my underthings," she sniffed proudly, still trying to keep a semblance of dignity.

"Your parents have no money to pay for anything, so don't you dare ask them for anything," snapped Mother St. Peter.

She pursed her lips against any further outcry so Margaret swallowed hard and took a deep breath. Mother Louise smiled gently at Margaret and sent her on her way.

Several days later, a sneaky girl named Jackie appeared at the dormitory door, her face full of mischief, as usual. She liked to drape her arm around Margaret's neck and talk about sex when there were no nuns in sight. Margaret had little interest or liking for these one-sided conversations and often made an excuse to get away. On this day, she sat on her bed, her back to Margaret, and announced to all present that a parcel had arrived, and that inside it contained a girdle, some underpants, some sweat pads and some "huge" brassieres. The girls in the dormitory giggled and she continued, "And they aren't from her parents either. I opened it and it came straight from the Eaton's Catalogue." She turned her head and asked Margaret with a sneer, "Are the nuns paying for everything for you?"

She had hardly finished her sentence when Margaret leaped up and pushed Jackie from behind and sent her sprawling across one of the beds. She banged her head on the railing, raising a welt above her eye.

"Be sure to tell the nuns how you got that shiner," Margaret announced, "and I'll tell them how you were sneaking around opening other people's mail."

Mother Mary Agnes came primly to the dormitory at that point and shrilly directed the girls as usual. "You girls will line up in a straight row and pass out in the hall."

Margaret stepped out into the hall with the others and promptly fell forward on to the floor, sending everyone sprawling ahead of her.

"Is something wrong with you?" the nun asked, grasping her by the arm.

"No, I'm alright. You asked us to pass out in the hall, so I did."

"Bold lump, you didn't used to be so mischievous. You were so meek and mild when you first came here. You'd better watch yourself or you will be right out of here on your ear."

The other girls stifled their giggles, clearly enjoying the afternoon's entertainment. The bells rang as they made their way to the refectory hall for supper.

Bells were always ringing in the convent, bells for meals, for school, for attendance at the chapel, and for the Angelus at noon. The students lived and performed by bells ringing out the time for duties. To be prompt was a must and no excuses. That was the rule. It was, without a doubt, the most effective way of gathering the flock of boarders, and most responded like a well-disciplined herd of sheep. Some of the children were raised by the nuns since early childhood and so would be absolutely lost without the bells. It instilled a need in most of the students to be on time, indeed, there were some who would enter adulthood with a great dread of being late, the gongs and chimes echoed in their subconscious for the rest of their lives.

They walked two by two down the hall to the refectory for their meals, no talking allowed. They stood still while Grace was said, then as quietly as the scraping chairs would allow, they sat for the meal, each at her allotted place. Partly to discourage chatting, they were read excerpts from the Bible or Lives of the Saints. Occasionally, just to make sure the students were paying attention, a question concerning the reading would be thrown at an unsuspecting student. A correct answer would merit praise from the nuns. An incorrect answer would result in a scolding, and most likely, acute indigestion.

Margaret could not complain to her parents about anything that happened at the convent because the nuns censored all correspondence leaving the convent and coming in. Naturally all letters were most discreet. She was able to tell them everything when she was sent home during Christmas, Easter and summer breaks. It made no difference however, every fall she was sent back to the convent. The treatment meted out by the teachers at the convent was not so different than other schools of that era, however. Teachers were stern and children were expected to obey.

Margaret, who lived by strict standards for herself was often shocked by the behaviour of those who didn't, until she learned that some people are simply sneaks and scoundrels.

Jackie, the sneak, had unparalleled skills in seeing the weaknesses in others. She was without conscience, a con artist, clever at concealing her real intentions in order to get exactly what she wanted. She was gifted in her ability to fool the nuns. The other girls both admired and hated her for this.

One evening she dared to do what none of the others would even think to do. She had heard that the janitor's wife had returned to him, and was sporting a fur coat from her new boyfriend. The woman was in the building with him that very evening. Jackie was a terrible gossip and yearned to hear all of the juicy details. She sneaked out of study hall to find and interview the couple. The couple, being rather unsophisticated, satisfied her with their story. Jackie hurried back with the story and related it with great relish to all the girls. They were amazed at her gall. They whispered about what would happen to her if she were found out.

She was found out. The janitor told Mother St. Phillip of her visit. She was summoned to the office of Her Majesty the Reverend Mother. The rest of the girls shuddered with anticipation. All expected the roof to blow off the convent and Jackie to be strapped within an inch of her life and thrown out of school. Jackie, the boldest lump of all, would finally be punished for all her deeds and Margaret was glad of it.

Not one hour later, Jackie returned, smug as the cat that ate the canary, and was accompanied by the wrathful Mother St. Peter. "Our dearest Jackie," she exclaimed, "has told us about you girls. How dare you all turn against her!" The veins popped in her neck, and her evil eyes bulged. "She, who had the humility to come forward and tell the Reverend Mother about her quick temper, she, who is striving to overcome a human frailty, is shunned by the rest of you. For shame!" Spittle flew out of the nun's mouth at that last exclamation. "You pour scorn on the poor young girl, oh, the grave injustice of it all!"

The girls sat dumbfounded by what had just transpired, but not one dared to open her mouth. As punishment, they were to lose all privileges and recreation for two weeks until they had learned to appreciate dear Jackie. No one could figure out how Jackie was able to deflect all blame and appear the victim of an imaginary transgression. Margaret was furious with the injustice of it all but knew that there was absolutely nothing anybody could do about it.

*A*fter Easter holidays one year, Margaret returned to school, suitcase in hand, somewhat hesitant but resigned to her fate. It was a lovely spring day. Only patches of snow remained on the grass. The streets were slushy and muddy. She walked from the train station carrying her suitcase. It wasn't very heavy. She didn't have a lot of clothes, but all the same she was fatigued by the time she reached the convent. She walked up the path and rang the front door bell.

Mother Mary Agnes received her at the door with her arms open, but not in a welcoming manner. "What do you think you're doing, coming to the front door?" She shook her arms menacingly at Margaret. "Go around to the back, where you belong!" Some thicker-skinned girls may have shrugged this encounter off, but Margaret was overly sensitive and desperately wanted to be loved and accepted. She bowed her head and slunk to the back door.

*O*nce a month, Daisy sent Margaret a shinplaster. It is a long-obsolete form of paper money worth twenty-five cents. On it was the figure "Britannia," a woman wearing a helmet and leaning on a shield. She held a trident and a shell to represent Britain's dominion over the seas. Margaret had to use this small sum to buy scribblers and pencils for school. She knew what a sacrifice it was for her parents so she used the money very carefully. She couldn't buy treats and candy like the other girls who were sent several dollars every month. The girls usually shared the candy between them but when Margaret was offered candy she rarely accepted because she had none to give in return. She envied her classmates' ability to be so carefree with their belongings. They wasted their toothpaste, scribblers, pens, pencils, everything.

One day, Margaret was sitting in class when one of her classmates turned around and grabbed her scribbler. The girl tore two pages from the center to write silly notes to pass to another student. Margaret tried so hard to conserve everything and to see her paper wasted upset her terribly and she started to cry. The girl noticed Margaret's distress and stared incomprehensively, "She's crying about two sheets of paper, can you believe it?"

They couldn't believe it. "Don't have kittens Margaret. It's only a bit of paper."

Only Margaret knew how careful she'd have to be to conserve the remainder. The line between the rich and the poor was drawn clearly in the small world of convent school.

Mother St. Peter had drawn a caustic observation. "I have always noticed that it is the poor who waste things." To Margaret, adults were becoming more and more complex. She tried to ignore the inconsistencies and the injustices but was unsuccessful.

After the nightly ritual of prayers, face washing and teeth brushing the girls filed down the hall to the dormitory to sleep. Mother St. Peter stood at the doorway of the sleeping quarters to ensure everything and everyone was in place. Every girl, as she filed past the nun, said in turn, "Goodnight Mother St. Peter." One night, Margaret's mind was on her parents and how they were getting along and failed to give the appropriate salutation.

Mother St. Peter appeared not to notice but later that night, about eleven o'clock; Margaret was shaken awake by the nun. "You are a rude and arrogant child to not bid me goodnight. Do you think you are so much better than everyone else? You should be ashamed of yourself!" Margaret was glad it was too dark to see the nun's face. She had no desire to look into those hostile eyes, or see her gaunt face grow red with anger. She was hauled over the coals for several more minutes until she was shaking in her bed.

The next morning her classmates commiserated with her, but each was glad she was not the one taking the verbal beating.

*D*uring the day, the school was made up of boys and girls other than the convent boarders. There were tall gawky farm boys, good-natured mostly in patched overalls and girls in plain skirts and blouses.

One girl, a favourite with the teacher, always came well dressed and was as smug as a well-fed cat. Big boned, pushy and inarticulate, she did her homework in a plodding way, as the plough would turn the sod. She was insensitive and doltish and learned mainly by rote. Her father ran an experimental farming station. One day the parish priest asked her in a teasing way if her job on the farm was to dust the potted plants. She was quite offended by the suggestion. Freda was not used to slights or insults of any kind and regarded her place with Mother St. Peter as her just desserts.

When the School Inspector came to call, all had to be on their best behaviour. It was important to demonstrate to him that they had learned their lessons well. Margaret was a good student who worked hard and could be depended on to answer questions correctly. Mother St. Peter called on her to answer a question and even managed a limp smile and a piercing glance that meant, "You are not to let me down."

In a fleeting moment of mischief, Margaret redirected the question saying, "Freda knows the answer to that." She didn't of course, so Margaret contritely gave the answer while a barely perceptible smile crossed the Inspector's face. Mother St. Peter was not to let this bit of defiance go unpunished. The line had been crossed. Margaret would pay the price for her insolence.

Her eyes were downcast as usual, while she endured yet another scolding from this imperious little teacher with her turned-up toes. Slender feet clad in pointy-toed black leather, severe little shoes, not a jot of compassion was apparent in her appearance. How she disliked her students. Even her feet disliked them — waggling like twin black noses at their mistakes and lack of maturity. They danced towards the children with unmistakeable rage at any infraction of her many rules — some well known to the students, others only evident when they were broken.

Margaret hated her, and wanted to love her, with all the inconsistency and fragility of her fourteen-year-old mind and heart. The nun's feet, like the sharp prows of canoes, warned her to keep her place, to cringe and submit, and never to dare let her eyes ascend to observe that turned up nose. Mother St. Peter was a dainty creature, full of anger and intimidation.

She set her course to break the spirit of her students. Her feet were the only part of her with which Margaret communicated, because her terror of the nun forced her eyes down and turned her nature to sponge. Margaret was always ready to soak up the ever-flowing punishment. She was like a puppy with its nose glued to the ground under a constantly reprimanding master. Margaret held counsel with those toes for nearly two years. She felt oppressed and impotent.

Mother St. Peter taught the students well in academics but nearly destroyed their self-esteem. She gave Margaret false hope one day, of beginning friendship, by inviting her to accompany her for a walk to the post box. Then she cast her eyes down to Margaret's feet, demanding why she had no rubbers on. Dismayed at the realization that the august honour of her intended walk hung on the slender thread of this oversight, Margaret made a frantic rush back to the boarding school for her rubbers. She should have known it was a ruse. The nun was nowhere in sight when she emerged, so she brushed the stinging tears from her eyes, and realized another truth about life. Even if it isn't raining, one must have one's rubbers on.

Margaret won in the end though. Those curling, impudent toes in their little black shoes were finally stilled the day Margaret got the strap.

Mother St. Peter rolled down the world map in front of the chalkboard and told the students that they were to trace the prevailing trade winds of the world, an assignment that she had already given for homework.

Margaret raised her hand and ventured to correct her mistake. "Mother, we have already done this for homework."

She glared at Margaret, her anger rising, "How many of you agree with this bold lump that I made a mistake in the assignment?"

Most of the boys and some of the girls raised their hands. Others sat mute with fear and frozen in their seats.

Mother St. Peter was now ripe with indignation and wrath. "All who raised their hands will stand up and hold out your hands."

She rose up and down, up and down on her toes, a strap in hand, to give them a warning of their impending doom. With dramatic rising of the strap, she swept down the aisles of extended palms. As soon as a child began to cry, she moved on to the next, until every boy and girl, big or small, was sobbing in their seats. Her toes did their demonic dance, twisting and turning, skipping and hopping along the schoolroom floor, until at last she came to Margaret.

One emotion and one resolve flooded her being as the enraged nun made for her, waving the strap and telling Margaret to hold out her hands. The emotion was terror. The resolve was not to appease her by crying. The toes danced and jumped and twisted as she hit Margaret's hands again and again with the leather strap. Not a murmur passed the young girl's lips. Harder and harder she hit. The physical pain cracked in Margaret's brain but she was no longer afraid. The final day of reckoning had come. Margaret's furious eyes blazed into hers and at last the turned-up toes touched the floor. She dropped the strap and her weary body, exhausted by her tantrum, told Margaret that she had finally won. She no longer needed to appease Mother St. Peter. She no longer needed her love. She had survived the scourge of the flesh without a whimper, now perhaps she could also survive the much more terrible scourge of the spirit.

Not all of the nuns were cruel and heartless. Mother Aloysius Joseph, or Mother Ali Joe as the girls liked to call her, was the most beloved of all the nuns. She was as Irish as Paddy's pig, a humorous and an outrageously plain spoken person who curried favour with no one. Her charm was in her rough hewn manners. She was not offensive but completely honest. She saw through layers of pretence and defensiveness to see each person's real character. She stayed out of the inner strife among the nuns by following her own head in contrast to some who seemed to draw their life's blood from rules and regulations.

She was as spare-limbed and bony-faced as a ghost. She was accepting, unpretentious and full of love for the children in her care. One day, the girls were seated for lunch when the medals for charity were being passed out. To encourage charity and charitable talk among the girls, they were to vote for each other in order to qualify for a medal. Margaret looked about and saw that Sheila was not in her place. Sheila was not uncharitable, but outspoken, like Mother Ali Joe. Margaret found Sheila in the study hall and discovered that she did not receive a medal and was devastated. Margaret put her arms around her friend to console her. Sheila was a girl who would have everyone know how tough she was and now her heart was broken. Mother Ali Joe found them weeping together and no one had to tell her why. She gathered both of them in her skinny arms and spoke soothingly, then fetched them each a meal to eat together, away from the crowd. This was one of many small acts of charity demonstrated by the old nun.

The girls in the convent saw the true, unembellished love Mother Ali Joe had for them. She never struck them and was rarely angry. She taught and encouraged them with love instead of the strap and in a way became a "mother" to children who were so far from home. The girls were drawn to her like a magnet.

It was due to the self-less work of dedicated and single-minded individuals like Mother Ali Joe that hospitals, orphanages, schools and universities were built.

In the evenings, after their homework was done, the girls got together to socialize. Some evenings, the girls congregated in the furnace room to polish their shoes and curl their hair. Margaret and the girls chatted and giggled in the close confines of the furnace room. The curling iron was placed in the open door of the furnace to make it hot. The iron was usually wielded by one of the older girls who turned hair into ringlets and waves. Margaret enjoyed having her hair curled but there was a problem in that her hair was incredibly thick. She was inevitably left with masses of curls and wild, impossible to manage hair. The following mornings she often cried with pain and frustration as it was next to impossible to get a comb through the jungle of hair.

Sometimes, the girls were invited to spend the evening at a neighbour's house. On one such evening, the older girls plodded behind Mother Angela, on their way to a monthly supper at the Stein's. There were twelve altogether, clad in winter coats and buckle-up overshoes, sliding and stumbling on the frozen ruts and giggling in fits and starts. Jeanie kept close behind Margaret. In that position she could skilfully kick snow down the back of her overshoes. Most of the girls bore Jeanie's small persecutions silently, because the nurse had explained that Jeanie had a medical condition, St. Vitas Dance, properly known as Sydenham's Chorea, and explained that she couldn't help what she did. Margaret wasn't convinced in her lack of will in these things, but had been warned not to retaliate. As the snow piled up between Margaret's black stockings and overshoes, her feet became increasingly wet and cold. Jeanie's aim was far too accurate to be accidental.

"Stop that, will you?" Margaret hissed.

"Stop what?" said Jeanie innocently, sidling up to Mother Angela with mock injury in her voice.

"Stop kicking snow in my boots!" Margaret said angrily.

"What's going on?" inquired the nun. "I've warned you to be kind young lady. Remember charity begins at home." She looked severely at Margaret and put a protective arm around Jeanie. Jeanie looked up at Mother Angela with wide-eyed innocence and then back at Margaret and stuck out her tongue.

Margaret had the impulse to rub that smug little face in the snow, but wisely resisted.

Mrs. Stein kindly dried out Margaret's stockings on the oven door and slipped a pair of her husband's wool socks over the frozen feet. After a plain but wonderful and filling supper the group embarked upon some parlour games. Parlour games were the rage in the thirties but did not take place in the parlour. Parlours were almost like chapels, quiet, clean, damp and impersonal. They were reserved for visits from priests, nuns or the bishop. Instead, the huge kitchen with a table accommodating twelve to fourteen people was the playing field for indoor games.

In one game, each plate was piled high with mashed potatoes. One person would put a bit of food on a tablespoon and pass it to the right. Each diner would add a little, until the spoon could hold no more. The toppling mess had to be eaten by whoever dropped some of it. The girls squealed and laughed long and loud at whoever had to swallow the huge spoonful of potato in one mouthful.

When the weather was warm the girls played in the straw stacks or played games of tag. The nuns taught the girls more civilized games, such as crocket and cricket. The object of crocket was to hit a ball with a wooden mallet and direct it through a wire hoop. It was a bit too tame for young, lively bodies but did provide some challenges since the lawn amounted to scraggly clumps of dried prairie cut with a scythe. The balls tended to bounce erratically, so it was mostly an exercise in frustration.

Cricket was a bit livelier. It required the girls to bat a ball and run between goal posts. Injuries sometimes occurred when some of the girls were a bit too rough as they worked out their frustrations on the playing field.

One of the diversions the young girls had was dancing with each other to Bing Crosby records on the gramophone. All the girls squealed about how handsome he was and sang his songs as well as tunes by Artie Shaw and Rudy Valley, all of the girls except Margaret. The songs all sounded pretty much the same to her. She was never much of a hero worshipper anyway. The thirties had their share of heroes and movie stars like Fred Astaire, Greta Garbo, Ginger Rogers and the Marx Brothers, but Margaret didn't have much opportunity to go to movies and so didn't join in with the girls' excited talk of Clark Gable and Joan Crawford in "Dance, Fools, Dance," or that handsome Johnny Weissmuller in "Tarzan the Ape Man."

Country music was plaintive and lonesome, and this had more appeal to her. Margaret was very aware of her reputation as a country bumpkin and didn't want to encourage any more taunting, so when the others weren't listening, she might sing country tunes, such as, "Yellow Rose of Texas" by Gene Autry, softly to herself.

> *She's the sweetest little rosebud that Texas ever knew.*
> *Her eyes as bright as diamonds, they sparkle like the dew;*
> *You may talk about your Clementine, and sing of Rosalie,*
> *But the yellow rose of Texas is the only girl for me.*

Fall fairs were a favourite with the girls. They were each allowed to make something to submit to a contest. Margaret's submission was a still life drawing of flowers in a vase, for which she received first prize. She climbed the small stage to receive her blue ribbon. The man presenting looked at Margaret in a way she found disconcerting and held her hand for such a long time she was wondering if she would ever get her ribbon.

She had no money to spend at the fair but Mother Regis generously gave her fifty cents to spend. She gratefully took the money and walked about the fair putting great thought into how to spend it. One of the booths displayed the most beautiful doll she had ever seen. The sign read, "Name the Doll and Win Her!" Margaret coveted the doll with all her heart and longed to hold it. She thought for a long time and finally came up with the name Rosalind Theresa. She truly believed that the name was so beautiful that she couldn't fail to win the prize. Margaret was thirteen years old, but still a small child at heart, and that heart was broken when she did not win the doll.

However, she still had forty-five cents and envisioned the many ways she could spend it. She could buy this or that, but not altogether of course. She had learned to be careful in her purchases by watching her mother shop. Daisy agonized on how to spend five dollars. Five dollars could buy a warm blanket, or two pillows or a small rug for the floor or a tea kettle, or some mixing bowls. There were choices to be made. What was the most indispensable item and what could wait a little longer? As long as the possibility of acquisition was there, each item could be bought in imagination, and savoured. The joy of the true acquisition lasted only a few minutes, so it was best to take your time and savour all of the possibilities. Perusing the Eaton's catalogue before Christmas was a cherished activity for the family, even if precious little was actually purchased.

Margaret showed the kind nun her purchases and the ribbon she won. Mother Regis had a kind and warm manner and she had remarked one time that all Margaret needed was a little affection and encouragement. It's too bad that the good and perceptive people of the convent did not exercise more influence in the policy making.

The children were sent home during Christmas, Easter and summer breaks. For Margaret they weren't actually breaks. She spent the time at home helping her mother and helping the neighbours. During one of Margaret's summer breaks she was sent to help out in the home of a neighbour, an old woman whose husband was dying.

Margaret sat primly on the kitchen stool that afternoon in Mrs. Messer's house on the farm, and watched the old woman curl her lip as she talked about Margaret's dad. "Yep," she confided to her lady guest named Wilma, "Bill thinks he's the only one knows how to plough a field. Figures he's doin' me a big favour. Guess he is, in a way, since I can't pay him. Since Jim's bin sick I got to depend on my neighbours and that ain't no fun. Want another cookie kid? I declare did you ever see kids so skinny as them MacCallums? This one ain't so skinny no more since she bin away to school. That family! They keep on havin' kids and they can't afford to feed the ones they got. Mrs. Daisy Mac sent her oldest one here to keep me company and I'm glad she did. Not much fun puttin' up with that dying old bag of bones over there. At least this one talks."

Margaret watched as she grabbed her cane and hobbled on her crippled leg to the small bony form on the living-room couch. The old man opened his empty, hopeless eyes to her, and then closed them again. He rubbed a fleshless index finger across his jaw. The whiskers stood out on his cheeks like the stubble on the fields outside.

"Want somethin' to eat?" she yelled at him. "No? Don't know why I ask! You just lie there day and night you old crow! Doesn't matter what good meals I cook. You see people eating and you turn your head away.

Well, it's your tough luck, eh Wilma? We won't let roast beef and gravy go to waste or pie neither!"

Her cotton dress hung a little crooked on her wide rear-end and the bad leg sent the flowered material sweeping across Margaret's legs where she sat near the doorway, sending a shiver down the young girl's spine.

"God a-mighty a person gets tired carin' for the sick! If only he weren't so darn ugly. Even worse now that there's no flesh on them bones. I remember when our first boy was born. I took him to the photographer to get his picture taken. 'This picture ain't no good,' I told him. 'What do you expect?' he says, 'with such an ugly baby? Too bad he takes after his father!' Ha Ha Ha!"

Her witch-like cackle sent another shiver down Margaret's spine and she looked at the forlorn heap on the couch to see how he took the insult. The sick man was beyond caring and a fly made a lazy meandering journey across his sunken cheeks. He couldn't brush it off, so Margaret made her way timidly toward him to shoo the fly away.

"Stay away from him girl or you might catch what he got! Pour me and Wilma some more tea and make yourself useful for a change!"

She backed away from the old man and poured the tea like she was told and watched with great distaste as the old woman loudly slurped her tea. The wart on her chin seemed to get bigger everyday and Margaret noticed with disgust that two or three grey hairs were sprouting from it. "Why do some farm women have so many warts on their faces?" She had the sense to keep her thoughts to herself. If her face was kind Margaret certainly wouldn't have cared about the warts. Then the old man gave a sigh, and it startled everyone because he'd been so still.

"Did you want somethin' Jim? Are you too warm or somethin'?"

Her sudden kind tone horrified Margaret, probably because she sensed the awful meaning. A rattling, gurgling sound suddenly emitted from the shape on the couch. A hand clutched up as if reaching for an unseen object on the ceiling, then it fell limply, and the body began to shudder.

"Take the girl outside Wilma. No use her seein' more than she has to. Go home girl and get your mother. Go on now! I need her to help me. It's only a short run, so hurry!"

Margaret did run home to her mom. She ran away as fast as she could.

$\mathcal{S}$ometimes it seemed that the drought of the dirty thirties would never end. On one particularly hot day, the MacCallum's good friend Jake sat at his kitchen table. The fried egg had lost its appeal so he scraped the remainder of it and the bacon rind into the slop pail outside the back door. The hot, dry wind blew his face as he surveyed the weeds in his yard. The summers seemed to get hotter every year in this dry little town, but lack of rain never seemed to discourage the weeds; dry raspy thistles, which snarled around Jake's thin, bowed legs. The burrs stuck to his socks whenever he made his way across the yard. Good thing he had the scythe! He planned to use it as soon as the sun went down. Meanwhile he returned to the house to get the dishes done. He dipped a small quantity of water from the reservoir on the side of the coal stove and splashed it over the dishes. Then he dried them and placed them carefully on the shelf overhead. Then he gave the bare board floor of his one room shack a sweep with a lop-sided broom and settled down to fill his pipe from a tin of Ogden's pipe tobacco.

It was the summer of 1935. Jake Clemens was getting old and that's all he was getting. He turned this thought over in his mind as the smoke leaked out of the corner of his mouth. He didn't have many friends either except for Bill and his wife Daisy and four kids who lived across the street. They were almost as poor as he was and Daisy was expecting another baby. He really shouldn't let her do his washing. Scrubbing on the board was hard work in her condition. Still, he was getting pretty weak and tired. Bill had to take him home yesterday when he was on the way back from the post office. He had taken a dizzy spell and would have fallen off the sidewalk if he had not grabbed a telephone pole. He went round and round the blame thing. "Laws Moses!" He didn't know what got into him, just circling that post as if he didn't know the way home. He sure wasn't the Rough Rider he used to be, who rode with Teddy Roosevelt up San Juan Hill when he was young. The thought of his youth set him to rummaging in the old round-topped trunk beside his bed. Kneeling on the floor, he pulled out an old picture of himself in uniform and held it out to squint uncertainly at his past.

Jake had not planned to be a big shot — hadn't planned to end up this poor either. Seventy years old and too proud to go on relief. He had a nephew on a farm north of town who managed to drop off a bag of groceries when Jake wasn't looking. He wasn't much of a one to take handouts if he could help it. Bill and Daisy invited him for supper most nights. That was all right because they exchanged good turns, especially in the past when he was stronger. He wished one of their kids would come over to see him for a while. He would tell them again how he rode as a Rough Rider for Teddy Roosevelt in the Spanish American War.

"Si," he would say, "there I was just a-doozin' along, just a-doozin' along, si." His recollections took him along many a trail. In the heat of summer many years past, his horse, startled by a jackrabbit, threw him over the saddle. "Si! And in the dead of winter, si, I would find my pant leg frozen to the horse's side owing to having to attend to nature as best I could."

Funny, he mused, how he came up to Canada to live and ended up in a little shack with a yard full of weeds, blown in as it were, with the most meagre of supplies. He really must cut the weeds with his scythe as soon as he felt better. Maybe Bill would help him. He didn't think he would bother with supper. He wasn't hungry and it was too hot. He felt kind of dizzy so he put his pipe down on the table. He thought he had better lay down until he got his breath. He headed towards his bed.

Jake didn't hear one of the kids knock on the door the next day. George wanted to borrow the scythe. The weeds had grown waist high in their yard too. The knocking persisted and the childish voice called, "Hey Jake, are you in there?" Then a pause and, "Hey Jake, I want to borrow your scythe!"

Jake was past caring about weeds or anything else, wedged as he was between the single bed and the round-topped trunk. He was in a half sitting position, his elbows propped up by the edge of the cot and the lid of the trunk. His fists were clenched across his chest, eyes staring; the summer heat intensifying the heavy smell in the room. The air in the tiny cabin smelt sickly sweet as the hot July day dealt with his lifeless body. He was just stuck there, like a weather beaten, leafless old tree. Bent and grey and hard, fists clenched, his thin arms bent at the elbow but slightly raised and rigid, as if he were asking someone to help him get to his feet. He died alone as he had lived. If he had cried out for help in his last agony, no one heard him and his staring sightless eyes gave no clue. Outside, the scythe lay inert among the defiant weeds.

They reached out to touch him, gingerly at first. George was thirteen and Margaret fourteen years old and they stared at his dead face, barely able to believe it. They were speechless for a time and then wondered if they should pull him out and lay him down in a more comfortable position. He looked like someone in a trap and they wanted to help. That he was past any help or comfort finally took hold in their stunned brains, so they ran to tell their parents.

Jake was buried a day or so later after a small church service. The air in the church was hard to breathe in that confined space as Jake hadn't been found soon enough for the undertaker to perform the usual treatment to the body. They buried him in the village cemetery and his nephew had a small headstone placed to mark the spot of his final repose.

Jake was a great friend to the MacCallum family. Seven years earlier he had done them a great favour that was never forgotten. They were three months behind in the rent and Bill was out of work. The landlord had demanded that all of their goods and chattels be sold at public auction. It was their friend Jake who in a loud voice commanded that the sale be stopped and handed the landlord enough money to pay back the rent. This proud, independent man, who would rather die of starvation than ask for a favour for himself, had traveled the countryside to save them. This act of love was never forgotten by any of them and he was as surely a member of their family as if they were related by blood. When the family moved to the town where he lived they rented a house across from his. He was invited to many meals and Daisy did his washing every week on her washboard. When she was expecting a baby she considered telling Jake that it was getting too much for her, but she never had the heart to do so and when he died she was thankful that she had never refused.

He owned two horses and a wagon and did odd jobs for neighbours, hauling stuff from place to place. The MacCallum children were always honoured guests in his little shack. They would not be at his home long before he would bend over the edge of his open trunk looking for some long stored candy for them. Who knows how many years that candy had lain hidden in the trunk? It was as hard as granite but they sucked on it anyway. Meanwhile he would sit on the edge of his cot and grin at them in his toothless way, so pleased that they were enjoying his buried treasure. He would sit and listen to their views on life as if they were adults and they left with the idea that they had impressed him. He had little formal education, but much wisdom.

He was a part of their life, a rambler of tales of bygone days, tales he traded with Bill who traded stories with him while the kids lay

Old Jake, in the Drumheller river valley.

draped across their dad's knees, half-asleep and half-listening to tales that sometimes began, "By Gee, I mind the time the old geezer would never take a bath, but we got out the old Fels Naptha soap..." While the children dozed the stories meandered across prairie blizzards, driving old Maud and Bette and just by the time they were nearly all as frozen as pikestaffs, the faithful old horses would deliver them to some homestead or other, where the occupants would thaw them out and feed them. Old Jake's eyes would glaze over as he recalled "dozin' along" on his old nag until nature called. Then he would leave a pile of icicles by the side of the road. "Beggin' your pardon Ma'am", he would apologize to Daisy, his toothless mouth agape.

One evening Margaret nearly scared poor Jake to death by delivering his white bundle of laundry to him in the evening. She came around the side of his shack, her burden aloft and called out, "Jake, are you here?" Both hands clutched his heart as he thought an angel was addressing him, and she had to spend five minutes reassuring him.

Jake didn't have much in the way of worldly goods. There was a narrow bed, two wooden kitchen chairs, a small wooden table, a washstand and basin, a pail for drinking water and one for slop, a small coal and wood stove, a coal oil lamp and his precious trunk. That old wooden chest was his life's memories, the repository of his simple treasures, his private wishing well for children. Jake spent a goodly portion of his life plumbing its depths to find little treats for others.

*B*oarding school was a difficult adjustment for Margaret, but coming home for holidays was also difficult. She tried to keep up her friendships with the girls back in Munson, but it was difficult since she saw them only occasionally. She was also a shy child who had difficulty in social situations. The girls in the church got together once a week to socialize. Margaret was only able to attend meetings when she came home for holidays, so she never contributed much. Mostly, she sat in the corner and bit her lips.

The president of the Girls' Club rose to conduct the business part of the meeting. The subject was the Christmas hamper to be given to the poor of the village. Eighteen or twenty girls turned their faces toward the president with interest. "This year I would like to suggest that we give a hamper to the MacCallums," she said. "Mr. MacCallum has been out of work and they're pretty poor."

"Yeah, and I hear they're expecting another baby!" trilled a voice from the back. The speaker was a girl of Russian heritage who had suffered many times from unkind remarks. Some of the girls called her "Bohunk."

Margaret squeezed as far as she could in the shadow of the china cabinet. It was evening and the living room of the postmaster's house was crowded with girls she had known since grade one. She had lived in this town for so many years but had never felt one of the gang.

"Could we have a vote on that?" asked the president. "All in favour of giving the MacCallums a hamper raise your hand."

One hand did not rise. Both of Margaret's hands were gripping the edges of her chair. With an unhappiness that bordered on despair she struggled for the courage to speak up. No courage surfaced, only shame. It was terrible to be timid and afraid of everyone. Terrible to be fourteen and not accepted by the gang. Things were bad enough, and now a hamper.

Not long after Christmas though, came the best present of all. In the winter of 1936, Eddy was born. He was named Edward after Edward VIII. The family went wild with joy.

Margaret exclaimed, "I feel like standing on the rooftops and shouting about Eddy so that everyone can hear!"

Bernie chimed in "I'm going to feed him his bottle and carry him everywhere."

Daisy was forty-seven years old and Bill was fifty-nine when they had Eddy. He was a blessing to the whole family.

At the convent, nothing much had changed, except that screechy voiced, irritating Mother Mary Agnes became an ally of Margaret's one day following another incident of snow kicking by the ever present Jeanie. It was true that the child was sick, but Margaret suspected that some of her behaviour was put on. A nurse told the girls that the condition would cause Jeanie to have jerky, uncontrolled movements in her body, but Jeanie would throw things at the other girls, or dump over a wastebasket, or suddenly push someone against a wall. It was pretty hard to ignore the sudden attacks.

On the class's next walk down the snowy road, Jeanie decided to repeat her trick of filling Margaret's boots with snow. She believed she could count on Mother Mary Agnes' support no matter what and began to torment Margaret by following her closely behind kicking snow with great accuracy. Margaret jumped and dodged to no avail, and the ordeal continued both to their destination and back.

Finally, back at the playroom door, Margaret stooped to empty her boots, and saw Jeanie bend down to pack a snowball. She sent it flying and Margaret ducked just in time. The snowball missed her by inches. It sailed through the playroom door and scattered all over the beautifully waxed floor. A very angry Mother Angela entered the room and ordered Margaret to clean up the mess. All protests of innocence were ignored. After cleaning up the sloppy wet mess, Margaret went with the other girls to supper, but just as she was about to sit down at the table, Jeanie kicked the chair away and Margaret fell with a hard thump on the floor. At that point, all reason departed and Margaret flew at Jeanie, screaming with fury. With both fists flying she thumped and pummelled Jeanie until she cried for mercy.

Mother Angela pulled Margaret off Jeanie and restrained her. "You! Off to bed without your supper!"

Margaret obeyed, and left the room with her head held high, triumphant that she finally had some sort of justice. About a half hour later, Mother Mary Agnes appeared with a tray loaded with food. She said nothing, but smiled and winked at Margaret.

Chapter Six

Girl to Woman

_A_er victory over Mother St. Peter released Margaret from a childish need to be accepted and loved by her. However, the experience left her troubled and defiant. She developed a perverse need to be punished and sought to irk her teachers and even extracted a little pleasure in their attempts to punish her. It was a way to shield her from the shards of their belittling remarks and insults.

Though part of her remained a little child, another part became a fledgling adult trying very hard to understand what she should be and do. By the age of fifteen Margaret became increasingly aware of her passionate urgings. The knowledge of her growing sexuality was tempered by innocence and strict morality dictated by society and the nuns at the convent. The girls had few opportunities to talk to boys without an adult present. The nuns would rather have died than let their charges be subjected to any moral danger and the girls were guarded like sacred vessels. Most of the girls were not bothered by the censorship and protectiveness, in fact, few were actually aware of it. It was simply the way things were in the 1930's.

Over time, Margaret came to realize that the nuns at the convent, in particular Mother St. Peter, were human beings, who had faults and imperfections like anyone else. She would hold individuals responsible for her mistreatment, not the Church. Margaret loved her church and she loved her God. She did not lose her faith in either.

After graduating from the convent at age sixteen, she returned to Munson for high school full of feelings of impatience and defiance. She felt trapped in a bleak, dull town devoid of opportunities and asked, "Is this how I will spend the rest of my life?" In her mind the answer was a definite "No." No silence, no complacency, no patience with things as they were.

She resented her lot in life and though she loved her parents, for a time she held them responsible for her situation. What had they done wrong to deserve to live in poverty? Why were they so poor when others had money? Try as she might, she could not find the answers to her questions.

Her father was a very hard worker and was willing to do any kind of work that would bring some income to his family. He did odd jobs for farmers and local business men, and finally, in about 1938, he took an opportunity for steady work. He became the caretaker of Munson School, where his children attended. There was some discrimination in the town hurled against the MacCallums because some thought it was a lowly job, but they tried not to pay attention. The children helped their father out with the cleaning after school. It gave them money for groceries anyway, and a few other things.

Margaret was very close to her dad. He was a very generous, tender and gentle person, but in typical teenage, bigheaded thinking she thought she knew more than he did, and they sometimes argued. As she matured she blushed to think of what she said in her teenage wisdom, telling her dad about life.

Bill's only consolation for his years of being unable to find steady employment was in his children's progress at school. In them he found his hope and his joy. The children had every incentive to do well, because they wanted to get out from under the crushing weight of poverty.

The dirty thirties were almost at an end and the economy would soon experience another boom, but the people of the time did not yet know that. There were still many families on relief and wide-spread unemployment. Margaret spent many years watching her worried father try to scratch out a living. She worried along with him and grew to become a great worrier herself.

The passage from childhood to adulthood is never an easy one. Young people yearn to be treated as adults, but fear that they will be held accountable for the bad decisions they make. How sweet it would be to pass the buck to mom and dad. "It's not my fault. I didn't make the mistakes that brought us to this place in these circumstances." But with the knowledge comes culpability, and Margaret came to recognize that she was to blame for the mistakes she would make. That painful day of reckoning came when she realized that she must grow up and be responsible for her own life.

One of the least liked girls in the town was Maryanne. She was devious and cruel, and loved to strike fear into the other children. On a Sunday afternoon a group of the schoolgirls, all in their early teens, decided to go for a stroll. Maryanne was with them of course, but none of the girls was suspicious of the dark thoughts that lurked in her brain though her tendency to be unpredictable was no secret. She always had the element of surprise on her side. Suddenly, with a war whoop that struck terror in their hearts she lunged for the girls and they sprang forward like a herd of antelopes in instant flight, while this crazed wild girl shrieked at their heels.

A feeling of shame overrode prudence on Margaret's part, and she turned to face her attacker. She was soon to realize that a show of bravery must be backed with some realistic means of defence, and Margaret had none.

"You can make the others run," Margaret breathed heavily, "but I'm not afraid of you." What a lie, and it was to be her last one for a while. She pounced on Margaret like a wolf on a sheep, pounding, slapping, biting, scratching, kicking, enjoying her sport, not angry at all. The blows rained on Margaret like hailstones while she flailed her arms in impotent fury at the injustice of it all. She burned with a desire to teach Maryanne a lesson, to punish her for her monstrous behaviour, but inflicted not one telling blow. Instead, Maryanne finished Margaret off by flinging her to the ground and rubbing her face in some ashes that had spilled on the dirt road. Margaret felt like she was the victim of an attempted murder, and rose from the ashes of her defeat, literally, with only humiliation for company, and dragged herself home.

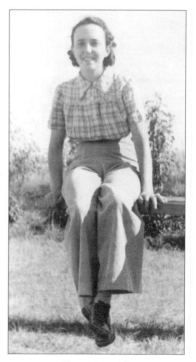

Margaret, age 16.

For weeks she nursed her pain and shame and withdrew from her peers. She put up with Maryanne's contempt in front of all her classmates. She dreamed of the day when she could get her revenge. She waited and schemed.

One day, Maryanne decided to court Margaret's friendship again. She sidled up to Margaret and asked her if she would come to her house and curl her hair. She possessed some mastery of psychology. Why not ask some favour of one you have injured? Gain their trust, so that you can stab them in the back again! Margaret would not be so easily fooled. She lusted for justice.

It was the days of rag curlers just before the advent of pin curlers and a cheap alternative to heat permanents. Margaret tore some old rags into thin strips and went to work. Maryanne's hair was thick, fine and silky, freshly washed in rainwater. Margaret took small strands of her hair and wound each strand tightly on the rag, securing each with a hard granny knot. When her head was covered with dozens of these bandages, Margaret left her alone, to spend the night on her crown of thorns.

The next day Maryanne came to school an hour late. Her hair was standing in a tangled mass of tight corkscrews with bits of thread from the rags peeking out of the mess. She looked like the victim of an electric shock. She announced in an aggrieved voice that she was late because Margaret had curled her hair and it took two hours to remove the rags. She couldn't put a comb through it and furthermore, she had been unable to sleep because of the hard lumps on her head and her head was still aching.

"Isn't that too bad," Margaret said, but inwardly her heart sang like a bird.

Financial conditions were very tough for her family the fall when she was to enter grade twelve. This was more than usually serious because there were books to buy and other unusual expenses with no source in sight to fill the need. That was when Margaret decided to go cooking for threshers on a farm. It would mean missing the first few weeks of school but it was better than not being able to go to school at all.

The farmhouse turned out to be a series of shacks with adjoining doors. Her narrow bed seemed clean enough but the board floors had the smell of recently applied water sloshed over layers of years-old mud. The owner was a bachelor who had a housekeeper of twenty-one years of age named Betty, who had a three-year-old child but no husband. She was friendly enough but seemed far more concerned with entertaining the seven or eight hired men than in getting the meals on time.

Mealtime was a despairing time for Margaret. "You'll find the knives, forks and spoons scattered around the yard," Betty said. She did not consider it at all unusual to let her little daughter play with the dishes and utensils as long as they were gathered up before the meal. This involved a search under the porch, in the weeds, under the stove in the kitchen and wherever her imagination would lead her. While Margaret dashed around frantically making sure that the vegetables were put on the stove on time, Betty would be sitting holding hands with one of the boys or lying stretched out with them on the couch. She explained to Margaret that they weren't feeling well and she had to look after them. There seemed to be a lot of sickness among the men that fall. The boss was a very nice man, but Margaret wondered how Betty got away with speaking so boldly to him. She told him what to order from the Eaton's catalogue and in general, how to run his farm.

One day it rained too hard for the men to work in the fields so Betty took Margaret to town for the afternoon. When Margaret enquired anxiously how they would be able to get supper on the table Betty shrugged and hustled her into the truck and away they went. Although she seemed to be very cozy with the men, she protected Margaret like a mother hen and quickly discouraged any leering cast in Margaret's direction.

The first place they headed for when they got to town was the hotel. She met some of her friends at the door but told them that she couldn't bring Margaret in because she was too young. They smelled strongly of beer and Margaret recognized some of them as men her dad had known for years.

Next Betty took Margaret across the tracks to see her sister who was still in bed though it was past noon. They talked together about the man whom she had spent the night with. This seemed rather odd to Margaret who was exceedingly naïve even for seventeen. The nature of the girls' profession did not register for several days.

About five o'clock they returned to the farm to make supper. This was done with considerable haste by cutting the vegetables in small pieces and adding lots of salt. The stove was stuffed with kindling until the lids were red.

Margaret found it difficult to sleep that night because one of the men, a plump, red-faced fellow kept peering in her window and making signs for her to join him outside. She was too frightened to yell for help, so instead covered her head with blankets and prayed for morning to come fast.

As the bacon and eggs sizzled in swimming fat the next morning and the men sat leering at the women over their food, it all became too much for Margaret. Everything went black before her eyes and she crumpled in a heap on the floor. She was carried to the car and taken home by the man who owned the farm. She had worked for four days and had four dollars in her hand as pay. It did help toward buying her books but she was not proud of her endurance on her first job.

*O*ne summer night, Margaret and her sister Bernie made their way down the wooden sidewalk to the town hall. Their summer dresses drooped from their thin shoulders, and revealed their skinny legs below the knees.

"Some way to go to a dance, without a boyfriend," Margaret said.

"I know," replied Bernie, "I feel sort of silly."

"We probably won't get a dance anyway," they choused, and then broke out in nervous giggles at the coincidence.

They were still giggling as they entered the hall, and found a space on a bench beside the wall and sat down, squeezing their hands together to gain control. Shoulders shaking, legs crossed, they waited out the giggles. Bernie started to cough a little, in a sort of bronchial wheeze.

"Should have brought your sweater," Margaret said.

"Then I really would look like a sad sack."

The hall became more crowded so before long, lines of young people, mostly girls, were standing in front of them. For a while it was sort of

Bernie and Margaret

comforting to be hidden behind a line of other hopefuls. It also gave a temporary excuse for not being chosen to dance. After a while, it got boring and anxiety began to creep in.

"Roll out the barrel…" thumped the piano accompanied by a frenzied violin, and several couples whirled off. Big, fat Mr. Benson made his way across the floor. He liked picking smallish young women to dance with because he could support them partly suspended on his huge belly. Their feet would hardly get a chance to touch the floor, so he never stepped on their toes. He picked Margaret, and away they went, accompanying the music at a spinning pace. Bernie averted her eyes when she saw "Nick the Arm Pumper" coming her way. His idea of dancing was to swing his partner's right arm up and down, in a wide arc, and leap and turn erratically all over the floor. To her surprise he picked the girl next to her, just as she was getting set to refuse him. She felt slightly miffed for some reason.

The most desirable men all had steady girl friends. Those couples would whirl and swoop to the music in a close embrace. They danced as one body in perfect time, no doubt accomplished after much practice.

"I wouldn't let someone hold me that close anyway," said Bernie proudly.

"Would you care to dance?" someone asked her suddenly. She rose to dance with the tall young man who smelled strongly of beer. He was a little unsteady on his feet but they made a few rounds without incident. As he directed her to her seat he suggested that they go outside for some fresh air.

"No thanks," she replied, "it's plenty fresh in here." The young man departed and Bernie turned to her sister. "I wonder why we bother coming to these stupid dances."

"It's okay if you're one of the popular ones, and I think you have to be fast to be popular."

"What's fast?"

"It has something to do with relations with boys. Never mind, just forget I said it."

"Whatever it is, we're sure not popular."

Some girls got up and danced with each other. It was better than waiting forever for some guy to issue and invitation.

Margaret and Bernie looked at each other and again said in unison, "I'd rather die than dance with another girl."

The sad part was always the time when the band played, "I'll Dance the Last Dance with You," or "When I Get Too Old to Dream," all hope that some dreamboat would walk them home faded away. It was such a short distance home that it made sense to walk. There was no reason to get into a car with a man, unless they wanted to kiss or something. Sleepy and just slightly disappointed, and with wilted rag-curls sagging with their spirits, they walked home once more, without a man.

Small town girl, thin, shy, pale,
Weeping a little inside,
Shoulders slightly stooped.
Sad
No one came to ask her to dance.
Large eyes, shiny black hair
Silently hoping, maybe now,
No, another girl.
Ashamed to sit, afraid to stand,
Invisible girl.
Resigned to loneliness,
A misfit.
Good-bye dancehall,
Snappy music
Bong, bong, bong,
Chords throbbing
Tears, quick exit.

Chapter Seven

School Teacher

$\mathcal{M}$argaret left Munson and entered Normal School in Calgary to begin her teacher training at age nineteen. She enjoyed her new found independence and made some good friends. The only down part was that the Second World War had started and many young men had to go away to fight.

Men seemed to be a vanishing breed, due to the war, and many girls forgot their pride in the shameless pursuit of any male available. If he happened to fill out a uniform he was virtually irresistible. Hence, the song, "Bless 'em all, the long and the short and the tall..." There was urgency, an excitement; a romance must develop before it was too late! "Getting a man" took precedence over "getting a school" upon graduation, for many of the teachers in training. As one cartoon of the day portrayed it, a girl says wistfully that she isn't so concerned about getting a "job" in a certain school, it's just the "principal" of the thing.

Sad and deplorable as the war was, it had a way of hurrying along the youth in their desire to savour life while life exists. There were no long engagements or taking time to get acquainted. As for the women who were preparing to be teachers, they had to compete with the girls in uniform, who like their brothers, had entered that enchanted world by enlisting in the armed forces. The plainest wallflower newly attired in a uniform became a woman of mystery. Margaret and the other new teachers had to stay put in their country schools when they were finally placed, while the girls in uniform travelled to far away places to serve their country in a far more glamorous capacity. They were able to follow the men and maybe get engaged over seas.

Margaret's yearbook from 1941-42 repeats the refrain over and over again, in the short remarks under their pictures. They liked to "make their own clothes," "go to dances," or "get a job teaching somewhere." Most of all, oh shameless hussies that they were, they were very determined to "get their man," no matter what.

It took the outbreak of World War II to pull Canada out of the Depression. Europe was in great need of materials to fight the war, and an increase in demand of raw materials was a boon to Canada's economy. The mining and manufacturing industries picked up until there were more than enough jobs for everyone. Farmers found the price of their goods also rise and thanks be to God, the drought had finally ended. Prosperity was everywhere.

The Canadian people listened to the radio to hear Sir Winston Churchill's voice booming over the airwaves. To Canadians, it seemed very remote and far removed from their everyday lives. Most people in Canada were not affected by the suffering of so many people far away, until September 10, 1939, when Canada entered World War II by declaring war on Germany. Canada's role was to defend the British Isles. They also defended Hong Kong against the Japanese invasions. Canadians took part in the Battle of Dieppe, and many other battles on mainland Europe. Many thousands of Canadian soldiers lost their lives or were wounded or taken prisoner.

Out of the thousands of Canadians who lost their lives were five young men from Munson. One of these was the druggist's only son. Margaret's brother George joined up as a pilot in the Royal Canadian Air Force and served overseas. He was one of the lucky ones who came home unharmed.

The war was brought close to home when Alberta built three internment camps to hold German and Italian prisoners of war in 1942. The sites chosen were Kananaskis, Medicine Hat and Lethbridge. By the end of the war there were close to 38,000 POWs in Canadian camps.[5]

On May 7, 1945, the German forces unconditionally surrendered and in August, 1945, the United States dropped atomic bombs on Japan and they too unconditionally surrendered.

Officially, the Great Depression ended in 1939 with the start of the Second World War, but it took some time for the province to regain economic stability. During the 1930's and 1940's, teaching jobs were hard to find, and Alberta's Normal Schools produced a surplus of teachers. Teachers faced difficult working conditions and low pay, as many school districts paid below the minimum wage of $840.00 a year. Rural school trustees had the most trouble raising local taxes to pay teachers. Schools fell into disrepair

[5] www.collections.ic.gc.ca/courage/canadasroleinwwii

and had few teaching supplies. Books and teaching resources were few or nonexistent.[6]

It was not easy to be a teacher in the 1930's and 1940's. Young women and sometimes men, nineteen or twenty years old, were sent to remote rural areas to teach. They were often responsible for grades one to eight, and sometimes even grades one to eleven, all in one room. In rural schools there was rarely indoor plumbing and drinking water had to be ported in. A potbellied stove provided heat and it was the teachers who had to chop the wood and start a fire before the children arrived at school in the morning. They were expected to do the janitorial work as well. They were often housed in a teacherage or boarded with local farmers and teachers could be dismissed from their positions for any reason.

Margaret, age 21.

Teaching methods of the time emphasized memorization and drill. It was a long time before Alberta adopted more progressive methods such as learning by doing and taking into consideration the interests of the child.

In 1935, the UFA (United Farmers of Alberta) passed the Teaching Profession Act, and introduced a number of improvements for teachers. Former Premier William Aberhart, who died in office in 1943, was a former teacher. He was succeeded by Ernest Manning who served as premier until 1968. Major advances were made in the status of the teaching profession during this period. Teachers were at last given job security and better living conditions.

*A*fter completing Normal School in February 1942, Margaret became a certified teacher. Her first teaching position near the town of Youngstown,

---

[6] www.teachers.ab.ca/Albertas+Education+System/History+of+Public+Education

Alberta paid her the pitiful sum of $65.00 a month, well below minimum wage of $84.00 a month. Teachers were not paid during the months of July and August. She arrived at the beginning of March to complete the school year for a teacher who left. She was able to acquire room and board from a local resident, whose farm was within walking distance of the school.

Margaret stood in the middle of the kitchen floor looking at him. The farmhouse was big and unpainted outside. Inside it was functional, clean and drab. One bare electric bulb glowed dimly from a wire hanging from the ceiling, powered by a farm generator.

The stark light from the bulb shone on the bulky figure in front of Margaret. He said, in a joking manner, "I'm the Lord and Master of the ranch," but Margaret sensed that he meant it. "I just put in the power last year so we have electric lights."

He looked her over and Margaret flinched a little under the scrutiny. She said, "How many children do you have?"

"Twelve. You will teach the younger six. The rest are grown up. Two are married and live on other farms."

"Where do I sleep?" she asked, wondering how all those bodies that can recline under one roof.

"Upstairs," he answered, indicating a steep flight of steps behind her, "The wife fixed up a room for you."

His eyes were dark and bold and she winced at the words "the wife." She always hated a man to refer to his wife as if she were an old cow or a piece of machinery.

His two older sons, who brought her there in an old truck twenty-five miles from town, looked at him, then at her. They appeared to be too old to be still living at home. They seemed to have a child-like respect for their father, or perhaps it was subservience.

He had a thick Dutch accent, and bragged as he talked about his farm. Margaret was unimpressed. She didn't care what a big boss he was. She was nervous about starting her teaching new job at age twenty, and was just looking for reassurance that she would be treated well.

It was dark, about four o'clock in the morning. The train didn't reach the town until two o'clock a.m. She was tired and allowed herself to be led upstairs to a small room that would be hers for four months or so. In the room was a homemade dresser of apple boxes covered somewhat inadequately with a flowered cotton flounce. A small mirror was tacked on the wall. Beside the dresser was a wooden chair. The narrow bed was covered with a patchwork quilt and had plain iron posters at the head and foot. Underneath the bed was a chamber pot, and on another apple box was a basin and pitcher of cold water. There was no indoor plumbing.

He pointed to a book of notes on the chair in Margaret's bedroom, "The teacher before you made lots of notes about the kids' work. She sure was good. Better read the notes so you know what to do."

"You're not a subtle man." she thought.

He descended the stairs heavily and Margaret climbed between the icy sheets.

In the morning she looked out the window and saw that the snow had drifted onto the narrow ledge outside her window. She heard him yell orders to his boys near the barn. The "Lord and Master" was keeping everyone busy carrying pails of milk, bringing horses out of the barn, and bringing eggs to the house. His stoop shouldered wife tramped like a Clydesdale through the heavy snow.

Margaret came downstairs unsure of what to do with her night offerings sloshing in the chamber pot. She saw an outhouse to the north of the house but had a hard time bringing herself to appear for the first time in front of his wife and children carrying a chamber of wastes to dump in the toilet hole at the back of the house. She wondered if her predecessor has anything in her notes to cover these circumstances. Feeling a little embarrassed, she ducked outside to the outhouse and came back in again, watched constantly by the children. She resigned herself to the fact that she would have no privacy in that house.

"Hello," he greeted her as she took her place at the long table. He then recited the names of all his children. Two of them ducked under the table and peered at her shyly or slyly, she wasn't sure which. They appeared distrustful, like wild kittens that disappear under the wooden sidewalk at the approach of a stranger. The family didn't see many people in this dried out country where farms are so far apart. Early settlers, less hardy than these, had already left the country, leaving him with six and a half sections of land, over 4000 acres, that he bought "cheaply." The cattle roamed the land dotted with alkali sloughs and gopher holes. It would take more than six sections of land so sparsely grassed to feed the cattle and horses.

How he swaggered as he told his children what to do. Even the grown up ones bowed their heads and obeyed his commands without question.

His wife sat sullenly as he stroked her legs under the table while they ate their meal. A long-suffering, apathetic look froze her features. She didn't smile when he spoke to her or return his caresses. The girls seemed not to notice but the young men, his sons, averted their eyes and looked ashamed. He blew out his stomach with great importance as he sat at the table.

"Hill Billy," Margaret thought with distain, except that there were no hills in this part of the country, only flat prairie. "What should I call a fat man like you, who has been isolated on the prairies too long, maybe, 'big frog in a dried puddle'?"

His wife came to life momentarily when he chided his children about not getting up early enough. "Why don't you get up early yourself?" she said with undisguised bitterness, "you and your bad heart."

"I'm not worried," he answered her smugly; "I have enough kids around to do the chores."

"Some accomplishment," Margaret thought to herself, "to raise a large family to be your slaves on this barren hell of a farm."

The road that led to the schoolhouse was no more than a well-worn track. The area's small population did not warrant the laying of gravel for a proper road. The word "School" was printed on a sign that hung unevenly by chains over the door. The small wooden building stood forlorn by the side of the road. The paint was chipped and wild grass grew knee high in the quarter acre or so of land that was the children's playground. There was no swing set or any other kind of playground equipment.

Margaret opened the door of the school and entered the cloakroom. The wall of the cloakroom was lined with hooks for the children's coats. Rounding the corner she saw rows of wooden desks of various sizes and a chalkboard. A map of Canada hung on the wall beside the Union Jack flag. She would be responsible for a class of twenty-eight students from grades one to nine. She would also be responsible for chopping the wood to feed the pot bellied stove in the corner of the room, but because spring was approaching, it was unlikely she would have to light it very often. A broom and mop and pail also stood in the corner, indicating she had to do all the janitor work as well.

She opened various cupboards and found a sparse but adequate supply of paper, pencils and books. Things were still scarce in the 1940's, though the country was slowly pulling out of the depression. Opening the right hand drawer of the teacher's desk she found a leather strap. She had never before held a strap in her hands, though she had certainly felt its sting. She smacked it soundly on the top of the desk, and the sound reverberated in the quiet room. She replaced it in drawer and decided she would use it sparingly, if at all.

The students filed into the classroom the following morning, and looked at their teacher with curiosity. They were a rag tag bunch of kids, all from local farms. The youngest was a tiny girl of six, who spoke little English. The oldest was a big fifteen-year-old farm boy who towered over Margaret.

She spent the first part of the morning trying to get to know the students and then attempted to start the lessons. It wasn't long before some of the bigger boys put the new teacher to the test by throwing pencils and wads of paper at each other. Their shenanigans escalated into shoving matches at which point Margaret brought out the leather strap. A hard crack on the desk of the worst perpetrator was enough to bring order to the room. Margaret could then get down to the business of teaching.

Margaret came home from school early one afternoon and hurried around a corner of the house too fast. There she saw the Lord and Master sending an arch of pee into the dusty yard, sending the chickens squawking and scurrying out of the way. She pretended not to notice but he turned around and leisurely did up his fly, not embarrassed at being caught. He leered at her and she concluded that she would be very glad to see the end of June.

Occasionally, Margaret would get a ride into Youngstown. There, she would do a little shopping and go to the post office. One day, a letter had arrived from overseas from her boyfriend Michael, a sweet, caring man who joined the army. He was overseas fighting in Europe. She was a little worried about what she would say to him in her return letter. He wanted her to wait for him so that they could get married. Margaret was torn. She had met someone else. Well, like it or not, it had to be done. She would have to break up with Michael. He would be sad, but he'd get over it someday.

Poor Margaret lived to regret the decision to break up with Michael. The parents of her new boyfriend objected to their son dating a Catholic girl and soon broke up the pair.

It was the end of June and the family gathered in the kitchen. The order from the Eaton's catalogue had arrived. The children had long been hobbling to school in their older siblings' shoes. Childish voices squealed with excitement and anticipation, "The shoes are here! The shoes are here!" Five year old Danny, sat on his father's knee, his face lit up with expectation. The parcel was opened but there were no shoes, none at all.

Danny said, "Daddy, you didn't buy me any shoes?"

"Why didn't you tell me?" his father said in a mock surprise voice.

Margaret fumed with fury, since he bragged not long ago that he bought the parish priest a car. She knew there must be enough money for shoes for the children. She thought to herself, "Do you think that will put you in good with the Lord? You had better rethink your priorities. Do you think that a place is reserved for you in Heaven just because you observe Sunday Mass and make sure that your wife polishes your shoes? Poor little Danny, no wonder he throws a tantrum at the supper table every night without fail." The family was at a loss to know why he did this, but she knew.

Billy, Margaret, George, Bernie, Eddy.

She knew he didn't care what she thought. Any man who would watch his wife lug a baby on her back while she poisoned gophers, and this after she worked all day in the house; would not be upset by an outside opinion, but she was no longer able to hold her tongue.

With fists clenched, she stood up and yelled at him. "Mr. Lord and Master, you are a dolt! Don't you love your children? I can't understand how you could treat them so badly! No, wait, I know the reason. You are pompous and selfish! You are bleeding your family to satisfy your need to feel important. Before I go away, let me ask you this. What are you Lord and Master of? You are nothing but a rotund product of these dried-out prairie lands. I'm glad I'm going now. Good-bye to you, dictator of your fenceless farm!" She turned in disgust and left the room.

*M*argaret's next teaching position was in an area called Drumheller Valley. It would later be called Dinosaur Trail, due to the rich cache of dinosaur fossils found there.

It was a difficult place for farmers to try to eke out a living, due to the lack of rain. In the days of the drought, the living was even more difficult. However, many hardy souls did survive there, people such as Jim Jenkins and his family.

Jim Jenkins knew what he was about and no one could tell him differently. He couldn't read or write but his wife Elizabeth could. She had finished grade three and, as he proudly told the various teachers in the one room school his kids attended, "Elizabeth, she does all the writin' that needs doin' around here."

He stood in the doorway of his two-room shack that October afternoon, watching his pregnant wife Elizabeth spoon jam into jars from a pot of boiling fruit on the coal stove. It kept her pretty busy, what with the kids getting in a lick of it whenever her back was turned. She didn't really worry about the flies that marched in steady procession, up one side of the jars, inside the jars and out. It amused him to see those darn kids of his, William, Edward, Daniel and Jennifer, outsmarting their mother. He always referred to his children by their full Christian names. To have called them by any nickname would have put him on a par with those dang foreigners who were his neighbours. His was the only English speaking family in this part of the Badlands and he needed no other qualifications. Though he sure had plenty other reasons to feel superior, if it came to that. Anyway, it was best to "git going over to that there school," to set the new teacher straight as to what he expected of her. With a satisfied chuckle at his spirited brood of youngsters, he climbed into his beloved automobile, the "Ole Gray-Dort." He guided its shaky chassis over the brittle ruts to the schoolhouse.

The school, named "White Star South," was a small wooden building perching on the thin rocky soil of the river valley. To Jim, it was an imposing edifice. He had supervised its construction free of charge three years ago, in 1939, and he felt considerable obligation to see to the quality of the teaching also. It was for the teachers' good, and besides he supplied the ten-gallon can of water twice weekly, plus the odd ride to town for a small charge.

The Gray-Dort rattled to a stop at the other side of a barbwire fence from the school.

Unhitching his long thin legs from under the steering column, he gave the steering wheel an affectionate pat, and pushed the canvas window flap out of his way as he opened the door. The top string of barbed wire yielded under the pressure of bony fingers as he stepped over it to the schoolyard. He walked bent forward, in an undulating gait, rather like a large angleworm. His bony knees appeared and disappeared through holes in the knees of his overalls. He gave a pull up on his overalls and adjusted the stiff peak of his well-ventilated cap. Sprigs of hair escaped through the holes like angry feathers. He tapped on the door and prepared to triumph once more.

Margaret was twenty-one years old when she got her second teaching position. She looked up at the stranger who entered the classroom. She had a broom in her hand and was ankle deep in papers and dirt. Jim saw that the school was getting a cleaning, and that was good. The other teacher, a middle-aged old girl, whom he had fired after a months' tenure, had been pretty dirty.

"Howja do Ma'am. I'm Jim Jenkins. Live about half mile down the road. Got a place down there by the river."

Margaret extended her hand to meet his. She surveyed his bib overalls, torn sweater, and big boots. He then fastened his beady brown eyes on her. Before she could say hello, he launched into a speech describing the many shortcomings of her predecessor, a grass widow named Mrs. Churchill. "We didn't exactly take to the old teacher who was here afore you," he said importantly. He pulled a toothpick out of his pocket and stuck it in the corner of his mouth. It seemed Mrs. Churchill hadn't really appreciated the fine points of his older children. She had disciplined them on a few occasions, and worst of all, had actually seemed to prefer the kids belonging to those unspeakable foreigners, who lived among the hills and worked in the mines. The unpardonable injustice of it all sent him into a frenzy of arm waving and fist thumping. Words could not express his indignation. "Fact is, I went to the school office and told them we wanted a new teacher."

He was about to set this young teacher straight on how the school was to be run. "Just thought I'd drop by and let you know a few things. First off, I supply the water every week and if things don't go right I can sure stop 'er. There ain't no way to get to town except I drive you in the old Dort. The road ain't passable for most cars. The municipality don't keep up the roads in the Badlands. Lots of rocks and sharp shale and washouts, tears the tires to pieces. You don't treat my kids right, you don't get to town, see?"

Margaret was still quite inexperienced and uncertain, but sensing a need to hold her own, she told him in no uncertain terms where she stood on the issue. She angrily replied, "I will not be blackmailed with threats of no water and I still have my own two feet to walk the six miles into town. You'll be very lucky if you can keep me as the teacher here for two weeks. The teacherage has no supplies, the school is dirty, and I have never seen such a lonely, desolate place to put a school in all my life! Listen, Sir, don't you dare give me orders about how to run this school! The day you fail to bring me water or give me any trouble, is the day I walk out of here no matter how bad the roads are. I don't need a job that badly."

Jim was not used to defiance, especially from a young woman, and he couldn't quite comprehend why she wasn't afraid of him and it rendered him speechless for a minute. "Ah, don't get excited Miss. You stay; we'll be good to you. Me and the Misses, Elizabeth, that's her name, we're glad they sent a young teacher for a change. You come to supper tonight and we'll get to know you. Good-bye Miss." He tipped his cap and returned hastily to his car.

He arrived as promised at five o'clock to fetch her. She climbed in the front seat of the car, and was bounced up and down on the springless seat while the thin tires of the Dort courageously fought the ruts of the trail to their shack.

By the time he arrived back on his porch with his guest, Elizabeth had managed to seal the sticky jars of fruit in which swarms of buzzing flies still took a lively interest. How many were entombed in the preserves one could only guess. It was of little concern to Jim Jenkins and his family in any case. The rough board table which occupied most of the room was set with a few chipped plates and old tin pie plates. A plate of bread and lard to spread on it lay in the middle. A long sticky fly paper was tacked to a wooden beam in the ceiling, coiled downward over the table, black with frantic, noisy flies, caught by the wings, legs, or head and fluttering helplessly in the glue. The walls of the kitchen, made of hard-packed mud did very little to reflect the light of the coal-oil lamp which Elizabeth had to light later in the evening.

Trying to ignore the showing-off of the four children, Margaret took her place on the rough board seat on one side of the table. The sight of thin stew, chuck full of garlic and onions, being ladled onto the plates, set off a new burst of energy in the children. They tore in mad circles around the table pausing only long enough to stir the food on each plate with grubby fingers. Jim chuckled and Elizabeth's eyes twinkled with delight, as their little devils added variations to the frolic by flinging bits of food back and forth. Suddenly, Margaret jerked upright as fingers playfully jabbed her in the ribs and pulled her hair from behind. Suddenly a shriek brought the clamour to a halt. Holding his round little bottom with both hands, Charles cried out to his father, "She pinched me!" Margaret did her best to look unconcerned and bent to her plate, and the meal progressed without further incident as the children eyed the teacher with new respect.

This was the first of many unavoidable visits to the only English speaking family in the area. The Jenkins would not accept refusal, so fair weather or foul, Margaret ended up there more frequently than she cared. One bitterly stormy winter night, Jim arrived with his wife to see how the teacher was managing. The battery on her radio had died and she was huddled in bed to keep warm.

"We came to take you to our house," said Jim. "Ain't right for a young girl to be alone on a night like this."

"But I'm not feeling well," she protested, "I'll be fine and thanks for coming. I just need some rest."

Her perfect alibi was ignored. Gathering her and the blankets, he hoisted her over his shoulder, and bore her, protesting, to the ole Dort.

She was shivering badly now and pulled the blanket tight around her shoulders as Jim opened the door on the driver's side and hopped in. The car had no heat and her teeth chattered all the way back to his farm.

Jim had dragged an old grain shed beside his shack two years ago, for a much-needed addition to his house. He had covered the floor with several inches of straw and put a pot-bellied stove in the middle with a bare stovepipe leading the smoke through a hole in the ceiling. He put Margaret on the straw floor where she slept fitfully with two of the children. She watched the stovepipe become crimson to within a few inches of the ceiling. Guardian angels were definitely on watch that night. She fully expected to be incinerated with the Jenkins family. Though she would have preferred to stay in her own home, she recognized the caring and generosity of the Jenkins and bought them some curtains for their bare windows, but it was as much a thank-you gift to God for their survival, as it was for their intended goodness.

For years, Jim and his family scraped a living from the barren, thin-soiled forty acre plot near Drumheller. He struggled daily to provide for his growing family. One day, an oil company found oil on his land and it was determined that he held the mineral rights. Afterwards, it was said that he was walking around smoking two cigars at a time. He and Elizabeth and their eight children left the Badlands and went on to live the good life.

*S*pring arrived in the Badlands and Margaret took her paycheque to town, to do a little shopping. It had been a perfect day for shopping. The sky had cleared after yesterday's spring showers leaving a fresh clean smell in the air. She had been glad to accept a ride into Drumheller from one of the town folk, and now with a box containing her new dress tucked under her arm, she walked back to the road that connected Drumheller to her teacherage. Margaret had no car or horse and there was no public transportation. Her only options were to walk or accept rides from people. The farm and town people were generally accommodating and she usually didn't have to wait long for a ride.

She heard a vehicle approaching, turned around, and put out her thumb.

"Where ya headed Miss?" the driver of the truck asked.

Margaret didn't recognize the man but assumed he was a local farmer. "To the school, about six miles down the road. Do you know it?"

"Sure. Hop in. You the teacher there?"

"Yes, until the end of June anyway."

They made pleasant conversation for the next mile or so until suddenly the driver turned off the main road, onto a path that led into a farmer's field.

"This isn't the way to the teacherage," Margaret said, a little confused.

The driver turned to her, suddenly very angry. He shoved the gear shift to park and growled, "Okay Miss, this is where you pay for your ride." He roughly grabbed her arm and tore at her clothing.

"No!" Margaret screamed. She looked all around her but there was not another car or person in sight. She slapped at his face and pulled his hair, but he was very strong and pushed her back on the seat. As he held her down with his right hand he used his left to tear again at her dress. She was able to raise her right leg and knee him hard in the chest. He hit her hard across the mouth and shouted obscenities at her. Margaret would not give up. She struggled and screamed until the attacker found her to be more trouble than she was worth and pushed her out of the truck. She landed on her back on the dirt path. The driver threw her box after her and her dress fell out of the box and into a murky puddle. He backed up onto the highway and sped off, leaving her frightened, bruised and horribly humiliated.

She picked her dress out of the mud, tucked it under her arm, wiped away her tears and waited for another vehicle to take her home. She went directly to her cousin's house and tearfully relayed the horrible experience, but instead of sympathy her cousin remarked, "Well, it serves you right. Girls like you are asking for it."

"What do you mean, 'girls like me' and why would I ask for a man to treat me like that?" she retorted.

She left her cousin's house shaken, embarrassed and saddened. Margaret washed her new dress but was never able to wear it. It reminded her too much of that terrible experience.

A dear old friend of Margaret's was Nell. Nell was a kind lady who lived on the edge of town on a farm with her husband. She had watched Margaret grow up and the two became good friends, though Margaret was forty years her junior. Nell was a patient, loving woman who became the victim of some unfortunate circumstances.

Nell was feeling tired and discouraged with her garden work. The afternoon sun grew hotter and her knees grew stiffer as she knelt between the rows of beets. John had promised her some new linoleum for the kitchen if she did more vegetable canning this summer. He might even buy some fruit to can if she could soften him up a little when he was in a good mood. The weeds reared their ugly tough stems and drew moisture and nutrients from the soil, stubbornly refusing to let the vegetables have a chance. Nell strained and pulled on their heads but the weeds tenaciously held their ground. Then Nell straightened her aching back and surveyed the amount of labour still ahead. She wiped her sweaty brow with the back of her hand. The work was difficult and goodness knows she was not as young as she used to be.

Margaret

The screen door slammed and Nell rose to her feet and wiped her dirty hands on her full apron. She'd forgotten the time and John was probably looking for his lunch. Nervously she stepped over the rows of vegetables and hurried as best she could for the farmhouse. She heard his grumbling before she reached the door. "Gol darn it Nell, when are you going to get some food on the table? A man works hard and what does he find to eat?" She tried to ignore his whining while she set the table. Once dishes and cutlery were out he calmed down a little.

She sliced some cold cooked potatoes into a pan to fry and cut some roast beef from last night's dinner. There were some pickles and fresh tomatoes and bread, so that should do. John's wiped his face with his sleeve to remove the grime from the fields but his frown remained. He grabbed his chair roughly and sat down, elbows on the table and glared at Nell.

"Look at the state you're in Nell. Least you could do is put on something clean when I come home, and you better have supper on time tonight you lazy good-for-nothing. And one more thing I won't have you doin' is givin' Jack any more food. We need it for ourselves."

"Now John, he worked here all day yesterday for no pay. He can't keep a wife and children with no food."

"They ain't my kids. I don't owe them nothing!" He stabbed his food and ate greedily. "Just watch yourself is all."

Jack's parents died of tuberculosis fifteen years previously and he was left orphaned. Nell and John adopted him when he was ten years old. Nell wanted to give the poor child a home. John wanted free labour on his farm. There was no doubt the boy was strong. He could harness the horses, milk the cows and do other work on the farm almost as well as a grown man. John rode him hard, letting the child know that no matter how hard he tried it was not good enough. Jack left home when he was fifteen years old because of John's ill nature. He married when he was twenty years old and lived on a nearby farm. Nell was not able to have any children of her own and she loved Jack and now the little ones she called her grandkids. John loved no one but himself and drove everyone away with his poisonous nature, everyone except Nell. After forty years or so of marriage she had long since given up trying to change him. Mostly she tried to cajole him and avoid confrontation.

John had been such a gallant suitor in his younger days. She was charmed away from a good teaching job to marry him. He smiled and brought her flowers. He treated her like a princess, until they got married and everything changed. He became rough, domineering and demanding. A person just never knows what lies ahead.

One afternoon, Clara, the postmistress of the village, and Margaret, came to call.

Nell loved company and quickly gathered the wisps of her grey hair into a knot at the back of her head and changed her dress. They sat in the parlour that, despite the aging wallpaper, had an old world charm. Nell had framed prints on the wall and a tall cabinet containing her best china and knick-knacks. Her ancient furniture was well cared for. Her lace curtains were faded but carefully mended and showed no signs of neglect. One could sense the gracious sophisticated atmosphere of a lady in this room. If truth be known, Nell was not content as a farmer's wife. She would have better fitted in the city with its libraries, universities and museums.

Years ago, Margaret used to introduce Nell as her grandmother. She would lift Margaret up to look at the paintings that hung on her wall in the farmhouse. With a charming detail that would enthral any child, she told her about the artist and what the painting was all about. She also loved to explain what she was cooking and how the various ingredients combined to make something taste good. She would patiently explain how soda and cream of tartar could work together to make a cake rise because they were so different. She took Margaret out to her garden and explained why she planted some vegetables and flowers in the sun and some in the shade because they would grow better that way.

John came in the kitchen door and when he saw the ladies who had come to call, he quickly made for the bedroom to wash up and change his clothes. He was always the charming host when Nell's friends came to call. He saved none of his graciousness or smiles for his wife though. He flirted with Margaret and poured her tea. Margaret was uncomfortable with John's attention and kept glancing in Nell's direction. Nell watched and said nothing, remembering the many niggling remarks and put-downs she suffered. "If they could see the real John they would be out of there quick as a wink," she thought.

"How are you doing in that school of yours? Those kids you teach given' you any trouble? You ain't too big, but I bet you could whip 'em into shape, eh? My grandson is doing real well. He's smart ain't he Nell?" He turned and sneered at his wife. "Nell here, she used to be young and pretty like you, now just look at her."

Nell's eyes grew wide. She was used to the insults, but this was the first time he had referred to any of Jack's kids as grandchildren. She knew he was putting on a big show for the guests and her anger started to rise. She got up and headed for the kitchen. "Jack and Mary haven't got much in the way of groceries in their house. Maybe I'll just round up a few things to bring over there, for the grandchildren, you know John, growing kids needs lots of good food to eat." John's smile disappeared and he gave his wife a threatening look. She knew that he dared not do or say anything with witnesses present.

The postmistress and the teacher helped Nell carry the vegetables and a couple of live chickens over to Jack's house. Margaret glanced behind her at John who was standing at the door of the house. He had a white-knuckle grip on the doorpost and his face was crimson with barely controlled rage.

Jack warned his mother not to go back home, knowing John's temper and tight-fisted nature and he invited her to stay with him and his wife. Margaret and the Post Mistress agreed. Nell wouldn't listen. She insisted that everything would be okay and walked across the fields back to her husband.

John had never been so angry. He was not used to having his wife stand up to him and he berated and degraded her more that ever, but Nell knew that she had done the right thing by her son and grandkids.

Nell did as much canning as she could, considering her arthritis was acting up again and she just didn't have the energy anymore. Everything was so hard now, not like when she was young, "By golly, I could work all day back then," she liked to say. It wasn't good enough for John though. He wouldn't buy her the new linoleum for the kitchen.

The following winter Nell died of a stomach ailment. John's loud sobs at her funeral filled the church. "Why did God take my wife? Now I'm all alone!" He was inconsolable. Jack said nothing to his adopted father at the funeral or ever again for that matter. John died alone on his farm fifteen years later.

Chapter Eight

The Baby Boom

In 1947, a major oil discovery was made at Leduc, Alberta. As time passed, more and more oil discoveries were made, and oil money flowed into the provincial government's reserves. The oil and gas industry was about to overtake farming as the main industry in Alberta. The Canadian Government wanted to encourage immigration to aid in its economic development, and post-World War II Alberta attracted a large number of European immigrants. There were British citizens who hoped to gain a better way of life in Canada, persons who had been displaced by the Germans, and veterans who had fought against the Germans.

The petrochemical industry brought many jobs to Alberta and as a result, all sectors of the economy experienced a surge of prosperity. The oil discoveries in Alberta made Calgary and Edmonton boom towns which attracted many skilled labourers. Unskilled and menial labour was still required in the farming industry. The government took advantage of the displaced persons and Polish war veterans and viewed them as a source of cheap farm labour. Some of them were made to live in shacks and labour in the sugar beet industry.

The British immigrants between 1946 and 1966 made up one quarter of the immigrants to the province. Preference was given to residents of Britain, France, Ireland and the United States because it was believed they would be assimilated faster, being able to speak the language. Other countries in Europe were considered after that, but Asians and Africans were virtually excluded.[7]

Margaret was twenty-five years old when she began teaching in Black Diamond. She was very glad to get the job. Black Diamond was a good sized town with a regular school, where each classroom had only

---

[7] Peoples of Alberta: Portraits of Cultural Diversity, P. 36,37

one grade. She taught a class of forty-two grade three pupils. That would be something to get used to, and quite a step up from the isolated, one-room schoolhouses where she began her teaching career.

She was an attractive young woman. Her skin was smooth and clear. Her smile was bright with perfectly straight, white teeth, though she'd had a minimal dental care. She was excited for the first day of teaching at her new school and had arrived early to prepare her lessons before the children turned up.

She was stopped at the door by a teacher who held her gently by the arm and said, "Oh I'm sorry dear, school doesn't start until 9:00 a.m."

"But I'm one of the teachers here," Margaret told her.

"My word, I can scarcely believe it," she laughed, "you look so young."

She enjoyed teaching in Black Diamond but had always wanted to marry and have a family. By the age of twenty-seven she was well past the age when most women married. She held out hope that one day the right man would come along. That opportunity came one spring morning.

"Are you almost ready Helen? We don't want to be late," Margaret called from the kitchen.

Helen, Margaret's best friend, emerged from the bathroom. "What do you think?" she asked, showing off her new dress. It was short sleeved and knee length with a simple flowered pattern. She wore bobby socks

Margaret and her grade three pupils in Black Diamond.

with her shoes. Few women wore stockings since supplies of materials of all kinds were required for the war effort. Cotton, nylon, rayon, silk and linen were used to make parachutes and uniforms for the soldiers and were still in short supply, even after the war. People were encouraged to buy only the necessary garments.

"It's just beautiful," Margaret answered, and she disappeared into the bathroom to check her own appearance in the mirror. She believed she looked charming in her black and white suit. It showed off her lovely hourglass figure. She had done her hair in pin curls the night before and combed them out in the morning to form neat, even waves in her hair just like the famous actresses Susan Hayward and Vivian Leigh. The dark colour of her hair contrasted beautifully with her blue eyes. She applied a little red lipstick and that was all the makeup she wore.

It was a pleasant Saturday morning in May, 1948. Sparrows and robins fluttered to and fro in the few trees planted by the residents of Black Diamond. They chirped their mating calls to each other and set to work building nests. Margaret and her friend Helen walked the five blocks to the church to attend a function put on by the Catholic Women's League. The two ladies couldn't afford cars on their salaries, but a few passed them on the way, sending up billows of dust from the dry gravel road. The ladies turned their heads and shut their eyes against the thick, dirty clouds.

The church hall was decorated with paper flowers and streamers to welcome the new parish priest. Margaret and the other ladies of the Catholic Women's League served coffee, tea, sandwiches and cakes to the guests. People were dressed in their Sunday best, the men in suits and the ladies in their prettiest dresses and spring hats. Helen introduced Margaret to some friends who also attended the church in Black Diamond. The man was tall and slim, with brown-blond hair slicked straight back on his head. The woman was also tall and slim. Her brown hair was done in the same fashionable pin curls as the other ladies in the room.

"Margaret, this is my friend Louise and this is her brother Albert."

"How do you do?" he said. He smiled cheerfully as he shook her hand.

Albert wore thick glasses and Margaret saw that his suit was a little worse for wear.

"I was explaining to these people," indicating the small group of men and women beside him, "that Black Diamond is located on the

Cowboy Trail. It is a route that extends from the Alberta/ Montana border to Mayerthorpe, north of Edmonton. One hundred and fifty years ago a trading post was set up in Rocky Mountain House. At that time, the fur trade was the main industry in Alberta. Of course it wasn't called Alberta then. This land was part of the North West Territories. Later, in the 1880's, ranching families took over and it became cattle country.[8] Now, as everyone knows, ranching and farming is the main industry of Alberta, but I speculate that it won't be long before the oil industry takes over as the main industry. Just look at what has happened in Turner Valley. Alberta is likely sitting on vast reserves of oil and gas."

"He seems to be an educated man," thought Margaret. She could tell that his eyes were kind, and by the way he kept looking over at her and smiling, she knew that he was attracted to her. In fact, throughout the whole function, he never took his eyes off of her.

They found a table together and struggled to make shy conversation. His admiration for her was obvious in his eager but timid conversation. He smiled and showed genuine curiosity about her. She was pleasant in return but tried not flirt or even show a lot of interest. She learned that the following September he would be going away for a year to finish his studies at a university in North Carolina, and afterwards he would apply to become a professor of Mathematics at the University of Alberta, in Edmonton. She was very intrigued by this, as she was always attracted to intelligent men. "Would you like to go bowling with me this afternoon?" he asked nervously.

"I'd love to," she answered.

Albert was shy at first with Margaret, but he was cheerful, polite and respectful. After bowling, they walked to the local café. They sat at a small table covered with a checker table cloth. The waitress, a tall, skinny woman in her forties, approached them, carrying a coffee urn. Her hair was tied back in a bun with a few greying, scraggly wisps sticking out. A cigarette dangled between her lips. "Cup a' coffee?" she offered.

"Yes please," said Margaret.

The waitress poured the coffee and placed the pot on the table and slid in the booth to sit beside Margaret. "You don't mind me taking a load off do ya?" She took a long suck on her cigarette and stabbed it out in the ashtray. "Lord, my feet are as puffed as two balloons. Get a load of that."

[8] www.abheritage.ca

She pointed to her swollen ankles. "You both look real swell. You on a date or something?"

Margaret nodded, knowing it was impossible to keep a secret in a small town, and this waitress was the worst gossip of all.

A voice called from the next table. "Hey Mabel, what does a man have to do to get a cup of coffee around here? You just gonna sit on your arse all day?"

"Hold your horses, lord a' mighty, a woman can't get a minute's peace around here! I suppose I better get a wiggle on and serve up some more coffee to these folks." She gave Margaret a wink and ambled to the next table. "What the sam-hill is your hurry over here? You got a meeting to get to or something?" She laughed heartily at her own joke and coughed hard into her handkerchief, bringing up a load of phlegm.

Albert and Margaret continued to talk and get to know each other. She liked the way he furrowed his brow when he was concentrating and the way he glanced away self-consciously when he saw her watching him. He spoke calmly and politely and considered everything she had to say.

When evening came, Albert walked her to her door. "Goodnight Margaret," he said, "I had a very nice time with you today. Are you free tomorrow?"

"Yes I am. Call for me in the evening and we'll go for supper."

"Until tomorrow then," he said formally, and he shook her hand.

Margaret smiled at his overly serious ways. Later that same night, she told her friend Helen that she was going to marry Albert.

He proposed to her a month after they met, and of course she happily accepted. They were both on cloud nine. At last, she was going to get married, and to a kind, caring and interesting man, but their courtship would be cut short by his imminent departure to North Carolina in September. The day of their parting was fast approaching and then he would be gone until the following summer, so they savoured every moment. They walked hand in hand down the streets of Black Diamond laughing and discussing future plans. They decided on July 1 of the following year for their wedding day. It was an exhilarating and happy time.

The months that followed saw many letters flying back and forth between North Carolina and Alberta in which the couple professed their love and devotion to one another. Margaret couldn't wait to open her letters after she picked them up from the Post Office. Usually, she tore them open and read them on the walk home. Her heart beat fast when she read his sweet words. She practically skipped and sang on the way home. She would then dart to her room and put the letter with all the others, in a special box, and then get busy and pen her own letter. She read his letters over and over whenever she felt lonely for him. Sometimes they would plan to talk on the phone. It was lovely to hear his voice but they had to keep the conversations short and impersonal. Long distance calls were very expensive and the telephones in the town operated on party lines, where anyone could listen in.

One of the other teachers in the school, a lady in her 50's, was engaged to a man of the same age. They were also going to get married when he came back from the United States. Tragically, and unexpectedly the other lady received notice of her fiancé's death. The cause was rather obscure. Some believed it was suicide. It was heartbreaking because the woman had waited so long to get married. This threw a pall on Margaret's plans because the two women had discussed both of their upcoming marriages with so much happiness.

Albert and Margaret were married in St. Michael's Church, in Black Diamond. It was a simple but beautiful wedding. She was stunning in her white satin beaded dress and long veil and train. Bill and Daisy attended of course, as did Margaret's brothers and sister. Albert had lost both his parents at an early age, but his sister Louise was in attendance, and many other guests.

The couple was very happy and very much in love. During the ceremony, the priest lifted his hands over the couple and said as part of his blessing, "Let us pray that this couple has a fruitful marriage." He never knew how well his prayers would be answered in the years to come.

In the post World War II years of the 1940's and 1950's, the role of a married woman was to help her husband advance his career. He was the breadwinner. She did all she could to support him. She was supposed to keep house, raise the children, entertain his boss, and get along with the wives of his coworkers. As was customary, Margaret quit her job after she got married. She stayed home and kept house and wondered if someday she might become a mother. She did not have to wait long. One month after their marriage they were expecting their first child. She and Albert moved to Edmonton where he began to teach at the University of Alberta.

Albert had studied for many years to gain his position at the University of Alberta. He had also spent many years in the company of learned people and felt comfortable with them. Margaret, on the other hand, had little experience with the niceties of society.

She felt like the Great Pretender in the midst of the well-educated ladies of the University of Alberta Women's Club. As the wife of a professor, she was invited to an afternoon tea party on campus. Their conversations went over and around her that day, fluttering and palpitating in the well-modulated tones of the upper class. Her small town upbringing had not prepared her for this experience.

Someone spoke to her but she didn't quite hear what she said. "Pardon?" she said to the lady in tweed, who wore spectacles held by fine chains.

"Oh, I say, I believe you are Albert Shaw's wife, are you not?" Before Margaret could answer, she continued, "Ernest and I would like you to call on

Albert and Margaret on their wedding day.

us this Sunday-week-evening." Her accent was very English and she spoke rapidly. She was Dr. Agatha Preston, who taught in the Biology Department.

"I...I'm sorry. I don't quite know what you mean."

She regarded Margaret impatiently. "Sunday-week-evening...We shall expect you." She turned aside and Margaret noticed the hearing aid.

Speaking louder and enunciating carefully she said, "Do—you—wish—ME to visit you, or my—husband—and—I, and at what TIME?"

Looking a little vexed the lady in tweed said, "Come Sunday-week-evening." Then to forestall any further stupid questions she moved off, glancing vaguely around at the other ladies of the Women's University Club. Everyone was preparing to leave the gathering and Margaret looked frantically around for an interpreter. Three amused young women were standing near and one of them volunteered to come to her aid.

"What does she mean? What does 'Sunday-week-evening' mean?"

"Consider yourself honoured," said the woman. "You have been invited to the Preston's a week from this Sunday evening. She doesn't invite just anybody to her home. It will be well to find out if your husband is invited though. One time I thought that I was included in an invitation given to a group of people. When I got there she looked at me and said, 'I didn't invite you,' so I had to leave immediately."

This disclosure did nothing to boost Margaret's self-confidence, so she decided to talk it over with her husband. It was important to know if this was to be a ladies' get-together, a mixed affair or just a visit between Dr. Preston and herself.

Margaret thought seven-thirty was an appropriate time to arrive. It was late enough that Dr. Preston would have finished her supper, but not so late as to keep her up past her bedtime. The question of her husband's part in all of this was to remain unresolved for the moment. Margaret's ignorance on the whole matter of protocol in this affair brought her a great deal of distress. The only thing to do was to go to the source when the great day arrived. She would get their friend Geoff to drive her to the Preston residence, since she and Albert did not own a car or a telephone. He would go back for Albert if need be.

Sunday-week-evening arrived so Margaret got her ride to the Preston house. Geoff waited in the car while she ascended the stairs and knocked timidly at the front door. There was a scurry inside and finally Dr. Ernest Preston, a professor of Mathematics, poked his head out and said, "Yes, may

I do something for you?" Margaret knew him by sight, but evidently he didn't know her.

"I'm Margaret Shaw," she said nervously, looking at his white t-shirt and casual appearance, "Your wife invited me to come this evening, at least I hope it's this evening. Anyway, I want to know if Albert is invited."

He stared at her as if he did not hear her correctly. Then he said, with extreme British courtesy, "Of course, of course, I dare say!" With that, he closed the door and left her standing outside. She was beginning to think she would never understand the mysteries of social behaviour among university people. She stepped back down the stairs and delivered the news to Geoff, then returned to the front door. She knocked again and waited, and knocked again, and waited. No one came to the door.

Uncertainly, she opened the door and meekly called, "Hello?" and stepped inside. A flight of stairs ascended in front of her and to one side stood a table and telephone. It was a large house. The living room, to her right, was empty of people. It seemed obvious that she was the only guest and she felt very self-conscious. She hoped that her husband would arrive very soon.

Then, to her horror, she saw sights that were definitely not intended for the eyes of guests. She caught brief glimpses of her host and hostess dashing about partly clothed and calling back and forth to one another.

She then heard sounds not intended for the ears of guests, "My word, what could have possessed Albert's wife to arrive so early Ernest dear? I have not even had my bath."

"Not to worry darling, she was only asking if Albert was invited this evening. Rather a daft question don't you think? I'm sure she's on her way home to change. She was clearly was not dressed for the evening. Have you seen my razor? I need to shave."

"I'm eavesdropping on their preparations! I'm not properly dressed for the evening!" The need for instant flight was apparent. She made a sudden grab for the doorknob and was prepared to bolt, though where she would go she wasn't sure. Geoff had already left to pick up Albert. Then the phone rang. She watched it numbly as it rang and rang. It was the betrayer of her uninvited presence. Before she could collect her wits and disappear, Dr. Ernest came shirtless down the stairs. The expression on his face was one of complete disbelief when he saw her standing there.

She managed a weak smile and said lamely, "Um, what time would you like us to come this evening?" In view of the fact that she was already there, looking at his hairy chest and potbelly, it seemed a rather stupid question.

"We are expecting our guests about 9:00 p.m."

"Oh, I see. My ride has already left. Sorry."

He looked distressed and at a total loss as to what to do with her. She thought hard for a way to withdraw gracefully, but before she could say anything, Dr. Ernest said, "Please come in and make yourself at home."

Dr. Agatha Preston came down the stairs soon after carrying her husband's shirt and wearing a bathrobe. "Do excuse us dear," she said, "We have just returned from picnicking with our son. We'll need a little time to freshen up."

Neither smiled at Margaret and she felt a tremendous need to get away. Despite her apologies and offers to come back later, she was ushered into the living room and pressed to make herself at home. She was given magazines and a pack of cigarettes.

"I don't smoke, but thank-you anyway."

The rejection threw her host into such a state of nerves that he perched momentarily on the edge of a chair and regarded her in a manner bordering on panic.

"Look, I have made a blunder in arriving too soon. Please don't feel obliged to entertain me now. I will sit here and wait for my husband."

About an hour later Albert arrived, and still later, other guests. What is more, they arrived in semi-formal attire. They all looked smart and chic and Margaret felt positively dowdy in her plain skirt and blouse. In due time, Dr. Agatha Preston descended the stairs, looking elegant in her hostess dress and with one hand held gracefully out to greet everyone.

For the next three hours the conversation ebbed and flowed, but it was mostly over Margaret's head. She desperately wanted to contribute to the conversation, to help her husband in his university social life. After all, this was an opportunity for the staff to socialize with and get to know the newest faculty member and his wife. She wanted to make a good impression, but these educationally elite were discussing topics about which she had no expertise or interest, so she sat mute for the entire evening. She felt completely out of place in the room, until at one point, the conversation became dominated by Dr. Benson, an Oxford man, who was currently conducting a study of wildlife, particularly lemmings, in the MacKenzie Delta. Margaret yearned to show that Albert Shaw, of the Faculty of Mathematics, a teacher of advanced calculus and statistics, had a wife with a few brains. So she asked brightly, "Dr. Benson, when do lemmings fly south for the winter?" She glanced at the faces of those present and saw raised eyebrows and a few smiles.

In the stunned silence that followed he replied very brusquely, "Lemmings are rodents."

She had finally broken all of the commandments. She was now a confirmed social misfit. She had failed in her attempt to become an accepted member of the brainy club and did not help her husband in his university social life, but all was not lost; she gleaned two priceless bits of information from the experience, that lemmings are rodents and Sunday-week-evening means a week from next Sunday, in the evening.

Snobs are rude and full of pride,
They foster hurt and pain.
They view the rest of us,
With elegant disdain.
Perhaps snobs are full of hate,
And terrible dispositions.
They can't abide the sight of us,
Who hail from rude conditions.
They hold their heads above the crowd,
With arrogant display.
They offer us but a passing glance,
Then scornfully look away.

Margaret was very close to her father so when he died in 1952, she was devastated. She had nothing but admiration for that simple man and held him in the highest esteem.

Never saw a television, never owned a car.
Never had an income, above the price of bare necessities.
A Mister Fixit of things, mechanical or spiritual.
He cared for others with no expectation of gain or praise,
And received very little of either in his life.
Of unselfish character and humble self-regard.
He lived life simply and gratefully,
Doing what God expected of him,
And enshrining his gentle memory,
In the lives of his children.

Daisy and Bill

*D*uring the post-WWII era, between 1947 and the early 1960's, Canada, the United States, Australia and New Zealand experienced a sharp increase in their populations due to the great number of babies born. The men had returned from war and the economies were doing well, so people settled down to raise large families. Children born during that era became known as the "baby boomers." Margaret and Albert certainly did their part to contribute to the baby boom.

The soft light of dawn peaked into the bedroom of the little house. The blankets on the bed had been hastily thrown aside and pyjamas carelessly dropped to the floor. Margaret sat on the edge of the bed in obvious discomfort and rummaged through her suitcase, thinking to herself. "Oh dear, I forgot to pack my toothbrush…oh, never mind, there it is. Now where are my pyjamas? There they are. I will need some dimes for the phone…" It was the spring of 1950, just ten months after their wedding and her labour pains had become more intense.

Albert was downstairs in the kitchen nervously talking on the phone to the taxi company. He was glad he and Margaret had decided to have a phone installed. It was most helpful in situations like this. "How long before the cab arrives...Yes, alright, goodbye." He sprinted up the stairs two at a time, to gather his wife and her suitcase for the trip to the hospital.

A half hour later, Albert's footsteps echoed on the hard tile floor of the hospital as he pushed Margaret's wheelchair down the sterile, white corridors to the admitting desk. The waiting room was quiet and almost empty at this time of the morning, except for a few people who sat reading newspapers and smoking cigarettes. No sooner had he signed her in that he was given the bum's rush. "Nobody but medical personal is allowed in the delivery room with the mother-to-be Mr. Shaw. You can wait here, though I'm warning you, the birth of a baby can take a long time. I suggest you go home and get some rest. We'll give you a call when it's all over. Now don't you worry, we'll take good care of your wife."

The couple's anticipation of the birth of their first child was mixed with worry. Margaret had had no prenatal classes, because none existed at that time, so aside from what she had been told by her mother and other women, she really did not know what to expect when giving birth to a baby. The ordeal came as a shock to her. Nurses looked in on her from time to time to check her progress, but otherwise she was left alone. She lay on the narrow hospital bed feeling sad and abandoned as the contractions became more and more intense. No pain killers were offered as she lay on the bed, and she wept. Never before had she felt such pain. With no one to comfort her, no one to hold her hand through all her suffering, she was terrified.

"Don't be such a baby!" a nurse barked, upon seeing the tears. "You'd think you were the only one who ever gave birth."

"I hope you give birth to ten babies!" Margaret barked back.

The nurse's harsh words did nothing to comfort Margaret as she lay hour after hour in distress.

The couple needn't have been in such a hurry to get to the hospital, as it took thirty-six hours of labour before the little girl was born. Margaret was exhausted and traumatized and refused to even look at her new baby. Albert on the other hand, was beside himself with joy and marvelled at the beautiful baby. "We should name her Mary, after my mother," he said, and he smiled from ear to ear.

Margaret's curt response was, "You better enjoy this baby, because it's the last one we're having."

The couple moved, with their baby, from the rented apartment into a new house in Edmonton. Margaret loved her little home. It had all the modern kitchen conveniences, a refrigerator and a gas stove, and in the washroom was a bathtub where, for the first time, Margaret could lie back and have a good soak. It was most luxurious. She felt positively spoiled.

Nineteen months later, in the winter of 1951, a second child, Michael, was born. The couple was most pleased. They now had a girl and a boy. Both children were healthy, dark haired and bright eyed. It was the perfect little family. Some couples might stop at two children, but not Margaret and Albert. Their family was far from finished.

Seventeen months after Michael's birth, in 1953, Rita was born. Unlike her siblings she was blond and blue eyed. Only eleven months later, Patrick was born. Thank goodness for the new washing machine. It didn't have a spin cycle so the clothes had to be pushed through the ringer and then hung up to dry. Its purchase stretched the budget but it was a real time saver to not have to wash all those clothes, and diapers, by hand. The busy little house was quickly becoming crowded. While a family of six was not unusual in the 1950's, in the midst of the baby boom, Albert knew that with a growing family to clothe and feed, he should keep his eyes open for new job opportunities.

Albert was offered a job in Ottawa, Ontario to work for the Dominion of Canada in the Bureau of Statistics. It was a good opportunity for Albert and gave him a nice increase in salary, which was important for his growing family. So, a very pregnant Margaret and her husband packed up the family's possessions and moved to Ottawa where their fifth child, David, was born in 1955.

Soon after settling in, the family packed up again and moved to Kingston, Ontario where they promptly added three more girls to the family, Bernadette, in 1957, Elizabeth in 1958 and Madelaine in 1959. Margaret's heart burst with joy and love as she looked into the little face of each new arrival. She was pregnant during virtually all of the first nine years of her marriage and much to her dismay, her waist line increased with the number of children. She was once so proud of her lovely figure, and now it was gone.

They were then a family of ten living in a three bedroom house. It was increasingly difficult to keep order in the busy little house. Noise, confusion and mayhem ruled the day. Babies cried and soiled their diapers while toddlers pulled books from the shelves. Pandemonium became a way of life as small children ran up and down the hallway and in and out of the door. They played and squabbled with one another and scattered their toys from one end of the house to the other. The children slept two or three to a bedroom so it wasn't surprising that after Madelaine's birth the doctor commented, "Well, you have another girl Margaret, but goodness knows where you're going to put her."

The acidy odour of the diaper pail filled the home as Margaret trudged back and forth, baby on her hip, as she attended to the many chores. She looked longingly out the window wondering what it would be like to go for a walk or to lay on the grass undisturbed and uninterrupted by demanding children. It was not to be, not today, and not for a long time.

She set the baby in the playpen and set to work preparing the potatoes she had freshly dug from the garden. Fifteen to twenty potatoes should do it. She scrubbed off the dirt, peeled and chopped them and added them to the pot containing her browned stewing beef. She peeled the carrots and cut the beans, and added these to the concoction to simmer for an hour or so. Lastly, she prepared the flour dumplings that bobbed around like little white clouds on top of the stew. The warm, comforting aroma filled the kitchen as she ladled the stew into bowls and set them on the table.

Margaret was busy day and night caring for her large family, but she didn't truly know the meaning of the word "busy" until the day nine year old Mary came home from school burning with fever. Margaret promptly put her to bed and it soon became evident that the cause of the fever was chicken pox. The disease was exceedingly common in those days; in fact, all children were expected to get chicken pox at sometime or another. One would hope though, that not all of your children would be sick at the same time. This was precisely what happened at the Shaws' house. It wasn't long before the illness was spread from child to child until all eight children, including five month old Madelaine, were scratching and complaining. Over the next week, finger nails were cut short and liberal doses of camomile lotion was applied.

It seems that the Shaw house was rarely free of illness. It became most serious and distressful when little Bernadette's loud, barking cough woke Margaret in the dead of night. Outside the air was frigid, crisp and still. The stars shone down on the wintry landscape. All was quiet except for the little girl wheezing and coughing, struggling to pull air into her lungs. Margaret was extremely troubled. The little girl was only two and a half years old when a simple cold became a nagging cough, and the nagging cough worsened and became croup. Margaret brought her into the bathroom and turned the shower to hot. She sat on the toilet seat with Bernadette on her lap while the steam filled the room. It seemed to relax the child's breathing, and finally she fell asleep and Margaret placed her back in her bed.

The following morning was exceptionally cold. Mary and Michael were sent to school and Albert boarded the bus to work. She was alone now with the six youngest children who ranged in age from five years to six months. Margaret was glad that Bernadette was still asleep. The poor child needed to rest after her awful night. Margaret was also very tired, but sleep was out of the question with so many little ones needing her attention.

Finally, Margaret was able to sit down for breakfast. She poured milk on her Corn Flakes and had taken just a few spoonfuls when Bernadette's barking cough began again. Margaret hurried to the small girl and gently picked her up. Her little body was hot with fever. She was frantic for breath, wheezing as she tried to suck air into her lungs. Margaret carried Bernadette into the light of the kitchen and saw that her lips were blue. "Oh, Dear God!" she exclaimed.

She desperately needed a babysitter for her five little children while she took Bernadette to the hospital. She picked up the phone and began to call friends, neighbours and relatives. Finally, after an anxious half hour of calling, she was able to convince a neighbour to come over. The family still did not own a car so Margaret called a taxi to take her daughter to the hospital. The taxi pulled up, crunching the hard snow beneath its tires, smoke from its exhaust pipe filled the frigid air. He honked impatiently as he waited for a very flustered woman who emerged from her house carrying a bundle in her arms. She walked unsteadily to the cab, so as not to slip on the icy walkway.

After arrival at the hospital, it was decided that Bernadette should be put into an oxygen tent. The poor child was terrified as the plastic tent was wrapped around her bed blurring the outside world and muffling voices. She cried and reached her arms to her mother. "You need to go home now, Mrs. Shaw. Visiting hours are not until 6:00 p.m.," said a prim, unsmiling nurse.

"Please let me stay for a little while."

"I'm sorry ma'am, it's hospital policy."

When Margaret returned to the hospital in the evening she entered the room and looked into her daughter's forlorn little face. "Mommy? Up?" said Bernadette. Margaret could not resist unzipping the oxygen tent and picking up the little girl.

"There now my darling," she said, whereby Bernadette promptly threw up all over her mother.

"What do you think you're doing? You should not take that child out of the tent. She needs the oxygen, and look at this mess! Now I'll need to clean her up. I would appreciate it if you parents would just let your children be and let us tend to them." The nurse snatched Bernadette out of her mother's arms and placed her back in her bed. "What is the matter with these parents?" mumbled the nurse. "Don't they realize we have policies and rules in place, and they are there for a reason?"

Margaret said nothing, but meekly slunk away, her blouse sticky and wet with smelly vomit. Bernadette spent several lonely days in the hospital and her parents were mostly compelled to worry about her from home. She did however, make a complete recovery.

It is natural for mothers to worry and fuss over their children and when something goes wrong, mothers often blame themselves. Margaret was often filled with nagging worry and guilt that filled her with fear and ate away at her self-confidence. Over time the guilt grew to become self-loathing as she beat herself up for the times she felt she had failed her family.

Margaret (holding Elizabeth), Albert, Mary (far left), Rita, Patrick, Bernadette, David, Michael at Lake Ontario.

Margaret sat on the beach at Lake Ontario on a muggy summer day watching her children play. The cool water provided some relief from the hot sun and stifling Ontario humidity. For those who preferred not to go in the water, especially non-swimmers like Margaret, the trees that surrounded the lake provided some much needed shade. It was not a totally relaxing time for the parents who had to be constantly on guard. Margaret sat on the beach blanket doing her best to entertain her three littlest girls while Albert patrolled the beach keeping a watchful eye on the other five children. The hot, sticky sand clung to the soles of their feet and worked its way between the toes of the children as they raced up and down the beach and in and out of the water.

Madelaine was an inquisitive one year old and the sight of the waves washing up on shore fascinated her. She watched her five oldest brothers and sisters, aged five, six, seven, nine, and ten years old, splashing joyfully in the water and longed to join them. She toddled unsteadily towards the water only to be hoisted up again and again by mom or dad and brought back to the safety of the beach blanket. Frustrated but undeterred she tried again and for once, got away unnoticed.

She was startled by the cold water as it washed over her tiny feet, so much so she fell with a plop on her bottom at the edge of the lake. Still unnoticed by the busy adults and her preoccupied siblings, she ventured further in, crawling on hands and knees. The next wave knocked her over and she tumbled and rolled in the strong surf. Underwater she instinctively kicked her legs and pumped her arms and raised her head to the surface of the water. She gulped some air. Her baby fat made her naturally buoyant but the water kept pulling her further and further into the lake. The water was cold and her body started to relax.

"Ma'am! Your baby is floating away!" a woman called to Margaret.

Margaret gasped in horror and dashed towards the waves that carried her baby face down into the deep water. The chill of the water took her breath away and with every step she took, her baby was carried ever further away. Margaret was a non-swimmer and soon the water was at her waist, then her chest. The waves splashed over her face. She coughed and desperately stretched out her arms but just couldn't grasp her precious infant. She stepped even further out, the love for her baby overpowering her fear of deep water. The water was now at her chin. Her feet slid a little on the gravel floor of the lake so she was afraid that she too would be in need of rescuing. She made one final reach and she grasped a chubby leg and pulled it towards herself. She held the baby high over her head and turned toward shore. The baby was coughing and shivering with cold. "Why didn't I see her go into the water? I should have been watching. I'm so stupid, stupid, stupid!" she said to herself.

The children started elementary school one after the other until it was Patrick's turn. Margaret walked him to school for his first day of grade one. She held his hand as they walked across the green grass of the school field. Patrick glanced nervously around and tightened his grip on his mother's hand. He had played at this playground many times before with his brothers and sisters, but today there were so many children and so many big kids!

"This is your new school Patrick," said his mother cheerfully. He stopped short and looked in wide-eyed terror at the large building. He cried and held her hand, refusing to let go. Margaret talked to him gently and walked him down the wide corridor. The aroma of fresh wax and industrial cleaners filled the air. Excited girls in their new dresses and boys in starched shirts neatly tucked into their trousers waited with their parents at the doors of classrooms. Patrick held onto his mother with both arms wrapped around her waist when they arrived at the grade one classroom. Margaret ran her hand over his military-style hair cut and kissed his forehead in as attempt to calm the anxious child. "Go inside your new classroom dear. Everything will be okay. Don't worry."

"Come in and take your seat," said the unsmiling teacher.

He reluctantly let go of his mother's hand, looked back beseechingly one more time and entered the classroom. Margaret watched for a moment and then turned and walked home.

A half hour later, Margaret heard the creak of the front door and there stood Patrick.

"Patrick, what are you doing here?" she asked.

"I didn't like school. I wanted to come home."

"You can't stay home, you have to go to school." Margaret took him by the hand and walked him back to school. She knocked on the classroom door, and nudged him inside. She again walked the two blocks back home. She set to work feeding the younger children, when she heard the front door open and there was Patrick again.

"I think it's time to come home now."

"Patrick, it is not time to come home, you have to go to school." So for the third time that morning she walked her son to his first day of grade one.

It was no surprise to Margaret when a half hour later Patrick appeared at home again.

"I don't like school. I'm going to stay home."

"You can't stay home, I'm going to walk you to school again and I want you to stay there!"

Patrick did stay at school until the end of the day and when he came home at the appropriate time there were tears streaming down his face.

"Hi Patrick, how was your first day at school?"

"Bad." He held up his hands to show his mom. "The teacher gave me the strap because I kept running away."

Margaret took her skinny freckle-faced boy in a hug and held him tight. She was filled with guilt and remorse. "Why did I insist he stay at school?" she thought to herself. "I should have listened to him when I saw that he was so afraid. What is the matter with me?"

Margaret blamed herself again after Patrick nearly lost his life at Lake Ontario. The children were given swimming lessons in a roped off area of the lake. The water was often choppy and cold but the children became strong swimmers. Patrick grew to become a gangly nine-year-old child. While swimming at the lake he spotted an area of swirling water. To him, it looked like an underwater tornado. It was a most curious phenomenon. He foolishly swam closer to investigate and to his horror, he found himself being sucked under the water. Looking up, he saw the surface of the water disappear above his head while an invisible force pulled him further and further down and into an underwater mud hole. He felt with his hands the wall of the mud hole, for he could no longer see. Desperately he clawed at the mud wall, fighting the powerful whirlpool with every ounce of strength in his small body. Finally, through great determination he reached the surface of the water and gasped for air.

"Why didn't I watch the Patrick more closely? I don't even want to imagine the outcome if he wasn't able to swim back to shore," Margaret lamented.

Tragically, at school the next day, Patrick learned that a student at his school was drowned the day before at Lake Ontario. "He was caught in an underwater whirlpool," said the principal. Patrick felt sick to his stomach and looked down at his hands, at his fingernails that were still filled with mud.

Daisy and her sister Vera, in Victoria, B.C.

Margaret knew that it was impossible to foresee every danger or difficulty that her children might face, nevertheless, she felt responsible when something went wrong. In the years to come there would be others would hold her responsible for severe problems that afflicted two of her children, problems over which she had no control.

*M*argaret and Albert grew tired of the sticky, thick humidity of Southern Ontario. They longed for the wide-open skies of the prairies, the land of their youth. They were also lonesome for their families, so they decided that a move back to Alberta was what they needed. With the oil industry booming in Alberta, Albert applied for and landed a job with Imperial Oil Limited, as a statistical engineer.

So it was that in 1961, just prior to their move back to Alberta, Albert and Margaret finally made the decision to buy a much needed car. The automobile was, at one time, only a play thing for the rich. Over time it became available to the average person and gradually replaced walking, horses and bicycles as the primary mode of transportation. People were able to travel long distances in a much shorter amount of time. It was far

The Shaws and their new station wagon.

more convenient to jump in a car than saddle a horse and since gasoline was relatively cheap it could even be used as a form of recreation. Even the lay out of cities changed as a result of the automobile, with the advent of suburbs and shopping centers.

The family was in need of something large, but inexpensive, so a station wagon best suited their needs. The vehicle had no radio but it was in good working order. Best of all, it seated nine, which was almost enough for their family of ten. That problem was easy to solve. Smaller children could sit on the laps of the older children if need be.

Margaret believed it was time she learned how to drive so naively she asked her husband to teach her. She did not know the folly of this request. Albert was exceedingly nervous sitting beside a new driver. He behaved very much out of character and was impatient with her mistakes and shouted orders at her. "Margaret! You must come to a complete stop at the corner! Use your signal well in advance of a turn!"

Margaret, with her nervous personality, did not respond well to her husband's harsh teaching method. As a result, her skill behind the wheel worsened, which caused Albert even more anxiety, but over time she became a careful, but not overly confident driver.

They were excited about going home to Calgary and happily packed their possessions in boxes and crates and sent them on the moving van. While the van hauled their possessions across Canada, Albert packed the six oldest children and their yowling cat Sugar-Brown into the station wagon while his pregnant wife and two youngest children took a taxi to the airport.

Margaret was late arriving at the airport so she hurried as quickly as she could across the tarmac with two heavy bags slung over her shoulders. She had only minutes to board the plane before it left without her. Her eight months pregnant, swollen belly seriously impeded her progress. She held her little girls' hands, and waddled towards the stairs of the plane.

Elizabeth looked around nervously as passengers and airport personal bustled about and at planes taxiing back and forth. She heard the roar of the plane engines and went into panic mode. She squealed and squirmed and did her best to run away from her mother. "Elizabeth, no, stay with me," Margaret pleaded. Elizabeth bit her own hand, screamed and jumped up and down in her attempt to free herself. Margaret held her hand in a tight grasp and had to shift the weight of the bags so as not to lose her balance as she approached the narrow stairway. "Alright girls, you go ahead of me," she said as she pushed the two and three-year-old girls in front of her. They were suddenly pushed aside by a young man carrying only a briefcase who ran up the stairs without stopping to offer his assistance. "Rude, ignorant man!" she muttered under her breath. She took a deep breath and made the slow ascent into the plane.

It turned into a very unpleasant flight. Elizabeth, as usual, behaved very strangely, rocking back and forth in her seat, squealing and wailing in her tearless way, during much of the five hour flight to Calgary. Margaret had to restrain her wild child many times to prevent her running up and down the narrow aisle of the plane. Meanwhile, Madelaine ate her lunch and then threw it up again all over her seat and her mother. Margaret's only regret was that the rude man was not sitting next to her.

*M*argaret knew from the start that her baby Elizabeth was odd. Like her siblings, she was large and vigorous. Her hair was soft and curly brown, and her features were perfect, but she would not breastfeed. She bit and struggled when Margaret tried to nourish her. Her body became rigid and stiff when anyone tried to cuddle her. Seemingly without curiosity, she would not play, nor would she make eye contact or even look around or reach for objects. At the age of two she finally learned to walk and her speech was peculiar. She didn't speak in order to communicate like most children, but simply echoed words she heard, like a parrot. Her voice was expressionless and her vocabulary was very limited, even for her age.

It was a great concern to her parents. They brought her to a number of doctors but none could find anything wrong with her. "She is neglected, starved for attention. Give her what she needs, and she'll be better," the doctors said. She did not get better. In fact, her behaviour became more and more strange.

Elizabeth seemed to exist in a world of her own and was oblivious to the needs of others. This became evident during the time that all the Shaws were stricken with pneumonia. When an illness struck the Shaw house, it was not enough that one or two children got sick. Often the illness would travel from one to the other, so that Margaret and Albert spent many days tending to coughs, wiping noses or holding children as they vomited in the toilet. It was on just such a day, after a sleepless night spent listening to her children cough and wheeze, that Margaret called the doctor. He arrived at the door, black bag in hand. He pulled out his stethoscope and went from one child to another to listen to their lungs. He declared that all eight had pneumonia, wrote out prescriptions, and wished Margaret luck.

She dragged herself from one child to another for hours that day. She was hugely pregnant with her ninth child and could not will herself to move anymore. She coughed and blew her nose. "Oh no, now I'm catching it too," she thought. Finally, she collapsed with exhaustion on the couch as weariness filled every pore of her being. Her weary head rested on the arm of the couch. "I'll just close my eyes for a few minutes," she thought. Like a person drugged, she couldn't help but fall into a deep, blissful sleep. Not even the coughing and crying of her children would wake her.

"Crack!" A sudden pain startled her awake.

"Ouch!" she yelped and held her hand to a rising welt on her forehead. There stood Elizabeth, holding her doll upside-down by its legs, its hard head with a tangle of hair obviously the weapon used on this occasion.

"Don't sleep!" she ordered her mother.

"Elizabeth! Why did you do that? That hurt!"

Elizabeth retreated to a chair, put her thumb in her mouth and rocked herself back and forth, back and forth, all the while watching her mother with eyes devoid of emotion.

From that day on, when ever Margaret attempted to nap, along came Elizabeth and with the hard head of her doll she would whack her mother on the head, so that Margaret was afraid to fall asleep. Elizabeth never played with toys in a normal way but used them only as weapons or projectiles. Her siblings learned to be attentive when Elizabeth was around, in case they became the target of her rages.

Christopher was born shortly after their arrival in Calgary in 1962 and two years later, she was pregnant again. With great excitement she called her sister-in-law and relayed the news. "Isn't it wonderful? We're expecting another baby." She welcomed her tenth child, Robert, as she welcomed all of her children, with great joy. She and Albert looked forward excitedly to the birth of each child, not as another burden or mouth to feed but as gifts from God. She brought the baby home from the hospital full of anticipation, but had no crib for him to lie. That bed was still being used by Christopher. Albert pulled a drawer from his dresser and emptied it of clothing. He laid some soft baby blankets inside to make a temporary cradle for the newborn. In fourteen years Margaret had given birth to five girls and five boys.

It was in the winter of 1965 that Margaret experienced excessive menstrual bleeding and it was determined that she should have a hysterectomy, and that was the end of her childbearing years.

Elizabeth's condition did not improve with time. She often flew into furious tantrums that could be triggered by something as simple as her mother rearranging the furniture in the house. The tantrums included striking her parents or siblings or biting herself or banging her head on the wall. She could not be reasoned with. All forms of discipline were ineffective. Albert and Margaret were mystified. What could be wrong with their daughter? The doctors still didn't know.

"She's just spoiled," they were told, or the most stinging remark of all, "You don't give her enough affection. You must be a very aloof and distant mother." Her condition was blamed on Margaret's nervous disposition. Finally, after many years, they were given the label of schizophrenia that later proved to be incorrect, but at least they were comforted with the knowledge that Elizabeth's condition that was not their fault.

Over the years, many psychiatrists and paediatricians examined Elizabeth. Finally the diagnosis of autism was made in 1964. Little was known at that time of the condition, its causes or treatment so Margaret and Albert were left to flounder in the dark. They did all they could to familiarize themselves on the subject by reading books, going to meetings, sharing experiences with other parents and agonizing for countless hours until they were in danger of losing their own sanity.

*T*he house in Calgary was larger than their residence in Kingston, but with the number of people occupying the house, it was still too small. The children doubled up and tripled up in bedrooms and it was difficult for anyone to have any privacy. It was a crowded and busy house.

Margaret's days were filled with changing diapers, doing laundry, cooking meals, washing dishes, driving children to and from lessons, cleaning up clutter, shopping, keeping track of many expenses and solving the many problems that arose on a daily basis. She was busy all the time but had little mental stimulation. The drudgery and sameness of it all was stressful and her patience was worn thin. The situation was made worse because she was never allowed enough sleep. Babies or sick children frequently interrupted her sleep at night, and during the day it was nearly impossible to nap.

The tension gripped Margaret's body and what began as a stiff neck gradually developed to become a pain so severe that she required hospitalization. She had x-rays, but they showed no abnormalities. Her neck was put in traction for a time but she failed to receive any benefit, besides, she became bored with treatment and a low calorie diet that had been forced upon her, and she asked to be sent home. So, with muscle relaxants and a collar to keep her head supported, she was sent on her way. Because the doctors could find no cause for her pain, they indicated that there could be a psychological cause.

*S*aturday was grocery shopping day for the Shaws. Albert and Margaret and the children would climb into the car for the drive to the grocery store. They herded the children up and down the aisles while each parent and the eldest child pushed a shopping cart. Older siblings were enlisted to keep an eye on younger ones, but in all the confusion, the inevitable happened. On one occasion, little five-year-old David was a little too slow to exit the store. As he did, he saw the last of his siblings climb into the station wagon. His dad backed up and drove away leaving the little boy standing alone, confused and scared. Back at home, Margaret set to work putting away groceries while Albert bathed the younger ones and helped them put on their pyjamas.

"Where is David?" asked Albert. "Tell him to come in for his bath."

No one knew where David was. He could not be found in the house, or outside in the yard or at the neighbour's. Albert felt a little sick to his stomach, thinking that he may have left him behind at the grocery store. Quickly, he climbed into the car and drove back. There was David, standing at the front door of the store, waiting patiently for someone to come and get him.

The poor child was again temporarily separated from his family in July of 1965. Mary took her younger siblings, Michael, Rita, Patrick and David to the Stampede Parade. All went well until David got lost and separated from the group. Mary searched and called but eventually had no choice but to lead the others home and hope that nine year old David would make it home from downtown by himself. Margaret was sick with worry and sent Albert in the car to look for their lost son. David, the lost little lamb, eventually found his own way home.

*E*lizabeth ran away from home regularly starting at age two. Margaret and Albert met many people through her. She was an ambassador of sorts. Strangers were always carrying her home, or driving her home or calling them to pick her up. Her addiction for this pastime compelled Margaret to pin identification on her at all times.

One Sunday afternoon when the youngest child was a few weeks old, the family undertook a picnic to Happy Valley, which was located just west of Calgary, with a huge lunch in the station wagon and all ten children. As they sat down to eat they counted heads and Elizabeth was missing again. Then over the loudspeaker came the call, "Will the parents of Elizabeth Shaw please come to the swimming pool?" Without any fear, and no idea how to swim, she had leaped in the deep end, and someone pulled her out.

She loved trampolines and had a remarkable memory for the location of trampoline parks all over the city. Several times Margaret had to phone the police when Elizabeth was away for a long time, and they would find her bouncing up and down in ecstasy. The attendants were a little curious that she walked in and used the facilities without paying. One time Margaret found her in a corner store. The owner of the store was somewhat aggrieved that this strange child was helping herself to ice cream, chocolate and other goodies. Explanations never seemed adequate, so Margaret just paid and left quietly.

Elizabeth hated to see a baldhead and would scream indignantly at the possessor of one. One day Margaret drove to a service station to have her car checked. The mechanic sat down in the driver's seat to test the car when Elizabeth reached up from the back seat and smacked him smartly on his baldhead and scolded him for his imperfection. "Hey you, you have a bald head. You're a bad man!" The poor man was hurt and embarrassed and apologized saying; "I used to have a very nice head of hair when I was young."

The day came in September 1964, when Elizabeth was six years old when she should have been starting grade one. They had to prove to the Catholic School Board that she could not be educated in an ordinary school. This was in order that she qualify for Special Education or for an institution. The plan was to bring her for one day, so the only day of ordinary schooling that she ever had began at home with a bath. Margaret washed her soft brown wavy hair and dressed her up in a pretty dress. During the bath Elizabeth ate some soap and it made her quite windy. This amused her immensely and she giggled about these small eruptions all the way to school.

The principal met them at the front door as he had been forewarned of the ordeal ahead. He escorted them to the grade one room and began preparing Elizabeth for school. He took her by the hand and started to show her around the classroom. He introduced her to the teacher who looked most apprehensive. Elizabeth let go of his hand and quickly scurried under the desks, and pulled open drawers and cupboards with wild abandon. No one could catch her, and they waited, frozen, while she had her own way. The other twenty-five or so children were all out of their desks either laughing and running after Elizabeth or looking a little scared of her. One little girl started to cry.

Still hoping that he could handle the situation, the principal took her again by the hand, after a frantic scuffle, and led her to the window. "When you calm down young lady, you will like your bright classroom and your new teacher."

The new teacher, despite her youth, looked as though she was going to have a stroke. She couldn't speak, but appeared to ask how she could be delivered from this situation and quickly!

The principal bent down to talk to Elizabeth, now that he had her firmly in his grasp. "How do you like the room?" he asked.

She looked up at him with a twinkle in her eyes and said, "Would you like to hear me make a big fart?" She clenched her teeth and squeezed a loud discharge of wind into the room. Then she turned to her mom and said, "Did you hear what I said Mommy? Did you hear me fart?"

Choking with apologies about her language and explanations of her condition, Margaret left her with the teachers and went home.

The noise could be heard down the halls of the school coming from the grade one classroom. A small, brown haired girl in grade two wearing thick cat-eye glasses recognized the screams as coming from her sister. She shrunk a little in her desk and tried to hide her eyes.

"Hey Bernadette," whispered a classmate, "isn't that your sister making all that noise?"

"No, it's not," she lied.

"Yes it is. I saw your mom here at the school earlier. That is your sister," said another student.

"No it's not," Bernadette insisted. "I don't know who that is."

Just then Elizabeth ran by the grade two classroom, giggling and shrieking loudly. She was followed closely behind by two anxious looking adults, the grade one teacher and the principal.

"See, that is your sister!"

"No it's not! I don't know her!" Bernadette was determined that no one would associate her with that wild child.

Elizabeth lasted until noon when the school gave up and called Margaret to come and get her. It had been a wild morning.

*A*lbert was always looking for encouraging signs from Elizabeth that she may get better. After all, she had learned her alphabet and sometimes she wanted to play, and she certainly loved to jump. But, no matter how hard he looked, it was obvious she was not normal and never would be. When she played she was overly rough. She savagely beat her siblings, and especially her little brother, Robert, whom she pushed down the stairs on occasion. She threw tantrums for no obvious reason for which she often required sedatives. Her behaviour became the talk of the neighbourhood. "What's the matter with that Shaw girl? Did you see what she did the other day?"

The school board in Calgary did not have any programs suitable for Elizabeth. They believed her condition was too severe. In fact, there were virtually no supports at all in Alberta at that time for the treatment of autism or many other mental handicaps. Parents had two choices, keep your children at home and care for them yourself or send them to the large mental institution in Red Deer.

Margaret and Albert were faced with a terrible dilemma. Elizabeth had a tumultuous childhood so far, filled with tantrums and wild behaviour. At times she was overactive and at others she was practically comatose. They could not handle this unruly child in addition to their other nine children and the effect on the other children was quite undesirable. She required so much of their attention that the others' needs were neglected.

Elizabeth's doctors insisted that she be sent to Linden House in Red Deer, which was part of a complex that housed mentally and physically handicapped children. Albert and Margaret were very much opposed to sending their daughter away. They had more radical ideas that were, in fact, years ahead of their time. For example, they suggested a specialized day care for handicapped children be built in Calgary, but no one was willing to build such a facility in 1966. With no options available they took the painful step of placing her in the hands of the mental institution. They left Elizabeth in Red Deer and returned home. In addition to the pain and guilt they felt, they had to deal with criticism from others. "How could you do that to your own child? I love my children too much to ever send them away." Even as a young child, Madelaine knew these comments were mean and unfair. She felt her parents' pain but she also knew the home was a more peaceful one without Elizabeth, though she could never bring herself to say this to her parents, for fear she would hurt their feelings.

*A*lbert and Margaret continued to push hard for better conditions for the handicapped when many other parents were unwilling. They wanted to increase awareness so that some meaningful programs could be developed, even as they were told that a cure or chance for recovery was remote for Elizabeth, they continued to push hard for therapy or cure. Many of the doctors were impressed that they wanted their child helped as most parents just want their children tucked away.

"People need to know about autism and the problems all parents of handicapped children face," Margaret said. "I will contact that talk radio station and maybe they will put us on the air." The response to the radio show was very positive. They had conversations with their MLA, and discussions with Mental Health Association, to little avail. It would be many years before any changes were made. Margaret was heartsick and frustrated that her attempts seemed to lead nowhere.

Ten months after Elizabeth was sent away to Red Deer she had all but lost the ability to talk. Margaret and Albert were very sorrowful about the loss, but thought that perhaps it was the trauma of the move that caused her to lose her language. Over time however, psychologists were pleased and sometimes astounded with Elizabeth's progress. Not only had she regained the ability to talk but she had a large vocabulary and she had completed the grade one reader. Her behaviour however was a different matter entirely. For that she was given strong tranquilizers.

On her eighth birthday, Margaret gave Elizabeth two dolls, but as usual, Elizabeth's play was exceedingly odd. One of them became the "bad girl" which she treated as a patient and disciplined. She wagged her finger at the bad doll, "Sit down you and behave yourself!" The other became the "good girl". This one she praised. It became increasingly evident that she would never lead a normal life.

*T*ragically, in the year 1966, the Shaw household was turned upside-down again. This time the attention was focused on three-year-old Christopher. Beautiful little Christopher with his big brown eyes and sweet, gentle nature; who called his father "Daddy-Albert," was also starting to show signs of autism. Once completely toilet trained, he regressed to wearing diapers. He stopped walking and started crawling and he stopped talking and started parroting. Both autistic children learned to talk before the age of three but later their speech was robot-like and repetitive almost as if they found it easier to sing their requests. In both cases the speech would come and go, so there were periods when one or the other was virtually mute.

Then the tantrums began, the lashing out, the self-abuse, striking at a world he could no longer comprehend. Albert and Margaret were heartbroken. They sat in their bedroom at night, when they thought they wouldn't be heard by the children and discussed the bleak future and they cried. Their children laid quietly in their own beds engrossed in conversations they weren't supposed to hear. In their own childish ways they also tried to comprehend.

It also took years for Christopher to be diagnosed with autism. One doctor said he was of average intelligence and just needed more interaction with other children and then perhaps he could go to kindergarten. Ignorant doctors again put the blame on Margaret for his condition. She was told she was a cold and aloof mother and that is why her children were handicapped. She tried hard not to take to heart the opinions of these "experts," but it was difficult.

"Maybe they're right, or why would I have two autistic children? But they can't be right. The other children are not affected."

She lived with years of guilt and discouragement which ate away at her happiness. She was frequently driven to tears or she took out her frustration in bursts of anger.

The day had come. They could not put it off any longer. It was the spring of 1969 and Christopher was getting bigger and more unmanageable. Margaret and Albert had done their best to cope. Even the children tried their best. They could not handle the situation on their own because it put too much stress on the entire family.

"Perhaps the institution would not be that bad," Margaret said, "after all, Elizabeth had adjusted." She packed Christopher's suitcase, folding each item of clothing neatly and checking that each was labelled with his name. "I must be strong. It's for the best," but inside, she felt that something was dying. "Who would like to come to Red Deer with us to say good-bye to Christopher?" she called to her children, as cheerily as she could.

Four children volunteered and climbed into the car. They had all been to Red Deer many times of course, to visit Elizabeth, and the drive usually included a trip to the beach at Gull Lake or the trampoline park or a meal at a restaurant. It was a great treat. The conversation in the back seats of the station wagon was excited and animated. Christopher sat in the front between his mom and dad. Very few words were spoken between Albert and Margaret. There was little left to say. They both felt like they were abandoning their dear son to an unknown fate.

Albert drove to the head office of the mental institution to sign the various documents. His hand shook as he held the pen. He took a deep breath and let it out slowly. Above all, he must maintain control and not break down in front of his wife and children. He was given directions to the building that housed young boys and drove there with great trepidation. In general, he was an easygoing man who accepted with grace any curve balls that life threw at him. He did not have a poverty stricken childhood like his wife, but he had been raised by a distant, angry father and a mother who had been unable to protect him. She died when he was only sixteen years old, and then he lost his father at age twenty. Afterwards, he lived with his older sister until he went away to university. He loved his wife and children very much. They were the most important things in the world to him. Logically, he understood the need to put Christopher in the institution; on the inside, he felt like a betrayer.

In the back seat of the car, four of his children were laughing and playing together. He looked at them with love, and then at his wife. She nodded and took Christopher by the hand. The family went inside the drab looking building to see the place where Christopher would live.

They knocked on the door, several times. Eventually a young man opened the door. He looked Christopher up and down but did not greet him.

"Come this way, I'll show you around." He led them to a large room to the left of the entrance. "These are the sleeping quarters," he said in a dull, monotone voice, indicating two rows of beds, eight to a side.

A few children lay on the beds, listless, with blank expressions on their faces.

"Where are the pillows and blankets?" asked Margaret.

"We take them off during the day, so the kids don't get them dirty."

Margaret's wide eyes scanned the bare, white walls. "Why aren't there any pictures on the walls?"

"The kids would only take them down and break them. Come on, I'll show you the playroom." He led them across the hall to another room. These walls were also white and bare and along two sides of the room were long wooden benches. There was nothing else in the room. On one bench a child lay curled up, asleep. Other children wandered aimlessly around the room or sat rocking themselves.

"Where are the toys?" Margaret asked.

"They'd only break them, or throw them at each other."

"What do they do for fun?" she asked.

"Sometimes we take them outside, if we have enough staff. Usually we don't."

A boy about seven years old suddenly pulled his pants down and peed on the tile floor.

"Hey! What do you think you're doing?" the young man said sharply. "Get over here!" He hustled the boy to the toilet, and came back with a mop and pail.

Margaret looked around the room and noticed a boy, completely naked, lying in foetal position in a corner of the room. "Why doesn't that boy have any clothes on?" she asked. Her eyes became more and more sad.

"He always takes them off," said the young man.

The boy who was sleeping on the bench awoke and looked at Margaret. He jumped up and ran to her and wrapped his arms around her waist. "Momma," he said.

Margaret hugged him in return and stroked his hair. Her eyes filled with tears.

"We suggest not hugging the children," the young man said, and took the boy by the arm and pulled him away from Margaret. With his other hand he held Christopher by the shoulder. "You should probably go now."

Margaret hesitated, every maternal instinct told her to grab her son and run away from this place, but she knew she couldn't. She bent down to Christopher and kissed him. "We'll be back next week," she whispered.

"You can't come back for two weeks. It will give him time to adjust."

Margaret held on to Albert's arm tightly, trying to draw on his strength, knowing that he was also struggling for self-control. He put his hand over hers, and squeezed her trembling fingers. He bent also to kiss his son, and the family returned to the car. Margaret looked back at Christopher. His large brown eyes, blameless and bewildered, stared back at her.

Albert sat at the steering wheel and stared grimly ahead. He lit a cigarette and sucked deeply. Margaret sat in the passenger seat and sobbed. The four children in the back seat were silent now. A terrible black cloud of despair descended on the car. There would be no beach or restaurant today. "Why did we leave Christopher there? Why isn't he coming home with us?" asked Robert, who was only four years old.

Nobody answered him. Margaret cried all the way on the trip back to Calgary. She felt like Judas, betraying an innocent one to a terrible fate.

Sometimes the family would go on picnics, perhaps to Bowness Park where the children could ride the Ferris wheel, or the roller coaster or the paddleboats. It was generally a great deal of fun, providing no one got left behind. The children were each given a few dollars to spend. The older ones, Mary and Rita, went off together to enjoy the rides and it was assumed that David would join his older brothers, Patrick and Michael.

The younger ones, Bernadette, Madelaine, and Robert, stayed close to their parents.

Patrick and Michael took a turn on the paddleboat together, and since it only seated two, they left their little brother standing on shore. David was rather miffed. He stormed off to find his parents and tell them of the great injustice he had just suffered. He searched the picnic area, the fair grounds and along the banks of the creek, but they were nowhere to be found. Michael and Patrick didn't worry about him. They assumed he had gone back to their parents.

The time came to go home and the family gathered, climbed into the car, tired and exhilarated after their time at the park. Albert backed the car out and left. Ten minutes into the ride home, Patrick asked, "Where's David?" Albert turned the car around and for the first time in his life, he exceeded the speed limit in his rush back to Bowness Park.

David was standing in the parking lot, his cheeks wet from tears. The poor waif was overlooked once again. Forgotten, the embodiment of the middle child syndrome, he had no fun at all at the park that day.

The family usually didn't travel very far on vacations. They would travel around Alberta and sometimes British Columbia, camping or staying in cheap motels along the way. The perfect opportunity for a vacation came with the announcement that Albert's hometown was having a reunion. It sounded like a great deal of fun. Albert guided the station wagon along the highway that led from Calgary to his hometown of Youngstown, Alberta. Beside him was his wife and in the back were three of the children, Bernadette, Madelaine and Robert. Youngstown is located in one of the driest parts of south-eastern Alberta. Normally, by mid July, the grass would be coloured yellow rather than green, made dry and brittle by the heat of the sun. July 1971 was one of the rainiest on record, and the farmer's crops were tall, green and healthy. Best of all, on the weekend of the reunion, the sun finally broke through. It appeared to be a very promising sign for a wonderful weekend. Albert had not been back to Youngstown since he was a young man and was looking forward to meeting up with old friends and acquaintances.

The car was ten years old and a little worse for wear, but it still ran, so the family was off on their weekend adventure. The car was packed with clothes, food, a tent and sleeping bags for the children and pillows and blankets for the adults. The two back seats could be folded down to create a space large enough for two adults to sleep.

The children were free to scramble from the front to middle to the end row of seats without the worry of restraints as they meandered down the highway. Seatbelt and baby car-seat laws were non-existent which was fortunate because the car did not have seatbelts. The lack of seatbelts did result in a few bumped heads when Albert was forced to quickly apply the brakes, but this was considered normal for car passengers of the day. It is hard to believe that any of the Shaw children survived during the time when no seatbelts were required in cars.

They arrived at the Youngstown campground, which was nothing more than an empty field covered with grass. The children jumped out of the car dressed in their shorts and t-shirts and gleefully began to set up camp, that is, until the swarms descended. The unusually wet spring had produced a bumper crop for the farmers and more mosquitoes than the town had seen in a long time. The family was attacked unmercifully. Itchy and swollen they prepared their campfire meal. It was a poor beginning to the weekend.

When evening came, the family climbed into the car for a trip into town. There would be a get together for the adults at one of the local bars. The children were too young to join their parents inside the bar so it was decided that they would go to sleep in the car parked just outside. It should be perfectly safe; after all, it was a small town. What could happen?

It wouldn't be the first time the children slept in the car. Sometimes, on a Saturday night, the children would change into their pyjamas and load the car with pillows and blankets for a trip to the drive-in theatre. The children munched on homemade popcorn while the car filled with smoke from Albert's cigarettes. The smaller children hid their eyes during the scary parts of the movies and eventually fell asleep on the laps of their parents or older siblings. At the end of the evening sleepy children were carried into the house and placed in their beds.

After the get-together in the bar, Albert was to drive the car back to the camp site where the children would move into the tent and the adults into the back of the car. The three sleepy children closed their eyes and awaited their parents' return. They were startled awake by a loud banging on the windows of the vehicle. Four inebriated men stood outside, yelling, hitting the sides of the car, trying all the doors. "Come on outside sweetheart," they yelled to Bernadette, who was only fourteen. They made kissing noises and obscene gestures.

"Come on out, we have something to give you, Ha! Ha! Ha!" said a man with a cigarette dangling out of his mouth. He sat on the hood of the car and bounced it up and down.

"Open the door honey, we just want to play," begged one of the men. He wore a John Deere cap over his greasy hair, though it was the middle of the night.

"We should find a brick and break the window," said another.

The children's nervousness turned to terror and they began to cry loudly. They attempted to cover the windows with blankets, to block the view of those mocking, cruel faces that glared at them from all sides of the car. They looked hopefully outside for their parents to return. "Mommy! Daddy!" they called.

Outside the streets were dark and gloomy due to the absence of street lights and made the men seem even more sinister and threatening. The children huddled together, afraid to stay in the car and afraid to make a run for the bar.

"Don't cry honey. Come on outside. I can make it all better. Ha! Ha! Ha!"

The drunken men eventually gave up their game and stumbled away down the street.

Margaret and Albert returned to a tearful, shaken group of children an hour or so later, and couldn't quite believe what they were told. They calmed the children the best they could. "Oh, never mind. They were just joking," Margaret said, but on the inside, she was filled with relentless guilt. "How could I have been so stupid as to leave my children alone in the car? Why didn't I think? They could have been seriously hurt."

The station wagon took them on many trips but over time, the poor old vehicle decayed with rust. Brown spots slowly ate away the body and floor of the old car until it looked like a giant block of Swiss cheese. On the inside, the carpet was worn away by moisture and many scrambling feet until a hole was revealed in the floor of the car. Through the hole the children could and watch the road pass by underneath. Sometimes for fun they would throw objects down the hole, much to the consternation of their parents. On gravel roads the car filled up with choking dust emitting from the hole in the floor. When it would no longer run, the old vehicle was eventually replaced, but it could never be said that the Shaw family didn't get their money's worth from the old station wagon.

$\mathcal{A}$ most amazing invention arose in the 1950's called the television. No one had any idea, at that time, what an impact that invention would have on society. It began innocently enough with variety shows like "Jack Benny." Parents didn't have to worry about anything unseemly or inappropriate for their families. It was all quite tame fare.

It wasn't until the 1960's that the Shaws acquired their first TV. What excitement! It brought the family together. How wonderful! Children were called in from play to watch the "Lucy Show," "The Honeymooners" and "The Wonderful World of Disney." The television only had two channels and was in black and white, but the world was brought into their living room. Over time the shows on TV became more sophisticated and were often remarkable. The family gathered around to watch The Ed Sullivan Show, the lunar landing, and other news broadcasts.

> *I should never have made provision for television.*
> *It envelops your life, exacerbates strife,*
> *Complicates living, keeps insisting on giving,*
> *Excessive commercials and endless rehearsals*
> *Of dramas, musicals and comedy, sports, news and documentary.*
> *It baby-sits small ones but interrupts tall ones,*
> *From doing their studies and playing with buddies.*
> *It separates poppy who watches his hockey,*
> *From daughters and mama who must have her drama.*
> *To workouts and prances, disturbing the chances*
> *Of peace in this house.*
> *Why do I stand it? Enough is enough!*
> *The real reason is I love the stuff!*
> *This love of contention, this TV I mention*
> *Is a part of our life with foolishness rife.*

Sometimes TV broadcasts were very disturbing. People were able to watch footage of war for the first time, with broadcasts from Vietnam. The North Vietnamese attempted in the late 1950's to overthrow the South Vietnamese in an attempt to make the whole country Communist. The Americans became involved in the war in 1959, though they didn't officially declare war until 1964, in an attempt to stop the spread of Communism throughout Southeast Asia. It was the longest military conflict in U.S. history when it finally ended in 1975. In that time more than 58,000

Robert, Christopher, Madelaine, Bernadette.

Americans lost their lives and another 304,000 were wounded.[9] The reality of the brutality of war shocked the population, and a movement began in the United States to end the war.

Beatniks of the 1950's had grown to become conservative members of the workforce but a new and more radical movement began. The hippie generation emerged in the 1960's, and the people who had worked so hard to drag the economy out of depression found their beliefs, values and way of life challenged by a younger generation who thought they knew better.

The counterculture that arose in the United States was one in which young people believed they were going to create a better world. The Beatles sang, "All we need is love, love, love..." and many believed that through demonstrations and non-conformity they could end the violence of the Vietnam War and remove the threat of nuclear war. The civil rights and women's rights movements of the time also influenced change in society. Young people questioned and challenged many of the cultural norms of their parents and previous generations. Believing that the old traditions and beliefs were the cause of current world problems, they rejected the

9 http://www.vietnamwar.com/

wisdom of past generations and sought to find their own solutions. The counterculture quickly spread to Canada.

Young people dressed in ripped, faded jeans, bright tie-dyed shirts, leather jackets with fringes and they shopped at army surplus and second hand stores. The girls wore mini skirts and halter tops. Peace symbols were sewn onto clothes and painted on faces. Long hair was left flying loose and untamed down the backs of boys and girls alike. They were an enigma to their parents.

Some young people sought to "expand their consciousness" through drug use. It was a dangerous pastime and many lost their lives through reckless drug use. "Turn on, tune in, drop out," was a phrase coined by Timothy Leary in the 1960's to promote the "benefits" of LSD. Parents were at a loss as to how to deal with and protect their children.

Peace and love became the buzz words of the day, but the younger generation looked for peace and love outside of Judeo-Christian tradition. Many followed the example of some famous rock stars such as the Beatles, and turned to religions such as Hinduism, but more often they rejected

Rita, Margaret, Albert, David,
Mary, Madelaine, Michael, Patrick,
Elizabeth, Bernadette, Christopher, Robert.

organized religions completely. Nonconformity was encouraged. "If it feels good, do it," became the new belief system.

The invention of the birth control pill meant girls did not have to worry about becoming pregnant and pre-marital and extra-marital sex became much more common. Young people indulged in "free love," which meant sexual promiscuity. Along with sexual promiscuity came a sharp increase in sexually transmitted diseases. Some would argue that it also contributed to the breakdown of the family. With more people cheating on their spouses, divorce was on the increase.

Young people have always questioned the values of their parents, but in the past, most eventually they came around to accept and embrace those same values. These young people went further and brought about sweeping cultural changes. Illegal drug use and the rejection of restrictions on sexual behaviour were two powerful negative influences of the sixties generation. Subsequent generations carried on that self destructive behaviour and the result was a legacy of family break down, drug addiction and sexually transmitted diseases that continues to this day.

*M*argaret felt that the lump would never leave her throat. Elizabeth and Christopher would always be handicapped and so would she, caught up in her love for them, and wedded to their helplessness. Love can make you care but it cannot cure. Her handicapped children, objects of her love, were born into a world that didn't want them. They were burdens on the system.

She prayed that God would give her the grace to bear the pain of their afflictions, to deal with people sated with the best of life who told her sagely, "Leave them to their own kind." Margaret would not turn her back on her own children, handicapped or not.

Born without the ability to communicate with his fellow man, the autistic person is lonely beyond comprehension. He is like a spirit locked in a prison where none of the phones work properly. When the messages arrive they are often garbled. The human voice, with its many tones and inflections is sometimes incomprehensible to the autistic person. If by chance, he understands the message, he may be unable to reply. His signals to the outside world are not understood. The sense of touch may be amplified, so that a gentle touch feels like a hot poker. At other times, he can bite his arm until it bleeds and feel no pain. Ordinary noises, like a vacuum cleaner, may enter the autistic person's brain at ear-splitting volume, causing him great anguish and he will lash out at the object or person causing him pain. He lives inside his own confused mind. In an effort to shut out the over-stimulating world he takes comfort in his compulsive routines, repeating the same act or the same phrase over and over. He languishes in a kind of grave above ground.

Autistic son, why do you stare,
So vacantly into space for hours?
Then lash about in seeming agony,
and punish everything in sight,
With your terrible rage?

Silent, robot child,
My baby, gone wrong.
My ninth child, curly haired and perfect.
"Talk to me please. Christopher look at me."
But you won't.

I say, "I love you Christopher."
You answer robot-like, "I love you Christopher."
"No, no, you must tell me that you love me."
You meet my eyes at last and smile shyly,
"I love you…Mom"

I reach to hug you for I must be satisfied.
You won't let me.
I can't hold you.
You attack your own flesh,
And sometimes mine.

I want to save you from yourself,
But I'm not able.
I bore you gladly,
But I can't share your life.
No comprehension penetrates your mind.

You rage and despair.
I lash about too,
Against that peculiar world,
That keeps me from you.
What happened to my little boy?

My beautiful remote child,
Why did you go away and leave me,
Heartbroken and bewildered?
Scarcely able to comprehend this double tragedy,
First your sister and now you.

I want to hold my son.
But you won't let me,
You push my hands away,
You look at me with unresponsive eyes.
Don't you know how much I love you?

My darling brown-eyed boy,
Why did you change,
From little boy laughter,
To tearless crying,
And stony isolation?

Chapter Nine
Middle Age

a distressed neighbour called on Margaret to help deal with a difficult problem, and she reluctantly agreed to help. She was always ready to help a friend or neighbour in need, even when it involved something distasteful.

"Will you come with me?" she said to Margaret. "I want to make sure they don't suffer. Do you think they'll suffocate under the heavy blanket over them? I don't want them to feel cold on the way."

"She's taking them to the veterinarian," thought Margaret, "to have them put to sleep. What would it matter if they all perished on the way?"

They took the seven, one day old puppies in a basket in the front seat of the car. The seven furry, healthy pups, climbing and squealing over each other, opening pink mouths and stretching tiny paws, were about to pay the price of their mother's love affair. A Boston Bull Terrier and a Miniature Collie mix is what they were, with round heads and long thin tails. A purebred commands a healthy price, but a mutt is lucky to escape with its life.

The doctor held in one hand a needle twice as long as each small pup he held in the other. They struggled in his hand a bit, and then an instant's pain. The small tails twitched. As each one died he laid it down beside the basket he took it from. They laid limp and lifeless, death-composed, like commas in a row.

Margaret led her weeping friend to the car. "A drink or two will calm your nerves," she said.

Margaret was a giving and caring person, so much so that she had great difficulty saying no to salespeople who arrived at the door or called on the telephone. "How will they feed their families if I don't help them out?"

"Good afternoon ma'am, I am calling to offer you a free demonstration of our Kirby vacuum. If you will allow us into your home we will clean your living room rug or any other area. No obligation to buy of course. This is our way of advertising…"

Margaret felt "put on the spot," torn between a real desire to be polite to the caller and the knowledge that she must be firm, even brusque, but that was not her way, and she inevitably was subjected to home visits. "If I dare to be polite on the phone, and then say no to them later, I might emerge with my money intact but then I feel guilt ridden. It takes a few days sometimes to emerge from such an experience and regain my senses. I could cheerfully wring my own neck for my gullibility." She did not like to be taken advantage of but was not prepared for the reaction of a particular saleslady when she refused to buy her vacuum.

"I guess I'll never learn. I always trust people so much that they take advantage of me. Now it will cost me twenty dollars to get this vacuum cleaned after you have used it for two days." The saleswoman didn't seem to recall convincing Margaret to keep the vacuum for two days to try it out.

Margaret had no quarrel with salesmanship as a legitimate occupation. She was opposed to the "con-artist" type of selling which takes unfair advantage of the customer.

Her heart-felt obligation to help took on a much greater meaning if it was a friend doing the selling. Be it Amway, Tupperware, Avon or whatever, she consistently bought more that she needed or wanted. Understandably, there was some underlying resentment on her part, but she was mostly annoyed with herself for her inability to say "no." A telephone opening line that left Margaret feeling powerless was, "Hello Marg. Do you feel like an evening out this week? I'm having a few of the girls over."

Of course Margaret would quickly agree. She would jump at the chance to have an evening out with friends where she could enjoy a cup of tea and conversation. It then developed that the evening out consisted of a "party," a "home clinic", or a demonstration. It could be Stanley, Tupper, Amway, jewellery-making or a beauty products demonstration. The ladies who held these parties were given some reward for enticing their friends to a sale where most felt compelled to buy whether they needed the products or not. After all, how could you say "no" to your friends?

At the party, along with some delectable treats and a glass of wine, they incidentally slipped the guests an order form, no obligation of course, but how could they possibly go another day without this item or that? There was a feeling generated that these products were a necessity, like your daily bread. If Margaret did not order something her hostess would have been deprived of a stack of plastic canisters in her choice of colours, or a cake holder that will never store in a cupboard, or a bacon keeper where her bacon could go rancid undetected for weeks. One could not be so callous as to order so little that the total of the assembled ladies fell below $250.00.

Margaret could never forgive herself for attending a total of ten Tupperware parties in eighteen months. The kitchen cupboards at home bulged with storage containers. Maybe she felt guilt, or generosity, or maybe it was simply because her brain became muddled by the huge variety of Tupperware items available.

What truly made it all worth while for the assembled gaggle of women, was the speech given by the Tupperware distributor, who explained how Mr. Tupper changed her life in a short but spiritual rendering of his invention of the plastic dishes and their sealed covers. They always showed such religious-like fervour and dedication to the patron saint of the company, whether it was Mr. Stanley, Mr. Tupper or someone else. This technique of selling seemed to play on the naïve, the generous, the obliging and the friendly nature of people, and that made Margaret feel resentful.

*D*ue to the stress that Margaret was under on a daily basis and her excessive weight gain, her health was at risk. She was strongly advised by her physician to get some regular exercise, to help her get fit, to lose some weight and reduce her stress. All of her children had taken swimming lessons, so why not her?

The floor of the locker room felt cold, damp and clammy under her bare feet, and smelled strongly of chlorine. She pulled the curtain closed in the little change room, and wondered for the hundredth time how her children had managed to talk her into this. "At least there are no mirrors in here," she thought, remembering with great distaste yesterday's experience at Sears when she had to try on swimming suits in front of three-way mirrors. She finally decided on a black one piece that covered as much flesh as possible and supported her heavy bust. She pulled on her first ever swimming suit to go to her first ever swimming lesson at the age of forty-four. She looked down distastefully at herself, "I look like an overstuffed sausage."

She self-consciously adjusted the straps over her shoulders and snapped the elastics firmly over her buttocks and reluctantly pulled back the curtain and peeked out into the women's locker room. A few young children and some toned young women were getting changed out in the open, unabashed about their nudity. Margaret unfolded her towel and wrapped it around her waist and made a tentative walk towards the entrance to the pool.

No one had swimming lessons in the town where she grew up. There was no swimming pool. There weren't even any lakes or swimming holes, except for the odd pond that was home to weeds, frogs and bugs. Swimming was simply not an activity in which children of the prairie dustbowl of the 1930's took part.

She dropped her towel at the water's edge and stood at the stairs leading into the pool and greeted her instructor. Margaret dipped a foot into the pool and quickly withdrew it, "Oh, that's cold!" she exclaimed. Somehow, she had expected the water to be warm, like a bathtub.

Over time, she overcame her fear of the water and her shyness of wearing a swimsuit and learned some basic strokes. Mostly, she learned how to float. She was very buoyant and found it quite relaxing to lie on her back and paddle effortlessly around the pool, so much for doctor's orders to get some exercise. She just closed her eyes and let the stress float away. Most importantly, she gained some confidence and had some fun.

Margaret and Albert

$\mathcal{O}$ne of the pitfalls of Margaret's nervous disposition was a tendency to giggle at inappropriate moments. It inevitably reduced her to an undignified heap of quivering, shaking, unstoppable mirth, leaving her open to charges of rudeness by those witnessing. In her reduced state of helplessness, attempted apologies only heightened the frenzy. Her gasps for breath, the streaming eyes, and physical weakness all gave the impression of distressing lack of control. Unfortunately, solemn occasions made everything seem funnier because it was unseemly to be merry when one should be serious.

Margaret's earliest breach of etiquette, that she could remember, took place when she was ten years old. She was visiting at the farm home of her ex-grade one teacher. The lady was not overly endowed with a sense of humour or affection for little girls with a penchant for giggling. A whispered conversation between Margaret and her little friend Mary had taken place before supper. They were teasing each other about who would have to sit beside the hired man at the table. The lot fell to Margaret and as she caught Mary's eye, they were at once enveloped in a marathon of giggles. Despite heroic efforts at control and a deep shame at her weakness, the laughter went on with sad effect on their table manners, as they choked and coughed over their food. The hostess was not in the least amused and glared at the two of them.

During her fourteenth year, as a convent boarder, there was another case of merriment gone wrong. They were seated in chapel under the stern eyes of the nuns and the dignified older students. It was a religious ceremony that entailed a procession around the perimeters of the chapel. The priest led the group holding a large Bible with altar boys following behind. Walking behind the priest was a taller alter boy carrying a large cross. His eyes were fixed straight ahead as he concentrated on his important duty. As they neared the alter steps Margaret caught her breath with certain anticipation.

"He's going to trip and fall with the cross," she thought, and fall he did, right into the priest. The priest was knocked forward and tried valiantly to maintain a grip on the Bible but fumbled it, sending it flying. The altar boy, priest, cross and Bible all fell to the floor with a loud crash. The proceedings came to a standstill as the two stood and tried to regain their dignity.

Her nervous gasp turned into unrestrained but muffled laughter while her shoulders shook uncontrollably. She glanced up to catch a stern look from Mother Angela. Margaret's contorted face brought an unwilling response from the pious nun and she turned away quickly, but her shoulders shook like Margaret's, and gave her away. Soon row after row of giggles and snorts destroyed the mood of prayerfulness. Later, when Mother Angela reproached Margaret for starting the uproar, her heart was not really in the sermon.

Another event in the catalogue of her sins of giggling took place in her early years of teaching. It occurred at church too, of course. In those days, in that German community, the congregation was divided down the middle, with the men on the right as you went in and the women on the left. The rows of stout matrons in winter coats with big fur collars and squat felt hats looked curiously alike. One elderly soul though, caught Margaret's attention. She was seated just a row ahead. Every time she lifted her head from her prayers, her hat tilted jauntily to one side at a rakish angle. A closer inspection revealed the curved hook of a clothes hanger protruding from the collar of her coat. She must have been in a terrible hurry to get to church. Again the palsied giggling took over the rows, as one by one the people discovered the cause of Margaret's amusement. Poor lady, she probably never guessed the comic relief she provided.

The worst place to giggle of course is at a funeral. Why would such a sorrowful occasion stimulate unbridled merriment? Margaret paid a visit to Eastern Canada to attend the funeral of an elderly aunt. She was not really dearly beloved, but the solemn faces of her friends as they offered their sympathies had a certain unsettling effect on Margaret. When an old friend with a characteristically squeaky voice approached Margaret and piped her condolences, the dam of control gave way. Giggles convulsed her and perhaps because of the shocked reproachful glares sent her way by relatives and townsfolk, she persisted with her painful, almost hysterical giggling through the service.

There is a time and place for laughter. She has on occasion consoled herself that her sense of humour keeps her sane, but was also dismayed that it was so out of control. The giggles left her with small dregs of shame, but a sense of delight too.

Stress became a state of mind with which Margaret was very familiar in her child rearing days and Elizabeth and Christopher were not her only concerns. There were eight other children, including, in the year of Canada's centennial, 1967, four teenagers. Mary and a friend flew to Montreal to take in Expo '67. Alas, the first little chick was spreading her wings, readying herself to fly away from the nest. She was going away to a big city. "Dear God, what if something were to happen to her?" She worried about each of her children everyday. Would they get involved in drugs? Would a daughter come home pregnant? It was hard to raise principled, high-minded children in the midst of the 1960's social upheaval. It's doubtful that Margaret was able to sleep through the night in the first twenty years of her marriage.

Margaret was overwhelmed and over time, had more and more outbursts of anger and crying. She was showing such severe signs of stress that Albert decided to meet with doctors to discuss her needs. "She is sleep deprived. Is she a danger to herself? Is she taking too many pills? Does she need hospital care?" he asked.

He was encouraged by the doctors to provide praise, and indicate she was needed, appreciated and respected, in the hopes that this would boost her self-esteem. Those particular doctor's orders were difficult for Albert to carry through. His stern British upbringing had taught him to suppress emotions. He handed out praise sparingly and affectionate words or touches from Albert were rare.

Money was another issue the couple had to deal with. Albert's salary would have been adequate for the average sized family, but not for a family of twelve. Though they were not as desperate as people of the Depression, they certainly had to scrimp and save. Margaret bought stewing meat and soup bones instead of steak. They grew vegetables in the garden, rarely ate at restaurants and bought little in the way of junk food. The children may have felt deprived, but no doubt they were healthier than some of their neighbours. There was always enough food, but it was simple fare and there were no picky eaters in the Shaw family. The food was put on the table and if a child chose not to eat the food, that child went hungry. The table was large, set for ten to twelve people everyday. The furniture was beat up and shabby looking, but they could not afford anything better. There was little in the way of luxuries and every purchase, big or small, was given great consideration.

Madelaine looked enviously at the other girls at school. They all had such pretty dresses. She glanced down at her own drab, much washed dress, a hand-me-down from Mary, to Rita, to Bernadette, to Elizabeth, and now to her. It was a little too big. She pulled her dress down over her knees to hide the holes in her leotards, but it didn't really matter. Everybody already saw. She pushed her unevenly cut blond hair behind her ears but it wouldn't stay. Her mother wasn't much of a hairdresser and her parents couldn't afford to send the kids to a professional hair cutter.

"That dress is ugly," a classmate laughed.

Madelaine wanted to yell, "Do you think I want to wear this dress? Just because you have money you can't make fun of me!" She didn't yell though. She dropped her eyes to the floor, mute and filled with shame.

The large family was such a drain on Albert's salary that Margaret reluctantly decided that she should go back teaching after almost twenty years out of the classroom. Fortunately, due to the baby boom, the Calgary Separate School Board was in great need of teachers, and Margaret began teaching at St. Paul's School in Calgary to help pay the bills at home. Unfortunately, Margaret had less time to spend with her children and was put under even more stress.

If she thought she was busy before, it was nothing compared what it was like when she started teaching again. She was expected to teach all day, attend meetings, grade children's schoolwork, plan lessons, and attend to a multitude of tasks requiring strength of body, mind and spirit. In addition there was never ending housework including mountains of laundry, sinks full of dishes, dirty floors and hundreds of other chores. The kids had to do their part but it was still difficult. It was a perpetually noisy and messy house.

Margaret's frustration level was at an all time high. At a time when she most needed rest, sleep would not come. When everyone else in the house was wrapped in slumber's delights she laid awake and listened to dripping taps, the humming refrigerator and the creaks and groanings of the house. She enviously watched her sleeping husband and listened to his soft snores, while her mind raced with a thousand unanswered questions and concerns. Sooner or later, something had to give.

She threw a birthday party for her daughter Rita complete with balloons, candles and a made-from-scratch cake. Margaret always tried very hard to make birthdays and holidays special and memorable for her children. She planned a great party for her daughter, even though she was already worn-out from a long week at work. To make it more fun for the children, Margaret mixed dimes in the batter, so that the children could find little prizes as they ate their cake. It wasn't long before the dimes were discovered in the cake and six giggling and squealing girls dug excitedly with their hands, digging and clawing away at the pretty cake.

The party was finally over and the girls were sent home. Margaret sat at the kitchen table and surveyed the ruined cake spread across the table, chairs and floor. She was overcome with exhaustion and dejection and started to cry. Albert stood behind her with a hand on her shoulder.

"Those greedy children cared nothing about my hard work. Look what they did to my cake."

Albert spoke quietly in an effort to calm her, "Never mind, that's the way children are." He gathered the dirty dishes and filled the sink to wash them.

Rita entered the kitchen, glanced at her distraught mother, then at the destroyed cake. She spied a shiny dime poking out from the ruins. Smiling, she stuck her fingers in the cake and pulled it out. Her mother cried all the harder upon seeing this. Rita stood with eyes wide, unable to understand her mother's distress.

Margaret awoke mornings as tired as she was when she went to bed. Her weariness showed in her inability to remember the names of simple, everyday objects. "Where's my fluffy thing?" she demanded of her children.

"What's a fluffy thing?"

"Oh, you know!"

The children were very used to helping their mother search for lost articles. She was constantly misplacing her purse, keys, gloves and many other things. Many objects went A.W.O.L. in the Shaw house. It was the Bermuda Triangle of houses. Missing objects could be found anywhere. Cups and spoons found their way to the garden. Hairbrushes disappeared under beds. Important papers and homework assignments often disappeared forever. It was quite normal for Shaw kids to go to school with mismatched mitts and socks. Sometimes, they wore socks on their hands to school, when they couldn't find any mittens, and the only socks that seemed to find their way out of the wash and dry cycles were the ones with holes.

Margaret's obvious distress at not being able to find her "fluffy thing" evoked some pity from her children, and they tried to help her find the mystery object. Children scattered to look in bedrooms, under piles of clothes, and under couch cushions. "Is this what you're looking for?" asked one, holding up a pillow.

"No!" came the frustrated reply.

"Are you looking for your sweater?" asked another.

"No! You kids have taken it! Where is my fluffy thing?"

The children, with their warped senses of humour made a game of their poor mother's torment. They ran about picking up objects and showing them to Margaret. "Is this what you are looking for?" said one, showing her a newspaper.

"No!"

"Is this it?" said another, showing her a shoe, and giggling with delight.

"No!"

This went on for some time until the children and Margaret, were laughing themselves silly. Finally Margaret was able to calm herself enough that she could think clearly. "What I'm looking for, is my metal mixing bowl, so that I can whip some cream for our dessert."

The worst culprit of all, the one item that caused more grief than any other, was her purse. Margaret's purse, assuming she could find it, contained a variety of essential and not so essential items. It was to her children a treasure trove if they could get a hold of it without her looking. There was of course a hairbrush, a wallet, keys, charge cards, receipts and papers that were of no concern to a child, but if one was lucky she could find a stick of gum or a hard candy, or a tube of lipstick. None of these items were readily available when Margaret was actually looking for them, however. It was for this reason that she bought herself an "organizer purse." At last, it was the answer to all her problems. It had pouches and zippers galore, a dream purse for the orderly woman. The problem was that Margaret was not orderly. Was her wallet in the middle zipper or the back zipper? Was her Bay card in this pouch or that, and where were her damn keys?!

Margaret opened her wonderful new purse to retrieve her keys. She checked this section and that, but to no avail.

"Kids! Help me find my keys, fifty cents to the one who finds my keys," and the search was on. Money was always a great motivator for her greedy children, but no one was able to collect the money on that occasion. The keys were not to be found. It seems they were gone for good, until one day, two weeks later, she found them while at church. She reached into her purse to get some money for the collection basket when to her surprise, there they were, tucked right where she left them, in a small pouch in the center of the purse. She was so delighted that "the lost had been found" that she jogged Albert's elbow and whispered, "I found my keys. Look!"

Unfortunately she had interrupted his nap and he awoke with a loud snort, which caused several heads to turn around and look in their direction.

*C*hristmas was a time of great happiness in the Shaw house. Margaret loved the holiday more than any other. She loved the religious part of it, the commercial part of it, and the gift giving and receiving part of it. She inevitably became caught up in a flurry of planning for the day. She bought presents for her children, her husband and many relatives. She shopped for weeks in advance, and stayed up most of Christmas Eve wrapping. On Christmas morning there was always a most impressive mountain of presents.

> *There's no middle ground for old Santa and me,*
> *From sending out cards to bedecking the tree.*
> *I toil like a ploughman from morning till night,*
> *And shop until weariness stops me in flight.*
> *I gather my savings and figure each one,*
> *What gifts are most suitable, and what will give fun,*
> *To the children especially, the pride of my life,*
> *And all of my family, each man and his wife.*
> *The number of relatives grows with each year,*
> *With in-laws and babies to give Christmas cheer.*
> *The presents pile up and resources run out.*
> *Is this really what Christmas is all about?*
> *I worry so much about fairness to each.*
> *I add and subtract to each stack within reach.*
> *I count what I give, be it two three or four,*
> *And wonder if time permits getting some more.*
> *My anguish is mixed with much joy and elation.*
> *But Christmas is more than just anticipation.*
> *Though who can deny though his mind be steady,*
> *That half of the fun is in just getting ready.*
> *But does the birth of the Christ Child give us reason enough,*
> *To drink till we're stunned and our stomachs are stuffed?*
> *From His poor beginnings being born in a stable*
> *We've transferred his Word to a much-loaded table.*
> *Though this Divine Child came endowed with such gifts,*
> *And compassion for mankind despite all our rifts.*
> *With His teachings let's hope that there lurks,*
> *A Divine sense of humour as He views all our quirks.*

Photographs were snapped and wrapping paper flew as eager children tore open their gifts.

"Awesome! I got a cassette player!"

"That's radical! We can record some music from the radio."

"Look what I got mom, a Tonka truck!"

"Oh, look! It's a Monopoly game. We are going to have a gas with this."

"Ya, it's gonna be a blast!"

The children's intense excitement filled Margaret with joy.

There was little time to play after the presents were opened, and the children very reluctantly left their gifts behind to go to Mass.

"Aw mom, why do we have to go to church? Can't we just stay home today?" they whined.

Missing Mass on Christmas day was of course out of the question, so off they went, each child looking back longingly at his or her gifts.

Afterwards, Margaret spent all Christmas Day cooking. By the time Christmas dinner was put on the table she was so overtired she could hardly enjoy the meal. She sank into the couch with her plate on her lap, wearily eating away from the crowd.

Every year she resolved that next year she would have a hassle-free Christmas, and then she would fall back into her old ways. She remembered her own deprived childhood and was determined that her children would not suffer as she did. Besides, she loved Christmas, every budget-breaking, bone-wearying, nerve-wracking, diet-destroying minute of it, and no one could take that away from her.

There's a quality about Christmas that's hard to define,
Though many have tried to, there's really no line,
That satisfies everyone, it's so obscure,
A delicious involvement of senses for sure.
The carols that fill us with tremulous pleasure,
For centuries with us but still such a treasure,
The embrace of a friend, who forgives us our wrongs,
The children who see us to whom we belong.
As each Christmas begins and ends with Amen,
I cherish the happiness granted me then.
The smell and the taste of the turkey we savour,
And the Christ Child who brings us such peace and such favour.

$\mathcal{L}$ike all families, the Shaw kids sometimes fought with each other, and like all parents, Margaret sometimes lost her temper. In reality, sibling rivalry became a way of life for the Shaw kids. The children fought over the bathrooms. One could never linger long there. Someone was always knocking, gritting their teeth and crossing their legs, "Hurry up in there! I got to go." Long, luxurious soaks in the tub were out of the question. Bath time was a time of great competition to be first in before the hot water tank would run out. "Don't use up all the water! Other people want a bath you know!" They fought over the sweets and treats that occasionally found their way into the house. They fought over toys and the television and sometimes, they just fought.

The visitor stood at the doorway of the kitchen and watched the small horde of children who played noisily in the living room of the house. They were working together to build a fort from cushions and blankets, and though they were noisy, they were cooperating. There were four children in all who ranged in age from four years to thirteen. This group represented only some of Margaret's children. The four eldest were in their teens and were too sophisticated for childish games. The two autistic children weren't there either. They were institutionalized, punished for the crime of being different from the rest.

Margaret was in the kitchen, preparing yet another meal for the family. The visitor had no children of her own and was disturbed by the noise and confusion in the other room. She felt pity for her friend. "It's a shame what the Catholic Church has done to you Margaret," she said.

"What did they do?"

"They forbid birth control, and made you have all these children, and two of them handicapped. It's such a shame."

"I don't regret any of my children, not even Elizabeth and Christopher. No one made me have all these kids. I accepted each one as a gift from God."

A screech from the other room interrupted the conversation. Peaceful playtime had come to an end.

"You stupid idiot!" screamed Madelaine. "Just shut up! Shut u-u-u-up!"

She stomped her foot and marched into the kitchen.

"Mom! Tell him to stop bugging me!"

"Don't be such a tattletale," yelled David. "You're so ugly. I can't even look at you. Ouch, my eyes."

"Shut-up you idiot!"

"No, you shut-up you dunce!"

"Leave me alone. Quit bugging me!"

"Ew, leave me alone. Quit bugging me," he mocked in a high pitched voice.

"Mom! He won't quit bugging me!"

"Leave her alone. All of you go outside and play," Margaret ordered.

Mary, so serious and sensitive, closed her bedroom door to the uproar, and Michael, who was less quiet but equally sensitive, added to the noise by shouting at the youngsters, "Shut up!"

Patrick and David, being more mischievous, did their best to make the situation worse by relentlessly teasing their younger siblings. The louder the little ones screamed, the broader the grins on Patrick and David. Rita covered her ears to block the noise and stomped her foot, "I can't stand this family!" she wailed, and marched down the hall to the room she shared with Mary and slammed the door.

It wasn't long before the noise in the house had reached ear-splitting volume.

Margaret yelled, "Kids! Stop that right now! That's it! I'm getting out the wooden spoon!" She pulled the mixing spoon out of the kitchen drawer as children scattered in all directions. They knew their mother's patience had reached critical level. It was best to get out of the way, or feel the crack of the spoon on one's backside.

Margaret stood gritting her teeth, still holding the spoon threateningly in her hand, and then glanced at her friend. The visitor stood wide-eyed, with her mouth open. "Perhaps you could give some of your gifts back," she said.

Sunday morning was always a challenge for Margaret and Albert. They were devout Catholics who wanted their children to also embrace the faith.

Margaret shouted, "Would you kids get a move on? We're going to be late for church again!"

Two adults, five teenagers and three children rushed frantically around the two-story house that Sunday morning in March of 1969.

"Where is my blue shirt?" said Michael. He swiped his long black hair out of his eyes and stomped down the stairs in frustration.

"Where is my hat?" shouted Madelaine. Everyone knew it was unheard of for a girl to walk into church with a bare head.

"Why don't you kids look after your own things?" Margaret said.

"Yeah, why don't you look after your things you ditz?" said David.

"Shut up you idiot! Mom, David called me a ditz!"

"I can never find any socks that match in this house," complained Mary.

"Why do all my stupid leotards have holes?" asked Bernadette.

"Mom, please help me find my hat!" said Madelaine.

"Here, you can wear this on your head," said Margaret, as she pulled two sheets of Kleenex out of a box. She arranged it on her youngest daughter's head with bobby pins. "Where is Patrick? Patrick! Get out of bed; we have to go to church right now!" It was a little like herding cats to get the children dressed, out the door and into the car, but after many threats by the parents and much complaining from the children, the task was done.

The family entered the sacred confines of the church and Margaret realized to her dismay, that her fifteen-year-old daughter was not wearing a hat. "Rita, where is your hat?"

"I hate hats. I'm not wearing one."

"Don't be ridiculous, here, put this on your head," and Margaret handed Rita some Kleenex.

Rita looked aghast at her mother. "I am not putting Kleenex on my head, I would look like a total dork!" and with that, she stormed ahead of the rest of the family, into the church and sat down.

Margaret watched her obstinate daughter with concern, but said no more. Albert then led the rest of the family in and found a pew. Each child genuflected and made the sign of the cross before he or she sat down. The children were arranged so that the troublemakers, the boys, sat closest to their dad. They could expect a smart smack to the back of the head for any misbehaviour.

Rita sat upright in the pew and stared straight ahead. There was much whispering and pointing in her direction. "The nerve of that girl, coming to Mass without a hat!"

The time came for the family to receive Holy Communion. The children filed up the centre aisle of the church, Margaret in the front, Albert in the rear, as the congregation took turns kneeling at the Communion rail, hands clasped, tongues stuck out, just a little, to receive the Body of Christ. The priest trod back and forth distributing the wafers. His robes swished by the faithful as they knelt. Albert approached the front of the church, his head bowed in prayer and contemplation of what he was about to receive. He raised his head and viewed from behind a line of sorry looking children kneeling at the communion rail, all wearing old, ill fitting clothes and sloppy running shoes. He thought to himself, "What a bunch of messy, ragged kids they are." Looking again he had a sudden realization, "Oh, they're my kids," and a small smile crossed his lips.

The Sunday church ritual was repeated every week, without fail. Albert and Margaret did their best to ensure their children embraced the faith. Some did with great enthusiasm and others didn't.

*M*argaret was concerned about a great number of things, and not least of all was her weight. Starting in her thirties, Margaret began to struggle with her weight. As the pounds piled on with every passing year, she became more and more distressed.

What's the use of making promises that you know you'll never keep?
Beyond a day or two, at most; they're chiefly broken by a week.
Especially as one gets older, and sees beyond the hour,
An idea born days before, by week's end has gone sour.
An example is my hefty weight. A fact of life so grim,
I go on diets constantly, and never stick with them.
For years I was so tiny, so little and so slight,
And now I'm overflowing the bounds, and this is now my plight.
The pounds I mean, I've doubled them, or very nearly there,
I'm carrying the weight of two; my frame's not meant to bear.
I can't accommodate this mass. My spirit sighs and moans.
If the fat ever flees my body, you won't ever hear me groan.

"I used to be smaller than you girls," she said to her daughters. "I know you don't believe me but it's true."

"We believe you Mom, we've seen the pictures," Madelaine said, always trying to console her mother.

"I remember one day when I was teaching; I tried to discipline a big farm boy in my class, and he picked me up and carried me outside and sat me on the grass, just like that. 'You don't weigh any more than the newborn calves on my farm,' he said. Then he went back in the school laughing his head off. You know I weighed one hundred and five pounds when I married your dad?"

"Yeah, I know mom," Madelaine said. She'd heard the story many times.

"I have really tried to lose weight, and I eat hardly anything. I don't know why I'm so fat."

"Maybe you should try to get some exercise," Madelaine suggested.

The idea of exercise usually fell flat with Margaret, unless it was a leisurely walk around the neighbourhood. She did not eat large meals but oh my, she did love her sweets. "I know, I'm just like a kid. I never had much in the way of sweets when I was a child. That's why I love them so much. I don't ever want to feel deprived again."

Margaret was never able to forget her childhood experiences of the Depression, and for good or bad, they affected her behaviour as an adult. When money was tight at the Shaw house, her experiences from the Great Depression came in handy. Chicken and turkey bones were put in the refrigerator together with the water used to cook the vegetables, to be boiled later for soup. Food was purchased in bulk. Four of this item could be purchased for the same price as two of the other. Stewing meat was half the price of steak. One or two packages could feed the family if it was made into stew or soup. Above all, don't throw anything away that could possibly serve some purpose in the future. But what could be done with the scrapings from her children's dinners? It was so wasteful to put them in the garbage. "Clean your plate, there are starving children in India who would eat that food."

"Let's get a box and we'll put all the leftovers in it and send it to India," joked one of the children.

She turned suddenly and angrily snapped at the children. "That's not what I meant! You children have no idea what it means to be hungry!"

Indeed, they did not have any idea what it meant to be hungry. That was a difficult lesson to teach in a home where food was plentiful. Oh, but what satisfaction it gave her to open her cupboards and see them well stocked with food! To open one's deep freezer and see it bulging with meat, bread, juice and ice-cream was pure pleasure. The knowledge that one's family would never go hungry was extremely comforting. Yes, of course the grocery stores were full of food, and yes, she and Albert earned enough money to support the family, but it was important that the house be well stocked. What if another depression hit? You just never knew.

*E*lizabeth and Christopher came home for Christmas, Easter and also a week or two in the summer. The tension in the house always rose dramatically during those visits. The handicapped children threw tantrums on a regular basis and destroyed what little tranquility there was in the house.

Elizabeth lay sobbing on her bed, and Margaret climbed in beside her. "What's wrong darling? Why do you cry?"

Elizabeth didn't answer, she couldn't say why. She had a teenager's body, but she was a child at heart. Her mind was wild, filled with crazed images and fears, leading her anywhere and nowhere. Margaret sobbed along side her daughter. "Please God, rescue my daughter from this hell, but I know it is not to be. She must live on and endure, until He takes her home."

> *Dear Doctor of my ailing child, I implore you to take heed.*
> *I came to you for comfort, and to solve her great need.*
> *I took her to you at age two, she couldn't walk you see.*
> *"She wants to be a baby still," you say, "She'll surely walk at three."*
>
> *But she giggles strangely everyday, and bangs her head so hard.*
> *I've other children to attend. I'm constantly on guard.*
> *I'm so deprived from sleep from her, and my other babies too.*
> *Please diagnose her case for me, see what I'm going through?*
>
> *"You mothers are all alike, neurotic to the core.*
> *There's nothing wrong with baby, for you I'm worried more."*
> *"What's on your conscience lady? Is guilt your problem dear?*
> *What have you done to make this child behave so strange and queer?"*
>
> *Dear doctor she is four years old, she talks a bit but yet,*
> *It's mostly gibberish and her pants are nearly always wet.*
> *She won't stay toilet trained or neat. She screams the day away.*
> *She runs stark naked down the street. She won't go out and play.*
>
> *She bites her hands and runs around, and up and down the hall.*
> *She flaps her hands until I found, I'm climbing up the wall.*
> *I can't go on like this with her. I'm going slowly mad.*
> *Whatever have I done to her, to make her be so bad?*

"That question we can tackle now, to give this case some meat.
A psychiatric study should put you on your feet."
Put me on my feet you say? I thought I made it clear
My daughter is the sick one now. Where can we go from here?

"It's plain to see your child is ill, but you're the cause I fear,
You failed to give her love so now; you're paying for it dear."
Dear doctor, she is six years old, I'm analyzed to death.
She's mad and uncontrollable. I just can't catch my breath.

She went to school for just one day. She drove them all to tears.
They won't attempt to teach her now. I'll have her home for years.
"What's wrong with that, you loveless wretch?
Deal with your problems quick.
It's you we have to blame you know, environment's the trick."

I have to disagree with you. I've laboured long and been,
The best of mothers to them all. I've worn my patience lean.
I've suffered much from doctor's scorn, they have to pass the blame.
To mothers and to fathers too, we can't all be the same.

Dear doctor, it's been twenty years, my girl is far from fine,
At least you don't blame mothers now.
We've progressed a little down the line.
Treat the children with your skill, but don't guarantee success.
Care for my child and others now, and bring them some happiness.

Her pain over Christopher was no less. She wrote to him, knowing full well he could neither read the note nor understand it. "Christopher, you are so good to look at. Do you know that? We must presume you don't. You don't know pride. You can't deceive; there is no guile, no sin in you. Your road through life is rocky, dull and strange. You are constantly baffled, hating change, lost, dependent, and fearful. You live in the present, never caring beyond the moment. You are the silent one, occasionally allowing a smile to cross your face. When you smile the light of heaven itself illuminates your features. I live for those moments. You are loved so much, by God and us, your family."

Christopher's years of institutional care taught him to fight. "Shaw behave! Do you want us to put controls on you?" he would parrot, over and over. His behaviour was difficult to predict and difficult to control. He would lunge unexpectedly and unprovoked at who ever happened to be closest and attack by kicking or punching his victim. When Christopher was thirteen years old he was taller and stronger than his sixteen-year-old sister. He grabbed Madelaine's left wrist firmly in one hand and with his other hand he reached for one of her fingers. His goal was to inflict pain by twisting the finger backward. She curled the fingers of her left hand into a fist to prevent a finger dislocation. With her right hand she delivered a swift upper cut punch to his jaw, startling him enough that he released his grasp and she was able to free herself.

Institutional care for the handicapped was gradually phased out in Alberta in the 1970's. It was replaced by group homes and specialized care facilities. It was what Margaret and Albert had spent years fighting for. One such facility was Margaret House, a school for autistic children in Calgary. Christopher was taken out of the Red Deer institution in 1975. He spent some of his teenage years at Margaret House and he spent the weekends at home. It was important that Albert and Margaret were never left alone with Christopher on one of his weekend visits in case they became victims of his aggression. When he threw a wild tantrum at home he was sometimes disciplined by being sent to his room. When that method was ineffective, it often required several people to restrain him. The Shaw children felt terrorized by Christopher on a weekly basis and were probably the only kids in their schools who did not look forward to weekends.

Elizabeth also learned how to fight. Her weapons of choice were her teeth. She would deliver a hard bite to whoever got in her way. She was sneakier in her attacks than Christopher. Turn your back and you may get a punch to the back of the head. Everyone was always a little on edge when Christopher and Elizabeth visited. It is not uncommon for autistic people to lash out at the world around them, but with proper and humane treatment they can learn self-control and coping skills.

Margaret was suspicious that Elizabeth may have been sexually abused. How, when or by whom it will never be known, but it would have been relatively easy for abuse of all sorts to happen. Anyone who wanted to take advantage of the vulnerable people in institutions could do so with very little risk to himself or herself. They were hidden away from the watchful eyes of their families and society. But did society really care? The handicapped were the throwaway people, not given the dignity due to every human being.

It was a sad and disgraceful part of our country's history when handicapped children were separated from their families, presumably for their own good, and placed in institutions with people who may or may not have cared about their well-being. What was it like for Christopher and Elizabeth in the mental institution? One can only guess. They are incapable of telling about their experiences and for years the institutions could have acted with impunity. To be fair, there must have been loving, good hearted people who truly cared about the well being of the handicapped. We also know there are many who did not.

$\mathcal{E}$lizabeth also spent time with her parents in Calgary to help to prepare her for her eventual move, but she had a hard time adjusting to life outside of the institution.

"Mommy you take me back to Red Deer," said Elizabeth in her deep, low monotone.

"Yes, Elizabeth, after lunch."

"Mommy you take me back to Red Deer after lunch."

"Yes, Elizabeth."

"Take off your coat or I'll break your arm, ha ha ha ha," mumbled Elizabeth. "Mommy after lunch you take me back to Red Deer."

"Yes, Elizabeth, we'll take you back after lunch, ok?"

"Ok, hmmmm," Elizabeth lightly bit on herself on her upper arm. "Hmmmm. Take off your coat or I'll break your arm, ha ha ha ha." She paced the floor of the living room. "Mommy you take me back to Red Deer after lunch." Margaret didn't answer, being preoccupied with preparing the food. "Mommy you take me back to Red Deer take me back to Red Deer take me back to Red Deer after lunch."

"Yes Elizabeth, now go sit down on the couch and stop asking me."

"Hmmmm, take off your coat or I'll break you arm, ha ha ha ha." She sat on the couch and rocked herself for a minute then got up and began pacing the floor again. "Mommy you take me back to Red Deer."

"Yes Elizabeth, now come and eat your lunch."

Elizabeth ate her sandwich very quickly while smacking loudly. She pushed her plate away. "You take me back to Red Deer now?"

"Soon Elizabeth. Now be patient!" Margaret said.

"Now be patient, ha ha ha, now be patient, ha ha ha, now be patient, ha ha ha. Take off your coat or I'll break your arm. Eeeeeeee," said Elizabeth as she paced the kitchen.

"Elizabeth! Just sit down and wait until we're all finished our lunch," Margaret said.

"When we go to Red Deer you take me to a restaurant and I want fith and chips and orange pop and raithin pie and ithe-cream."

"Ok, we'll go to a restaurant," said Margaret.

"Eeeeee. Take off your coat or I'll break your arm."

Elizabeth paced more and more frantically around the kitchen. "You take me to Red Deer. Stop it you bitch, ha ha ha."

"Elizabeth! Don't say that word," said Margaret.

Elizabeth paced and continued to mumble as if she hadn't heard. Her anxiety grew as she watched her family finish their meals. Her pace quickened. She bit her arm hard and slapped her own face. The group prepared for the one hour drive to Red Deer.

"You take me to a restaurant and I want fith and chips and orange pop and raithin pie and ithe-cream."

"Ok."

"You take to a restaurant and I want…"

"Yes, Elizabeth, I know," interrupted Margaret.

"You get me fith and chips and orange pop and raithin pie and ithe-cream."

"Ok, now get in the car."

"Stop it you bitch, ha ha ha."

Albert started the car and headed for the number two highway north. Elizabeth rocked herself back and forth in her seat. She was seated between Bernadette and Madelaine.

"Eeeeee, Mommy! You take me back to Red Deer!"

"We are going there, see we're on the highway," Margaret pointed.

Elizabeth bit herself hard and banged her head on the seat in front of her.

"Now you stop that!" Margaret said.

"Now you stop that! Now you stop that! You take me to a restaurant and I want fith and chips and orange pop and raithin pie and ithe-cream!"

"Yes Elizabeth!"

"Now you stop that! Now you stop that! Now you stop that!" said Elizabeth. She rocked hard back and forth for the next hour, stopping every few minutes to repeat her restaurant order and demand that she be brought back to Red Deer.

Madelaine and Bernadette, who had wedged themselves as far as they could into the corners of the car to escape their sister's flailing body parts, also began to ask their parents in turn if they could go to a restaurant and have fish and chips and orange pop and raisin pie and ice-cream.

They arrived at the restaurant and Elizabeth delivered her order to the hostess who seated them and to the waitress as she set the menus on the table.

"You'd better bring her food right away," said Albert to the waitress.

"Hmmmm, hmmmm, hmmmm," said Elizabeth as she waited and rocked impatiently.

The waitress, assuming that the dessert would be eaten after the meal, arrived with Elizabeth's second lunch of the day, minus the pie and ice-cream.

"Mith, I want raithin pie mith," said Elizabeth.

"Yes, sure," said the smiling waitress.

Elizabeth bit her forearm, a clear sign of distress.

"Be patient Elizabeth. Your pie is coming," said Margaret.

"Now you sit down and be patient. Take off your coat or I'll break your arm."

A full minute passed and the pie had not arrived. Elizabeth looked around the restaurant searching for the waitress. She spotted her taking an order from patrons at another table.

"Mith!" she yelled, "I want raithin pie! Mith! I want raithin pie you bitch!"

Many heads in the restaurant turned to see who the rude individual was.

"Elizabeth! Don't say that word!" Margaret said.

"Mith! Mith!" Elizabeth was becoming more and more distressed, and yelled all the louder, "I want raithin pie! Damn it! You bitch!"

"Oh mom, somebody, please get her raisin pie," begged Madelaine, who desperately wanted to run away and hide from her sister and all the disdainful looks of the people in the restaurant.

"Hey Mith! I want raithin pie!" screamed Elizabeth.

A harried, angry looking waitress scurried over to the table bearing a freshly cut piece of raisin pie, but to Madelaine's horror, there was no ice-cream on the plate.

$\mathscr{S}$hopping for clothing for her children was a challenge for Margaret. She had to find clothes that were affordable, but luckily, in the sixties and seventies, it was fashionable to look poor, with ripped jeans and sloppy shirts. Margaret faced some extra challenges when shopping for Elizabeth though, because she could not take her out to any stores to try on clothes. Elizabeth's behaviour was too erratic. Margaret couldn't take the chance of her throwing a wild, screaming, flailing tantrum in the middle of the store. Bernadette was brought along on shopping expeditions instead because Margaret believed Bernadette was about the same size as her younger sister.

She searched through the stacks of shirts and pants, looking at sizes and styles. Bernadette followed behind obediently.

A perky, smiling salesclerk greeted the pair. "Can I help you find anything?" she asked cheerfully.

"Oh yes," said Margaret, "you see my daughter is autistic and she lives in an institution. She can't be trusted to behave herself in a store and I have such a hard time finding clothing for her." She picked a pair of pants off the shelf. "Here, let's see if this will fit." Margaret then held the pair of pants to Bernadette's waist and checked the length.

The salesclerk looked at Bernadette with a most pitying expression. Bernadette turned pink with embarrassment when she realized what must have been going through the salesclerk's mind.

$\mathscr{M}$argaret was a gentle soul whose heart went out to all those in need. This included the people whom society often rejected, the poor, the handicapped, and the elderly.

Margaret brought her seventeen-year-old daughter Madelaine to the hospital one evening because of a raging fever. The fever was caused by an infection which required two days of hospitalization.

The old lady in the neighbouring bed reminded Madelaine of a zombie from one of the horror movies she had seen. The old woman was emaciated. As she lay on the bed her loose wrinkled skin fell back to reveal her bony face. Her mouth hung open showing her toothless gums. Hair stuck out of her pointy nose. The eyes were no more than cloudy white balls sunken into her skull. A few sprigs of white hair sprung from her scalp. Her snowy white skin was patched with blue and purple bruises which covered her face, arms and legs. Her breath rattled and gurgled as she struggled for air.

Madelaine looked around the room and noted the bare walls painted a "sick yellow," and at the other patients in the room, "Just a bunch of old ladies, no one to talk to." She scanned the poor selection of magazines at her disposal as she lay in her bed, and felt quite sorry for herself.

"Oh Jesus… Oh my God help me. Oh God, oh my sweet Jesus…Oh, oh…" the old woman moaned again and again, rolling her head back and forth across her pillow.

"Jeez, why doesn't she shut up?" Madelaine thought. She turned her head from the old woman and tried to ignore the monotonous complaining coming from the bed beside her.

A nurse strode into the room. Her starched white uniform and cap spoke of her authority. The grim set of her mouth with its slash of red lipstick, told all that she was a force to be reckoned with. "Mrs. Anderson, it's time for your lunch," she announced in a loud voice.

"No, no…" she begged. "I can't."

The nurse filled a spoon with pureed mush and brought it to the old woman's mouth. "Now you open up and eat this."

"No, it hurts."

"Come on now. You don't want the tube again do you?"

"Oh, oh…"

The nurse pushed the spoon into the woman's mouth. The old lady coughed and sputtered, allowing the food to dribble out.

"Now you stop that! Eat your lunch or I will put a tube down your throat!"

"No, please…oh God." She opened her mouth and accepted a few mouthfuls, moaning with pain as she swallowed.

The nurse looked over at the teenage girl in the neighbouring bed. "I know this looks bad, but I have to do it."

Madelaine nodded. She wanted to turn away from the frightening scene but felt compelled to watch.

"Water, please, I'm so thirsty. Oh my God…" The nurse held the straw to the old woman's mouth. She drank, and moaned again.

"Oh Jesus, oh my God…God help me. Oh God…" The old woman tossed her head from side to side and muttered her prayer over and over.

Madelaine again turned her back on the old woman and tried to distract herself with the magazines. She would have got up and left the room if she had the strength. The muttering and moaning persisted hour after hour. Night came and the old woman still could find no peace.

The following day Margaret held the back of her hand against her daughter's forehead. "Are you feeling any better dear?" she asked.

"Yes, I'm just really tired. That old lady kept me awake last night," Madelaine said.

"Oh my God help me... Oh Jesus..."

"She's been doing that for hours and hours," Madelaine complained.

Margaret looked at the woman in the neighbouring bed and her eyes filled with pity. She took the old woman's hand and held it, "Shush now, God loves you," she said.

The old woman turned her cloudy eyes toward Margaret. "It hurts, she said.

"I know."

"I'm afraid."

"Don't be afraid. God loves you. Trust Him."

"God loves me?"

"Yes, you are his daughter."

"Oh God...Oh Jesus..."

"Shush. Tell Jesus that you love him."

"I love you Jesus. Oh God...I'm thirsty. My feet hurt. It hurts everywhere."

Margaret gave the woman a drink of water and then pulled the covers from the old woman's feet. The feet were sickly blue and the back of the heels were covered with bed sores. Without hesitation, Margaret gently massaged the old woman's feet.

A nurse entered the room and looked suspiciously at Margaret. "Are you a relative of this lady?"

"I'm her friend."

The nurse looked unconvinced, but said no more. She strode about the room, distributing medication and thermometers. She took blood pressures, and marched out again.

Margaret laid the woman's feet tenderly on a pillow and returned to hold her hand.

"Who are you?" the old woman asked. "Are you an angel?"

"No, I'm Margaret."

"Margaret...I'm scared."

"Don't be scared. Tell God you love Him."

"I love you God. I love you God. I love you God."

Margaret held the woman's hand until at last she fell asleep.

Visiting hours ended and Margaret kissed her daughter goodbye, promising to return the next day. The nurse arrived in the evening to again deliver medications, take temperatures and blood pressures. When she arrived at the bed of Mrs. Anderson, she lingered a moment and then drew the curtain around her bed.

An hour later Madelaine watched the bed bearing the remains of Mrs. Anderson being wheeled out of the room and into the hall.

Upon her return home, Madelaine searched the obituaries and found the one written for her former roommate. "…was predeceased by her husband, survived by four children, ten grandchildren and two great-grandchildren. She will be greatly missed." She cut out the obituary and put it in her scrapbook.

Unlike his wife, Albert got through life in a calm, logical manner. Mr. Spock, the half-human, half-Vulcan character of the popular 1960's television show Star Trek, was unemotional and very logical, intellectual, brave and loyal. The character must have been modelled after Albert, or perhaps Albert was part Vulcan. He was a Mathematician; so naturally, reason and logic played a huge role in his life. He was a self-described egghead and nerd who quoted Shakespeare and historical facts with ease. Complex Mathematical equations were child's play. Somewhat lacking in social skills, he preferred a good history book to parties.

His father, Lewis Shaw, quit school after grade three, and worked in England's coalmines from the age of ten until he moved to Canada in the early part of the twentieth century. Once in Canada he learned the trade of the blacksmith and settled in Youngstown, Alberta. Albert learned blacksmithing skills from his father but Lewis and his wife Mary wanted their children to be well educated. In a time when many people lost their entire fortunes in the stock market, Lewis made some wise investments and was able to save enough money for his children to go to university. He was a bad tempered man though and was very severe with his children.

Albert, on the other hand, was kind and patient. He would wait in the car for hours while his wife or children went shopping, though no doubt he enjoyed the quiet time it gave him. His patience was not without limits though. Noisy children sitting in the back seat of his car knew well how to dodge his hand as he reached back to slap at what ever head or body part he could connect. He was also known to pull over and order his older boys out of the car to walk home if their behaviour got out of hand.

Like Mr. Spock, he was not given to great shows of emotion. He acquired the "stiff upper lip" of his English ancestors, where self-control was considered an asset and emotional outbursts and affectionate displays considered signs of weakness. He was the one to whom his children could go for clear, grounded advice, but not to be comforted. Their mother was freer with her emotions so she was the one to whom her children would go when they were hurting. Due to their mother's anxious nature though, the children often held back what was really on their minds for fear of upsetting her. Thus, the stiff upper lip was passed down to the next generation.

Albert taught by example, teaching virtues such as honesty without ever saying a word. He was never known to tell lies, cheat or take anything that didn't belong to him. He even scolded Margaret one day after a motel stay when she wanted to take the miniature bars of soap home in her suitcase. He would never break a law, or even drive a car over the speed limit.

Everyday Albert took the bus to downtown Calgary to work. On his walk home from the bus stop he often heard loud yelling, screaming and fighting from half a block away, coming from his home. He would pause for a moment, take a deep breath and reluctantly enter the chaotic house. His job kept him very busy but that didn't stop him from helping around the house. He did dishes, changed diapers and vacuumed floors along side his wife. The children were also expected to pitch in and help, but only complied after loud complaints. His devotion to his family was evident, even if he did not express it in so many words. At one point, he chose not to take a promotion at work, because it would take too much time away from his family. He did it without complaining and without being asked.

One bad habit he had was smoking. It was a habit that he picked up at the age of ten. A minor heart attack occurred in his late fifties while restraining Christopher during one of his many tantrums. Albert finally quit smoking at age fifty-eight on the advice of his doctor, "Quit or die." He did quit and he took up jogging. His self-disciplined nature was an asset in that very difficult endeavour.

Albert suffered for many years from a variety of illnesses. Severe pain in his abdomen, vomiting, fever, and weakness left him debilitated for days at a time. Margaret was very concerned for him. Month by month, then year by year, the doctors could not discover the cause of the problem. Was it pancreatic trouble or was it internal bleeding? A blood transfusion helped him to regain his strength for a short while, but he suffered terribly for four years until a surgeon finally removed his gall bladder.

Completely without conceit, he was not particularly interested in his appearance. Most of the clothes he wore were gifts. He would have been content to wear thirty-year-old suits were it not for the pleading of his wife to wear something new.

Albert was a man who enjoyed, or perhaps took comfort in routines. He had a place for everything and wanted everything in its place. Everything about his life was measured; from the precise way in which he combed his hair or loaded the dishwasher to the way he cut his meat, in small, square, bite-sized portions. The birth of ten children must have greatly upset his orderly life and his disappointment and frustration showed when at times he became brooding and silent. He had an unsettling way of shutting people out and one could feel lonely being in the same room with him.

Margaret tried many times to break through the wall he built up around himself, which was very frustrating for her. "Talk to me," she would plead.

"I don't know what it is you want me to say," he would reply, with a hint of sadness in his voice. He truly did not know how to communicate on an emotional level.

He was the epitome of the strong silent type, not a blabbermouth by any means, but when he spoke, people paid attention. If his answer to a request of his children was "No", they knew not to ask twice. He considered every word before it came out of his mouth. He wrote daily in his journal, where facts, such as the weather and daily events, unhindered by attitude, were recorded. He would rarely display his personal thoughts and feelings, even in a journal.

He would, however, converse quite frequently in Vulcan talk, for example, "Do you think that the speed at which you are driving is excessive?"

In English this means, "Slow down."

He would say, "I suggest that you study the matter more thoroughly."

That was his way of saying, "I think you're wrong."

Another Vulcan expression was, "I would not recommend that course of action."

That meant, "Don't do it."

Sometimes as a passenger in a car, he would give the driver directions such as, "Merge into the left lane, when you feel it's safe to do so, and then proceed in a westerly direction."

On earth that means, "Turn left."

Unlike Mr. Spock of Star Trek, Albert possessed every human emotion. He loved a good joke, and learned to laugh more often as he grew older. Later in his life, when the stresses of raising children had dissipated, he mellowed and would occasionally talk about his own life experiences. He certainly felt joy and sadness as well as anyone, and perhaps in time realized that by bottling up his emotions he had created for himself an even heavier burden than ten children could provide.

> *If I touch your hand,*
> *Will you misunderstand?*
> *If I wish to join your space,*
> *Invade your face?*
> *You are Inscrutable, unyielding, still,*
> *With an air of stolid will.*
> *Do you think me weak?*
> *That I should ever seek,*
> *To break your silent introspection?*
> *Where is that lost connection?*
> *That warm affection,*
> *That bound us one to one?*
> *How lonely and deprived you make me feel.*
> *You travel on that even keel,*
> *So unperturbed, so self-possessed,*
> *So brooding that my soul won't rest.*
> *Until I find a soft nest,*
> *Of recognition in your eyes,*
> *And reclaim the love I prize.*

Chapter Ten

Depression

$\mathcal{A}$ hand pressed on her right shoulder and then a softly accented voice asked, "Want a glass of water?"

Margaret nodded in reply and looked distastefully down at the partly eaten pancake on her plate. It looked like a flat, soggy little pillow. The fried egg lay bleeding on the edge where she pricked it with her fork. She stirred the syrup around and wondered why there was a time when she liked sweet things.

"Here's your water," said the slim, brown-haired waitress. "Anything the matter with your meal?"

For some reason Margaret usually felt compelled to confide in strangers if they showed the least amount of concern. "No everything's fine, I just don't feel like eating breakfast at any time. Now I'm supposed to eat a big breakfast because I'm having x-rays done and my stomach is supposed to be full."

"See, I bring you two glasses of water," she said, "one with ice and one without."

"That's nice of you." Margaret tried to show her gratitude by taking two or three sips of each glass. Then she nibbled on a sodden bit of pancake, but it tasted like a wet sponge.

"Look, you eat every bit of that pancake and egg. I will stand here and see that you do." The waitress crossed her arms and smiled.

Margaret felt like a baby in a highchair, like the one in the corner who waved car keys in his hand while his mother stuffed his face with mashed potatoes.

"What you getting x-rays for?" she asked.

"I get cramps a lot. The doctor doesn't know what's causing them."

"You look depressed to me. I bet that when the doctor gets through with you he will find nothing wrong. I say it's just your nerves. Just like me! Last year I had the cramps so bad my tummy swell out to here with gas. Sometime I feel like taking the knife and cut my tummy right out!" She illustrated her past discomfort with such alarming accuracy, using a butter knife for emphasis, and contorting her face in a semblance of agony, that Margaret quickly swallowed a big chunk of food and some water.

"That's better, now another piece. Do it right this time or you have to do it all over again for the doctor."

"Are you new to this country?" Margaret asked, trying bravely to regain her adult status.

"Yes, I come from Belgium, and believe me we have a hard time at first. It bad even now. My father, he have a nervous breakdown or something. He blame my mother for everything and he doesn't work at nothing."

It was Margaret's turn to show concern so she tried to turn the tables and offer condolences as best she could. It was really a wasted effort. She was the patient and the waitress the therapist in this scenario.

"Good girl, you just finish everything. That is good. You remind me of my mother. She get so depressed she say she think she will kill herself. I try to tell her that is just silly. She is in her forties like you. That is why." Then she looked at Margaret with sublime compassion.

Margaret was so flattered by the last remark that she gave the waitress a one dollar tip when she left. She was touched by the waitress's kindness and grateful for her motherly attention. In a small but significant way, Margaret was uplifted by this experience.

In addition to the cramps, for which Margaret required a hysterectomy, she suffered from back pain. From the time she was a young woman she had back pain, the result of being thrown from a horse at age twenty-one, and the pain got worse as she got older. Even raising her arm caused so much pain she wanted to weep. She was in so much misery that some days she could do nothing but lay on the couch. She was filled with guilt that couldn't fulfill her duties as a mother, and had to depend on her husband and kids to make dinner and clean the house.

She sat in a chair at the General Hospital about to confer with doctors about her back. After a wait of nearly three hours she was finally ushered in to sit in front of three doctors. One held her charts, another a set of x-rays and the third was a silent partner, who looked at her and yawned.

Dr. Morgan began by demanding why she was still overweight despite his ordering her two years ago to lose her fat. The subject of her back pain took last place to a tirade of accusations regarding matters of diet and forceful contradictions to any comments Margaret made. Aggressive people often took Margaret unaware, and before she could collect her thoughts, she felt she was being verbally beaten to the ground. Filled with shame and embarrassment, she sat woodenly in the chair, hands clasped between her knees, like a fourteen-year-old accused of cheating on exams.

"What can I do about the pain? Aspirin does nothing for me."

"I'll prescribe something stronger. It's a narcotic. Take it only as directed," he ordered her, and she was hustled out the door. "I'll see you in a couple of weeks to examine you."

She thought glumly to herself, "That will be the day. If he thinks I'm fat with all my clothes on, he's liable to have a real fit when I have to take them off."

In the past, she rarely let anyone take advantage of her. Yet more and more, she felt she was losing the ability to defend herself. "How long does it take in our lives here, to rise from the ground and stand upright, to cease to be a frightened, craven creature? How long before we refuse to take mistreatment? How long does it take to recognize that we all have a God-given dignity to guard? It's not generous to turn yourself into a human doormat. It is not kindness to give away the rights that make us different from the beast. We must not fool ourselves into thinking we are showing love, when in reality, we are turning our soft sides into targets for cruel and unthinking ones to pierce and wound. We were designed to be uplifted not degraded. The flesh can be destroyed before its time. The human soul can agonize, and become so shrivelled, as to be unfit for heaven."

Her parents and educators taught her to always consider the feelings of others and hold back retaliation. "Blessed are the meek, for they shall inherit the earth." Her youth was long past but the force of the teaching was still present, and tended to make her impotent in dealing with the world. There were times when she rose to the occasion and taken on an aggressor, especially when it came to her children's welfare. She would always consider their interests over her own. Most often, she felt like the helpless victim and bore her insults silently, and then fumed afterwards about the injustice of it all. Angry thoughts and silent hopes for vengeance were not enough. Perhaps it would have been best not to dwell on the negative, and just get on with living, but that was not Margaret's way.

She was strong in many ways but her self-image was weak. She was taught to love her neighbour but not herself, and the cost of self-hatred is high.

She spent her life worrying about her children, all of them. Their childhoods were tumultuous and she felt terrible for them. Elizabeth and Christopher filled the house with tantrums and wild behaviour, demanding all of the attention of the parents. It is little wonder that the other children got neglected. So it was that they had to put the two of them in the institution. This was an exceedingly painful step to take, but the only answer to their dilemma at the time.

The whole process of dealing with the problems of Elizabeth and Christopher dragged the whole family, body and soul, into a tangle of hurts and emotional upheavals that took years to heal. Margaret tried her hand at problem solving, but often felt like a failure. She prayed for guidance. What did she need to do and what details should she leave to God above? While she tilled one field another was neglected. The choices dwindled and the ruin spread. There was too much work and too little time for one person, and too few willing hands to help. Her back was strained to the breaking point. Her hopes were dashed by grim reality.

Something always set her off. Often, it was the little things, like an argument with a son or daughter, a doctor or a relative. Perhaps someone stayed out too late at a party, or the mechanic had difficulty fixing the radiator. She was angry that the housework wasn't done, or that Christopher got half a haircut because he was scared by the barber's scissors. Maybe it was because David was not fast enough in getting the car out of the garage or that Bernadette wanted to be called by her given name, not Bernie. Someone was disrespectful. Someone was disobedient. Someone did not behave in the way she expected them to behave. The cause was not important, but the effect was always the same. She was offended. The offence simmered as it ran over and over in her mind. Her anger was stirred by past offences whether or not they were related to the current one. She remembered her anger at the people in Red Deer. She was angry at her brother for something he said some years ago. She was angry at a neighbour's snide remark and she was angry at male chauvinism. Anger, hurt, guilt, resentment, and embarrassment ate away at her until she could stand it no longer. The emotional dam broke and she was beside herself with grief and anger. All clarity was left behind along with any logical solutions to her problems. All was clouded by her extreme emotional reaction.

She felt herself falling into that dark pit again. It was hopeless. There was no way out. The blackness surrounded her. The light became ever fainter. There was no more happiness. She reached her hands towards the things that once gave her joy, her husband and her children, but they could not pull her out of the pit. Her burdens weighed her down. Stress paralysed her. A ceiling of despair ceiled her in, preventing escape.

She curled herself into a ball and the tears streamed down her face. The weight of the criticisms, the insults and the hurt simply couldn't be borne. The children needed her now. They needed her care, her strength, her wisdom and her comfort, but she could provide them with nothing. She lay on the couch, wrapped in a cocoon of misery. She wished she could get really drunk and mask the pain.

When her children arrived home from school, they immediately knew that their mom was in one of her moods again. The atmosphere of the house was charged with negative energy. They looked at each other and sighed. For the next few days they would tiptoe around their mother, so careful with their words so as not to set her off. It was better to say nothing than inadvertently say something that would further offend or upset her. It was best to find an excuse to be out of the house. Go to visit a friend. Go to the library, be anywhere but there.

"You kids come and help me!" she yelled. "Damn kids, I wish I never had kids!"

They came and stood by her, waiting and hoping that the situation would not worsen.

"Get busy and clean the house. Can't you see how much work there is to do? Why don't you kids ever help me? Albert! Albert! Come and help me! Why don't they respect me? Why am I burdened with this family? Why can't I be happy? I wish I could die. Why can't I just die?"

Albert stood behind her and placed a comforting hand on her shoulder. She sobbed, "Dear God, I can't take it anymore. I can't take another day. I need to be strong, but I'm not. I'm a miserable failure. I'm a fat, miserable failure."

The children moved about the rooms in silence, doing dishes, sweeping the floor and avoiding eye contact, while nervous tension emanated from all. They could never confront her or question her about her black moods or react to the things she said. It would have been like a knife through her heart. "You don't know what my life is like, you selfish children." They knew that words were useless. They would have to wait until the depression passed.

> *Restrain me with your sacred hands.*
> *Rebuke me when I hear commands,*
> *And don't obey, don't understand.*
> *Forgive my weaknesses and note*
> *My virtues and not my faults.*
> *Though one is greater than the other,*
> *Just like my sisters and my brothers.*
> *I look with envy at the saints*
> *Who worshipped You and stilled complaints*
> *About life's difficulties spread*
> *Through centuries of humans bred.*
> *Just love me my God and spare your rage,*
> *At the inconsistencies I stage,*
> *In many places through my life.*
> *Recounting times when I have tried,*
> *To kill the blight of sin.*

For many years Margaret held out hope that Elizabeth and Christopher would get better. She phoned Red Deer repeatedly, asking for more tests for Christopher and Elizabeth. "You must accept that the autistic are incurable and can only be given custodial care," the doctor explained.

"I can't accept that," she said. In fact, it took many years for Margaret to accept the fact that Christopher and Elizabeth would never be cured.

Margaret was extremely frustrated and angry that nothing she did seemed to make any difference to the treatment of her children in the institution. "I will burn down the villas in Red Deer. I can't live at home anymore. I will go away, get a job somewhere and leave this family. I feel so damn guilty. I've made such terrible decisions in my life. I think maybe it was wrong of me to send my children to that damn institution. I wish I could turn back the clock and take it back."

Margaret's frustration led her to turn more often to tranquilizers and pain killers. "I'm no good to my family when I'm like this. I'm incapable of taking care of them. I'm no good to anyone. They don't love me. How could anyone love an ugly old toad like me? I'm a burden to everyone. I can't stand the pain Albert. Get me my pills. This damn back of mine. The doctors don't want to operate. They just prescribe stronger painkillers. Look how many I'm taking everyday now. They say they're addictive, but what am I supposed to do? I can't live my life in agony."

*S*he needed sleep so badly. Night after night she lay on her bed, rolling and fretting, sleeping a little only to awake a little later with her heart pounding, panicked because of some remembered uncompleted task. Weariness hammered at her brain while her muscles ached from lack of rest. Daybreak came and she dragged herself through her chores until she dropped with exhaustion on the couch for an hour or two of fitful sleep. Her sleep patterns became more and more erratic and agitation built.

She considered ending it all, to finally put an end to the pain and anxiety. "Nothing is fun anymore. I feel bored and yet I don't feel like doing anything. Nothing is going right. What is the use? There is no relief from the pain, either physical or emotional. I am suffocated by the weight of my own sadness. Why won't it stop? I need release from the prison of my own sorrow. Maybe I should just swallow the whole bottle and be done with it. Why can't I be dead? I wish I was dead."

Margaret set her Tom Collins on the coffee table and lay down on the couch. She wiped the tears from her bloodshot eyes and stared blankly around the room. Albert looked closely at her face and then walked quickly to the medicine cabinet and found the half empty bottle of valium. Fearing an overdose, he calmly brought Margaret her coat and shoes and ushered her to the car. Ignoring her protests he drove her to the hospital where she was checked into the Psychiatric Ward. The doctor explained that a fragmented sleep affects the brain and can contribute to depression and her self-destructive behaviour was certainly a concern.

She was admitted and was supposed to undergo "sleep therapy." Margaret would have none of it. She lay in her bed and waited until the hospital staff was occupied with other patients. She quickly dressed herself, looked left and then right down the hallway and then tried to sneak out of the hospital by the back stairs.

"You come back here Mrs. Shaw. You are not allowed to leave the hospital," called an orderly as he ran down the stairs after her. He took her, not so gently by the arm and brought her back upstairs.

"I'm not going back to any damn psychiatrists. I've already been analyzed to death. What good did they do?"

To prevent further escape the staff took away her clothes, but Margaret was undeterred. A few hours later she tried again, and this time got as far as a taxi, wearing only her hospital clothes and carrying $5.00. The orderly again led her crying and complaining back to her room. Her condition became steadily worse and at one point she had to be restrained in her bed to prevent escape. She lay there, stripped of her dignity, feeling utterly alone, hopeless and unloved.

The following day Albert came to see her bearing a gift of flowers and cards from her children. She took no notice of either. She had no words to say to her husband. She could not feel joy. When he thought she could get no worse her depression reached the point where she was allowed no visitors at all.

It was a painful, difficult struggle but she improved enough over the next few days to warrant release from the hospital. She was in a panic and had to get home quickly. Her daughter's wedding was fast approaching. There were so many things to do, invitations, bookings, and bride's maids dresses to be sewn. She sat bent over the new sewing machine her husband bought her. The bright, flowery material skimmed under her fingers. The activity, at first, was good for her. She felt as though she was really accomplishing something, until, "Stupid machine! Why won't it work?" The thread snarled and tangled again and again. "Damn, damn, double damn, triple damn!" She slammed her fist on the table. "Robert! Help me with this damn thing!"

The stress of the wedding preparations led to further arguments between family members and Margaret again became depressed and was sent back to the hospital. It was again a crisis situation, with a real danger of suicide. It was decided she should undergo shock treatments to try to block the pattern of depression and explosive inappropriate behaviour. She was terrified, believing that it would be painful. The procedure was done under general anaesthesia though and afterwards she awoke somewhat confused and had a bad headache but remembered nothing of the event.

A month after her release from hospital Margaret became depressed again after spending a good part of the day on the phone with people regarding Christopher and Elizabeth. She went to her medicine cabinet and took several valium with a vodka and orange juice. "Drive me to Red Deer. I'm going to tell those people exactly what I think!" she ordered Albert.

"I don't think that would be in our best interests at this point," said Albert.

She was outraged. "If you don't drive me, I will hitch-hike to Red Deer and raise hell! I will make them shut down that institution once and for all. Everyone is against me. I will leave and go far away from all of you!" This time however, Albert was able to sidetrack her desire to go to Red Deer and took her on a trip to the zoo instead.

The depression cleared and Margaret had a few good weeks but it wasn't long before the same complaints arose again. She complained about finances, lack of improvements at home, the children, and that she had no one to turn to when she needed help. She again took valium with alcohol and declared she wanted to go to Red Deer. Albert adamantly refused to give in to her complaints and threats.

"Your attitude has changed towards me Albert. We are just not as close as we were a couple of years ago," she remarked.

"That's true," he said.

"Do you still love me?"

"At present, no, given your current behaviour."

At that she walked out the door, saying she was going to Red Deer. She did not take the car. Hours later she was brought back by the police who found her walking in the middle of the road.

They stood in the doorway and questioned Albert. "If you knew she was leaving the house in this state of mind, why didn't you try to stop her?"

"I admit my attitude towards my wife is harder than it was before and I have decided to become more outspoken and rejecting of unacceptable behaviour and demanding improvements," he answered, leaning heavily on the front door.

Margaret wrote, "I can't live with a thousand quandaries and still have peace of mind. I can't live without my husband telling me he loves me. If there is no way to read his mind or siphon out his thoughts, how can I find the truth? He guards his thoughts like royal jewels. When both of us are dead and gone and it doesn't matter then, I hope our children will not deny the love that has brought them here, or the labour pains I bore to bring them all to life. It is with great weariness and tearfulness that I write this note."

Albert discussed with her psychiatrist the possibility of her being committed again. The psychiatrist advised that she should continue the behaviour therapy method of the rubber band. The band is worn over the wrist and the patient is responsible for interrupting her own thoughts. The elastic band technique works by suddenly interrupting the repetitive and obsessive thoughts that are part of the pattern of depression. In this way, the person is supposed to learn new behaviour and discontinue the old. The ultimate goal is that the individual has to understand that she is the one in control of her own emotions. The method requires the complete cooperation of the patient, and Margaret would have none of it.

Despite everything, Albert did not want to end the marriage. He was eternally optimistic. He wanted to reassure her that he was not looking to end the marriage. He said, "My relationship with you has been eroded but it can be reconstructed."

"No, it can't. I just want to die, at least before age sixty. I can't imagine living any longer than that. I am not loved. I'm not given enough attention by you or the children. None of you appreciate me. I am not given the discernment or concern that I deserve. You are the one who needs psychiatric help Albert, not only me. You don't allow yourself to feel anything. There's something wrong with that."

"I agree that I could stand a lot of improvements and all of these things you mentioned can be improved."

"No, things will never improve. My life is hopeless. I am being degraded by you all and I will leave. I'm getting in the car and I'm leaving right now!"

"Margaret, you should stay home until you're feeling better. Given the state of mind that you are in now it is best that you don't drive,"

She put on her coat and shoes and stormed out the door and to the car. Sitting in the driver's seat she started the engine. With her mind racing in a thousand directions she backed out of the driveway and onto the street. She did not know where she would go or what she would do when she got there. She only knew she had to get away from the pain and the sorrow. She found herself on the highway heading west towards Banff, but it was as if another person was steering the car. She was only vaguely aware of the traffic around her and was driving by instinct alone.

She pulled into a parking lot beside a gas station and turned off the engine. She had no idea what she should do next, or where to turn for help. Her eyes were dry. She had cried too many tears already. She was numb, exhausted from years of trying to make a difference in her children's lives. She decided that her family was better off without her and she would not go home again.

"I must write a note to my family," she thought. She sighed deeply and rummaged through her purse. There was no paper, only an envelope that contained her Sears' bill. On it she scrawled, "I am going away and I don't care where I end up." She placed the note on the dashboard and reached for the handle to open the door, then hesitated. Where would she go? She needed some time to think. She listened to the distant drone of vehicles on the highway and watched the tree tops sway in the breeze. Many thoughts ran through her head as she sat alone for hours in a self-imposed exile.

"What would happen to me if I never went back home? What would happen to my family? They don't need me. They don't want me around. I'm a miserable person. Will I ever be happy again? It's hopeless. I wish I could die."

She thought about suicide. It seemed to her to be the only way to relieve herself of the emotional pain she felt, but as was her habit, she turned to prayer when she was troubled. Somehow, she found the strength and drove home.

Margaret avoided disaster on that occasion but her troubles with anxiety were not over. A month later, on her birthday, Patrick slept until noon and this triggered another outburst. Nervous tension built in all those present. David, Bernadette, Madelaine and Robert sat stiffly in their seats at the kitchen table, exchanged glances, anticipating what was coming next. That's when Albert came in the door and presented her with a dozen red roses.

"Thank you Albert. They're beautiful." She smiled gratefully and calmed down. The children let out a collective sigh of relief, believing that they wouldn't have to deal with mom's moods that day. However, as evening rolled in, Margaret became agitated again as she waited for each of her grown children to call, and unfortunately, Michael didn't call that day to wish her Happy Birthday. This sent her into a tirade of complaints, "Nobody gives a damn about me. I might as well go away and leave everybody. I might as well be dead."

Albert's jaw was clenched tight as he struggled to control himself, but after listening to her grievances for the better part of an hour, his patience finally reached its breaking point. He slammed his hand on the table and shouted; "Now that's quite enough of that. You settle down!"

Margaret and the children present were startled by this rare outburst and watched Albert warily, wondering what would happen next. She did settle down and what followed were several good days where Margaret was cheerful and could be a good wife and mother.

The ever hopeful Albert said, "Margaret seems to have taken a close look at the situation and concluded that her surroundings are not entirely to blame. She seems receptive to the idea that there are circumstances beyond anyone's control and no amount of complaining or ranting will change these. She seems to have gotten quite a scare from noticing the number of deserted and divorced women on the Psych. Ward. She seems, for now, to want to avoid inappropriate behaviour."

Margaret held a lofty goal in mind, and that was to close the Red Deer institution and move all the handicapped into group homes in their communities, to be close to their families. She spent hours on the phone speaking to government agencies, individuals and groups, to try to push the idea forward, but to no avail. Unfortunately, with her shattered nerves, the whole process was extremely hard on her. This was combined with a series of normal family upsets and disagreements. It was all too much and she fell into yet another depression.

"People tell me to 'snap out of it'. Don't they think I would if I could? They can't understand what I'm going through. I get so irritable and take it out on everyone and then I feel terrible about it later. I feel so lonely."

Albert wrote in his journal daily. In one entry he described how Margaret's depressions were affecting him. "It's starting to affect my work. People at the office are noticing that the quality of my work is not the same. Though they are supportive, I can't keep leaning on them to cover for me. Margaret makes life difficult by lecturing me several hours a day, as a rule, on her difficult life, lack of respect for her, place of women in society, and how she has been mistreated by men. She is upset when the children don't follow her advice. Yesterday we went out for supper but she was unhappy with the service, and because there was no celery for her Bloody Caesar. She insisted on driving home and that was frightening because of the booze and drugs. On a trip back from Red Deer to bring Elizabeth back for a visit for a few days she took her frustration out on me. She was rather hard on me on the way back, and showed her discontent in the usual way. She made a fuss about small driving mistakes I made which I found rattling and irritating."

On one December afternoon, Albert stayed after work for an office Christmas cocktail party. When he arrived home, about an hour later than usual, Margaret was sobbing. "You should be home to be with me. Nobody appreciates me. I should go away for a time when my depressions hit so as not to be such a burden on everyone."

Almost monthly Margaret entered a state of depression. One could guess that she suffered from a severe case of pre-menstrual syndrome and later menopause that sent her hormones raging out of control. What ever the reason, the depressions were extremely hard on everyone. The tension slowly crept into Margaret's neck and back, year by year, causing her increasing pain. The increased pain led to increased amounts of pain killers.

Her children, who witnessed the distress, and lived through the crisis in their own home, reacted in various ways. Some acted out by fighting, drinking, or smoking and became easily agitated and angry. Others simply became withdrawn and moody. No one came through the experience unharmed.

Creeping anxiety. It starts in the chest, just a twinge at first.
My heartbeat quickens. My imagination stirs.
Where could they be? Where are my daughters?
They should be home by now. It's midnight.
I fear for their safety. Maybe there was an accident.
Maybe someone has hurt them. I need sleep.
I can't sleep until I know that they're home safe.
I pace the floor. I look frequently out the window.
I am angry now. Why haven't they called?
They don't care about my feelings. Selfish girls.
They're not really girls. They're women now
Madelaine and Bernadette, eighteen and twenty-one years old.
I shouldn't worry. They can take care of themselves.
Or can they? Anything could happen.
They went to a party. Where is the party?
Are they drinking too much? Will someone take advantage of them?
It's nearly 1:00 a.m. I hear a car.
Look out the window again. It's not them.
Dear God. Where are my daughters?
1:30 a.m., and still no word. What will I do if it's bad news?
I imagine myself at their funerals. It's too painful. I couldn't bear it.
It's 2:00 a.m. I hear a car. It's them! Thank God!
Just wait until they get inside. I'll give them a piece of my mind!

"Anxiety, what a plague you are, coursing through my body and mind, holding my common sense behind, making me a fool for all to scorn. Why was I born, to live this life? While others go calmly along their way, competent and smiling in their lives, seeming to conquer without strife all the duties on their way. I'm forced to stay in hopeless indecision. My body trembles sometimes. I am torn. Come here. Go there. I plunge into action, then despair. Surely there's a way to find some peace of mind, before I die."

Chapter Eleven

Daisy MacCallum

*D*aisy often talked of the Old Country with her children and grand-children. She spoke about the beauty of the countryside, and Irish dancing. She told them many times about winning medals in Irish dancing competitions. She talked about street musicians and school at the orphanage, and strangely, the more she talked of her childhood home, the thicker her Irish accent became. Though she had forgotten most of the Gaelic she spoke as a child, she could still recite a verse or two of a poem in that melodic tongue. She also knew many Irish folk songs by heart and these she sang to her grandchildren countless times.

> *When Pat came over the hill, his colleen fair to see,*
> *His whistle low but shrill the signal was to be;*
> *'Oh, Mary,' the mother cried, 'there is someone whistling sure'*
> *'Oh, mother, it is the wind you know,*
> *that's whistling through the door.'*
> *With my fol diddle-laddle-la*
> *My fol-diddle-laddle-lee*
> *With my fol-diddle-laddle-la*
> *Hey fal-da-lol lol-da-la-lee.*

"Come on now you kids sing with me!" and she'd lead her grandchildren in loud renditions of the songs.

> *Up to mighty London came an Irishman one day,*
> *As the streets are paved with gold, sure ev'ryone was gay.*
> *Singing songs of Piccadilly, Strand and Leicester Square,*
> *Till Paddy got excited, then he shouted to them there:*
> *It's a long way to Tipperary*
> *It's a long way to go.*
> *It's a long way to Tipperary,*

To the sweetest girl I know!
Good-ye, Piccadilly!
Farewell, Leicester Square!
It's a long, long way to Tipperary,
But my heart is right there!

"Did I ever show you kids how I can yodel? Oh…a diddle and a doodle and a diddle adda do, oh…a dee die doodle and iddle addle ooo…"

The grandchildren were never once given the impression that she had a difficult childhood or adulthood for that matter. Daisy was not one to dwell on the negative. She loved a good joke and the occasional cigarette or snort of whiskey. Her fun loving nature must have endured through many tough times.

"Bill never liked me to show off how I could dance or play the piano. Do you remember I told you kids when you were small, not to tell him if you saw me showing off to some of the neighbours?" she asked Margaret.

"I sure do mom."

"My husband loved to sing to me. I'd say, 'Now Bill, you never could carry a tune.'" She would joyfully croon while swinging her hand back and forth like a conductor of music.

Daisy, Daisy,
Give me your answer do!
I'm half crazy, all for the love of you!
It won't be a stylish marriage,
I can't afford a carriage
But you'll look sweet upon the seat
Of a bicycle made for two.

"I remember when I left the old country. I was on the boat and a sailor tried to kiss me! Oh, but I wouldn't let him. I never let anybody kiss me on the mouth, not even my husband. I just can't stand all that exchanging of spit!"

Daisy often spoke of her dead husband, how they were married after a courtship of only three weeks and even so, she could never have gotten a better man. She said, "When I get to Heaven I'm going to say, 'Hello St. Peter. Hello God. Now where is my husband?'"

Her grandson teased her and said, "You never know, Granny, there's lots of single old men around, maybe someday you'll get married again."

She replied, "Oh! I couldn't stand to be married to an old man, not if he had diamonds dangling from his yackohula!"

She frequently asked her children and grandchildren if they suffered from constipation. That ailment was a complete mystery to her. She had a very healthy constitution. She could however, relate to bad feet. She would often say, "Margaret, do you have trouble with your feet?" Over time Daisy had all but lost her ability to walk.

Despite her good nature, Daisy was not always easy to get along with. She was stubborn and opinionated. Her views on life could be seen as a reflection of her limited life experiences. After all, she was born in an isolated Irish community in the nineteenth century, and then spent much of her life in a small, stagnant prairie town, with little or no stimulation. While sitting in a doctor's waiting room, Daisy watched with amazement as a little child played. "Look at that little black child; he plays just like a normal baby."

Margaret's cheeks reddened when the child's mother looked up. "Well of course he does mom, he is a normal baby."

Daisy was affectionate with her grandchildren but was suspicious of strangers, an idiosyncrasy that became more and more pronounced as she got older. Her paranoia made it nearly impossible for her grandchildren to bring friends to the house. She greeted newcomers with, "Who is that strange child? Get out of here!"

"She's my friend Granny."

She would lumber threateningly toward the intruder, hobbling on her bad feet, wave her cane and bellow, "You! Go outside!"

The poor startled child would then turn and bolt out the door.

Daisy never had much in the way of earthly possessions. All she truly had were her children. With little to inspire her, no wonder her children became the focus and the center of her universe. How embarrassed they were when she bragged to her neighbours of their intelligence and abilities. "Margaret, Billy, come and sing a song for the neighbours," she commanded, much to their mortification.

Inventions of the latter half of the twentieth century were most mysterious to Daisy. She loved to watch the television, especially music and dancing, but could never figure out how to turn it off and on or how to change channels. "You kids turn on the TV for me. Find me a show with dancing."

"Look Granny," they would say, in an attempt to explain this new technology. "You use this button to turn the TV on, and turn this dial to change the channel."

"Oh you do it for me. I don't have the head for it," she replied.

In the same way, Daisy never learned how to use an escalator; its movement confused her and caused her to fall. A shower was also beyond her comprehension, as was a roll of tape. She often forgot to hang up the telephone after a call, leaving the person on the other end of the line yelling in frustration, "Granny! Granny! Hang up the phone!"

Daisy was a woman of simple faith who viewed the world with a sense of bewilderment and a measure of paranoia, but she was also a possessor of great love and a grand sense of humour.

Daisy MacCallum, age 86.

*D*aisy lived in an apartment close to Margaret, in Calgary, until she became too forgetful and too feeble to live on her own.

"Don't worry Roma; I'll get to the dishes later. Let's sit and enjoy a good hot cup of tea." Daisy poured a cup for her guest. She looked with satisfaction around her cozy little apartment. She had lived there since 1962, and here it was already 1968. It had been sixteen years already since her husband died. "Never mind," she thought, "one day I'll be with him again in Heaven."

Daisy surveyed her neighbour over her third cup of tea. She pressed a chubby hand on her bulging middle and burped a deep satisfying "Ur... urp." The huge mound of meat, potatoes, vegetables, salad and finally pie topped with ice cream had disappeared down her throat in a most satisfying manner and no waste of time, as always.

"Ah, that was a fine bird, and lots left for supper," she crooned contentedly. Food was a great comfort. Her neighbour from down the hall was not a very good cook and looked pretty gaunt and wrinkled for it too. She needed a good feed and Daisy loved to feed people.

"Let's see now. How old am I?" she wondered rather absently to herself. "About seventy-nine or eighty, near as I can remember." She wasn't sure how old her neighbour was and Roma would never tell. Funny how some women kept their age a secret even though they had reached the stage when they were wrinkled as a prune and couldn't walk very well any more. This fleeting curiosity did not remain with Daisy for long. It was far too much trouble to wonder about anything much. It was much better to have a good sleep. Roma and she would talk about gardens a little, mostly about the flowers, then about the weather, past, present and future, and if she could still keep her eyes open, they might mention their kids.

Roma was never entirely sure if she had four children and fifteen grandchildren or the other way around. She always did have a hard time keeping track of things but it didn't matter. Long ago, when her husband was living, she used to get scolded by him for this, but it didn't bother her much. The memory of him had faded as she had buried him over twenty years ago. She did remember the day she called him for dinner. It was while they were still on the farm. There were fried chickens on the table and fluffy mashed potatoes, new green peas and young carrots and raisin pie just out of the oven. She had called, "Tom, come in to dinner now." She remembered that she had called him three or four times but there was no answer. Thinking that he must have gone out to the field she returned to the kitchen to eat alone. There was no sense letting a good dinner get cold and he would eventually show up. He didn't though, and she finally had to go out looking for him. She found him sprawled beside a granary. There he was, as dead as you please. Three days later he was buried in the graveyard beside the highway and she had a busy time introducing all the relatives on his side to the people from her church. Some of her children were crying but she really didn't see why they were so upset. These things happen you know, and everyone was so kind, bringing lovely food to the house. It was a grand funeral.

Roma was saying something about the old folks' home just outside of Calgary, in Midnapore. "It's named after Father Lacombe you know. I think they call these places Nursing Homes now." Roma went on to tell about her rheumatism and how she might have to go into the home soon. "I hear the food is never served warm. I have a hard enough time eating without having to face cold meals, especially the tea. I like a good hot cup of tea."

"Ah...yes, a good hot cup of tea," murmured Daisy absently. "Did I ever show you a picture of Bill and me when we were married?"

"No, I don't believe you have," answered Roma.

"I think I have it in a box in the bedroom," sighed Daisy, and she disappeared slowly into her bedroom. She glanced around her bedroom absently. My, but the bed looked inviting! What on earth did she come in here for? Oh yes, she badly needed a good sleep. That dinner had given her gas pains a few minutes ago and they might return if she didn't get a rest.

The living room looked strangely bare when Daisy came out of the bedroom. What made her think of a cup of tea? Oh yes, she needed a good hot cup of tea.

"Hmm, it's getting dark outside, that's funny. Didn't seem any time at all since Roma and she had finished the noon meal. Oh yes, where on earth did Roma go? She was a peculiar woman to just leave like that. Roma is getting pretty old and forgetful, more forgetful than me," she mused vaguely. Two chores needed her attention. She had to go to the bathroom and she needed to get herself some supper. She was nearly starved.

When Daisy could no longer care for herself in the apartment, she was moved to Father Lacombe Nursing Home, where she spent the remainder of her days.

Without a doubt this old Irish blessing applied to Daisy MacCallum.

> *May God grant you many years to live,*
> *For sure he must be knowing,*
> *The earth has angels all too few,*
> *And heaven is overflowing.*

At the old folks home she tottered down the hall, head down, pushing her walker ahead of her. Her pink scalp showed beneath her soft, white, downy curls and her puffy ankles ballooned over her sturdy black shoes. She was a wraith-like scrawny remnant of her former self. Her blue and white polka-dot dress hung on her now. Eighty-eight years old, she was resigned and a little sad. Her eyes showed that. "Will you help me find my room?" she said to some people who had just entered the facility, not recognizing her own family members.

"Of course we will mom, how are you?" Margaret asked. Daisy peered at her daughter through thick glasses, recognizing her at last.

"Oh Margaret, have you come to take me to your house?"

"Not today Mom, we just came for a visit."

"Who are these people?" she asked with a suspicious tone, pointing her bony finger at the two teenagers accompanying her daughter.

"This is Madelaine and Robert, your grandchildren, remember Mom?"

"Oh, yes, well, they're practically grown up now." She looked at Margaret beseechingly, "When are you taking me home to live with you? I could keep house for you. I could scrub your floors."

Margaret looked at her mother's frail, bent body and was filled with pity. "We'll see mom." She didn't have the heart to tell her mom that she would never leave Father Lacombe Nursing Home. Margaret was always loyal to her mother. She came to see her as often as she could and frequently brought her home to visit.

A number of old people were parked in their wheelchairs in front of a television set in the main entrance, but no one's attention was focused on the screen. Two were asleep, their heads slumped forwards, and mouths open, with thin lines of drool dripping down their chins. The other three sat silently, staring vacantly into space, seemingly unaware of the existence of others in the room. Other elderly people ambled aimlessly down the hallways. They sat in wheelchairs or leaned on canes or walkers. The halls were quiet, except for the persistent ringing of a telephone.

A middle-aged nun in full habit greeted the family warmly. "Mrs. MacCallum, I see you have visitors, how lovely."

Daisy gave the nun a toothless smile. Cataracts dulled her blue eyes and her skin was severely wrinkled. "I'm very tired. I want to lie down now." Margaret and the two teenagers walked her to her room.

An immense woman lay in the neighbouring bed. Mounds of rolling fat spilled around her. Her great thighs heaved as she struggled to right herself. The bed creaked and groaned under the weight. She wallowed and grunted with the effort to sit upright. She grasped the edges of her bed with chubby hands, while her mouth hung open as she gasped for air. Her eyes watered behind many folds of skin.

"That woman stole my teeth," Daisy pointed at her roommate. "Tell her to give them back."

"No one stole your teeth mom, you probably just misplaced them," said Margaret. She began opening drawers and cupboards in search of her mother's teeth. She finally found the teeth under the pillow on the bed.

The other woman looked incomprehensively at the strangers in her room. "Get to school. Get to school," she barked at Madelaine and Bob.

This wing of the old folk's home was reserved for those who were most dependent on others, those whose minds had weakened as well as their bodies. Some could recall stories of their youth, of the World Wars and of the Depression, but couldn't remember what happened the day before. They were forlorn humans, with their aged bodies, failing eyesight, and ears that could no longer hear the high-pitched voices of their grandchildren. They were paying the price of living past their prime.

"Get to school. Get to school," the obese woman said again.

Robert sat on the edge of his granny's bed, looking uneasy, as if the large elderly woman on the other bed might jump up and grab him. "This place smells funny," he said. It was the mixed odours of sweat, urine and strong industrial strength cleansers.

"Open my purse," said Daisy, "and find yourselves each a nickel. You can buy some candy."

"Thanks Granny," Madelaine and Robert smiled but did not open their grandmother's purse.

Daisy looked fondly at her grandchildren. "It's nice to see young people. I get so tired of looking at old, wrinkled faces. Don't ever get old Margaret. I can hardly walk at all now you know. I think I'll lie down. I'm so tired." Daisy lay on the bed. "Did you know that I'm getting married? I'm going to marry the Bishop. Yes, it's true. Priests are allowed to get married now. Didn't you know?"

Daisy continued to deteriorate, as is the way with Alzheimer's disease. It is a cruel disease that eats away at people's minds, slowly wiping out the memories that make them who they are. And finally, and most brutally, the victims forget even their loved ones, and they are left utterly alone in a confusing world. In the year 1978, Margaret received the phone call she had been expecting but dreaded. Her mother was dead, at the age of eighty-nine.

So a Limerick girl with long black hair,
Tied back with ribbons bright,
Set out from Cork on Ireland's shore,
To set her life aright.

Daisy barely said goodbye,
This eldest daughter fled,
Not knowing a mother's love, expecting none,
Nor where her future led.

Her little sister stood,
With hand outstretched to pout,
"A penny Daisy, if you please,
Don't let me do without."

And then without a backward glance,
The past she left behind,
The future must hold better things,
A chance she didn't mind.

To emigrate to Canada,
Held terrors undisclosed,
But leaving Ireland's poverty,
She felt not ill disposed.

Her shallow trunk was light,
And held possessions few indeed,
The purse clutched tightly to her breast,
Would scarcely fill her need.
The trip was long and difficult,

As sickness clutched and bore,
Her slender body through its toils,
To test her mettle more.

Finally, the ship arrived,
The new land wide with space,
Astonished Irish immigrants,
And men of every race.

Through hardships of a thousand kinds,
Daisy bravely tried,
To mark her life a useful one,
Though talents were denied.

Cleverness was not her gift,
Nor expertise nor skill,
The object of much scorn endured,
Integrity her will.

She loved her family selflessly,
And left to mark her place,
One hundred plus descendents,
In humanity's embrace.

Chapter Twelve

School Teacher Again

$\mathcal{W}$hen Margaret decided to go back teaching to help pay the bills, she received a series of temporary contracts from the Calgary Separate School Board.

Christmas time rolled about and all the teachers were invited to the Principal's home for a get together. A staff Christmas party sounded like great fun, and Margaret was eager for a night out.

They were all assembled a bit self-consciously, the members of the teaching staff. It was just the first round of drinks and everyone was so polite. The men were giving up their seats to the women, and everyone spoke in modulated tones. The men sat on the floor or leaned against the wall but most of them ended up in the kitchen where the liquor was. The principal leaned on the fridge talking to the gym teacher who was leaning on the sink looking bored. He picked a good place to get sick if either the topic of conversation or the drinks began to bother him. So far, everyone was being careful in his or her speech and the women were patting their hair and complementing themselves on their own glamorous appearance.

The supervisor was present and congenial and wondered if he would have a good time. He sucked in his bottom teeth and made little whistling sounds as he talked. This small speech defect had been the subject of amusement by the daring ones, at conventions and staff meetings. He was plenty smart though, and everyone connected with this profession realized how much power he had to hire and fire, so they were careful to keep their humorous observations to themselves or at least out of his hearing. He tended to play favourites, so he was a tyrant or a doll, depending on one's experience with him. He invited comradeship by calling everyone by his or her first name. This, the teachers regarded as mildly flattering and called him Jim in return. By the second or third drinks they were all buddies. Some of the women have found a knee to sit on, preferably not one belonging to her husband or boyfriend and they laughed it up in great style.

There were a few on the fringe like Marcy. A hundred years ago she would have been named after one of the virtues, like Prudence or Honour. She was neat and precise even at parties and even in the way she ate an apple. In the staff room at lunch break she invariably had an apple for dessert, nothing frivolous like a butter tart or a chocolate bar. Margaret often watched her eating in the staff room. She bit into the fruit with her sharp white teeth breaking the apple into crisp wedges, which she chewed most delicately. Any droplet of juice was dabbed up at once with the Kleenex in her other hand. At the party she sipped daintily at a glass of ice water. She would never allow even mild intoxication to interfere with her disciplined life style. Her carefully tapered dark hair clung obediently to a small lady-like head. Even her slim fingers betrayed no emotion as they moved up and down the stem of the wine glass she held. Margaret irreverently wondered how she would react if someone kicked her in the butt.

Then the Life of the Party came in, late as usual and noisy as a thousand firecrackers. She made straight as a shaft for a tall good-looking man at the back of the room. They embraced with considerable enthusiasm as their respective mates looked on impassively. Three or four drinks tend to make one more tolerant. Mabel and her husband always came to parties well loaded.

"Poor Mabel," said a voice near her shoulder. "You can't blame her. Her husband's a dink."

"What's a dink?" Margaret turned and asked the man standing behind her.

"Well, let's put it this way. It's the opposite of horny, which is what I am."

She didn't dare ask him what horny meant as he began breathing heavily on the side of her neck and was trying to kiss her. She got the message and edged away to the corner of the room. This was a strategic mistake if ever there was one. He was young and strong and she was trapped.

"Look, I have to find my husband, and besides you are young enough to be my son."

He looked solemnly into her eyes. "I think we could really communicate, you might really like a young buck like me."

Margaret didn't know whether to feel flattered or insulted and ended up feeling rather foolish with the proposition. It had been a long time since someone made a pass at her. She finally got a chance to duck under his arm and found her husband. She didn't tell Albert about the young buck because he was too busy advising two or three young women not to have ten children like he did because of the many difficulties for the parents. He was usually so quiet that they found this hilarious.

"Everyone keeps taking my drink," squeaked the school secretary. She ran around on tiptoes smiling coyly at everyone. "Have you got a pen?" she asked Margaret, her voice chirpy and a little too loud. "I want to write my name on this paper cup. I don't want anyone stealing my drink. See, now I've written 'Anne' on it and it's mine."

She clutched the cup to her breast and skipped away but no one paid any attention to her. She glanced about and tried to look cute, but at the age of forty, she only managed to look frantic and pathetic. Margaret was glad she was able to supply the pen though.

An immensely fat young man grabbed Margaret's hand as she went by him. "Hey, where have you been all evening, and what does that blue ring on your finger mean?" He was sweating in dripping patches and his eyes were bleary as he asked those rather inane questions.

She ignored the first question but answered the second. "It doesn't mean anything in particular. Are rings supposed to mean something?"

He tried to stand up but the exertion is too much for him so he settled back with a resigned sigh, took another swig from his drink and tried to get acquainted from a reclined position. He probably hadn't had much luck with the young girls and thought he might as well attempt flirting with an older woman. She smiled warmly at him and felt that he should get some reward for his effort. She also felt quite safe with this one since he had such difficulty getting up. She wondered vaguely at her strange new acquisition of sex appeal. The party wasn't turning out as dull as she thought it would.

After a few hours, it was time for the intense discussions that seem to be a part of many parties. Nobody wins such arguments or gets to the point, if there is a point. Margaret was amused to see brotherly love shown in such abundance as a couple of the male teachers draped arms around each other's shoulders and struggled to remain upright.

"I love you man."

"No man, you're the best. I love you."

Then, to her horror, along came the young buck, making straight for her as she waited her turn for the bathroom. She grabbed at her husband's hand, as he happened to be standing near her. She suggested that they go home. He didn't seem to hear her as he was deep in discussion about a matter too grave for the occasion, but then Albert was generally grave about most things. Margaret felt a sense of unreality as she was shoved backwards into the bathroom by Young Buck and was kissed and hugged with such passion that it took a moment for her to return to her senses. She was finally able to push him away and she rushed to find her coat and husband.

"Bye John," she said to the principal as she went by.

"You embarrass me," he said, "stay away from me."

She stopped in her tracks, puzzled by his harshness. "It wasn't my fault."

"You shouldn't drink, you are a nice lady when you don't." he said, reaching out to steady himself against a wall. He spilled some of his red wine onto the carpet, and Margaret feel a little sorry for his wife.

"I'm nice even if I do take a couple," she lashed back and made for the door.

Going back to the car she thought of all those silly people with their brains addled by booze. The tears streamed down her face and she knew she was part of it for a while.

"I hate parties, I hate, hate, hate them!"

"What's this?" said Albert. "I thought everyone was having such a good time."

She tearfully filled him in on what occurred at the party and wished she had just stayed home.

Albert and Margaret

$\mathcal{M}$argaret's series of temporary teaching contracts in Calgary reached an end, but the family's need for extra income was still great. Try as she might, there were no more teaching jobs available locally. She was able to find a job teaching for a few months at a Native Indian Reserve in Northern Alberta, about four hundred miles from home.

She packed her bags and left her husband to care for the remaining five children and off she went. Margaret was very lonely and disoriented in her small rented house near the school but kept in touch with her family by telephone and the odd visit.

While in Northern Alberta, Margaret was free of the stresses of home but was faced with a variety of new stresses.

Just on her way out to supervision at recess one afternoon, a young voice called out, "Hey Mrs. Shaw, how come you got ten kids? My mom she got ten kids too and she not old woman."

A hoot of laughter greeted his remark, but she left the question unanswered and pushed her way into the brisk March day. "So I'm an old woman," she thought. She was fifty-two years old, but in this community it was considered old. In that place, girls often started bearing babies in their teenage years and usually without the benefit of marriage. They became someone's "woman" and had a houseful of little ones by the time they were in their twenties.

The girls grew up in poverty and had no idea how to raise children since many were themselves raised by teenaged mothers. The children came to school runny-nosed, with lice in their hair and nothing in their bellies. Children walked to school in the dead of winter with bare feet inside of rubber boots. To the new teachers it was shocking but to most of the old-timers it was unfortunate but not unusual. The nurse came once a week to treat their heads and check for signs of illness while the teachers tried to teach them to read. Most of the children only spoke Cree when they arrived but they had the help of teacher-aides.

Their black eyes watched her and they followed her around the schoolyard, at a safe distance at first. "You speak Cree?" asked one.

She shook her head, "no." Out of the corner of her eye she saw a child with a snowball in his hand. He dropped it when he saw she was looking. She didn't know who the intended target was, but suspected it was her. He held one nostril closed and blew his nose into the snow.

Sometimes she got "absence notes" from the parents. "Excuse my Hilda from school today. She got the shits," said one. "Ben's boots were wet so he didn't go to school," said another.

The children who were well cared for at home usually learned quite well. Margaret was impressed by the level of love and dedication shown by some parents, but in many of the homes there was trouble because of the drink. The janitor of the school sometimes gave Margaret reports on the children's reasons for absence. "Rosie, she won't be coming this week. Her mother's hurt bad. Her man gave her a lickin' and Susie took the kids to her sister's for a while."

Rosie was one of her best pupils and Margaret was surprised her father could be so brutal. He was better educated than most, but that didn't make much difference when the drink was involved.

Marie was seven years old and was very mean and cruel to the other children. She was constantly in trouble for hurting others. Margaret asked her teacher-aide to enlighten her on the reason for the child's behaviour.

"Oh, her mother deserted her three kids for a week to run away with another man and Marie had to look after the two younger ones by herself. They ate flour mixed with water for a week. This happened last year. She was only six years old. She's been like this ever since."

Every two weeks or so, the principal would bring a movie to the school. Everyone in the community was invited for an evening of entertainment. The price was twenty-five cents and everyone came. Gradually, many of the adults would disappear where they would patronize the beer parlour and leave their offspring to make their way back to the reservation at ten thirty or eleven at night. It was truly survival of the fittest. The teachers were warned not to start caring for the children in these circumstances, as the job would be handed over to them without question by their parents.

The school fights that broke out were bloody and fierce and often involved chains and brass knuckles. Margaret decided that her involvement in this mayhem had better be minimal. In one case though, she brought a girl to the medical clinic after the girl lost half an ear in a fight.

At certain times of the year, many of the children disappeared. They went with their parents into the forest to work the trap lines and they sold the furs to make a little extra money.

The problems were so deep and horrendous that teachers like Margaret who came for only a few months felt helpless and horrified. They dealt with the children's needs day by day as best they could. The spring that Margaret left was marked by a man who returned to the community after five years incarceration for hacking his wife to death in a drunken rage. Margaret knew their problems were certainly too big for her to handle and left the job feeling sad and shaken.

*I*n June of 1974, Margaret returned home from teaching in Northern Alberta, but the cycle of depressions continued and lasted for many years, throwing the whole family into imbalance. It was hard for anyone to predict when or why the depressions would strike.

Life had certainly been hard on Margaret and as a result she grew fearful and insecure. She tended to spread the blame for her depressions to those around her. "My mother treated me unfairly, because I was the oldest," said Margaret. "When ever anything happened, it was my fault. My mother made me feel guilty and insecure, and Albert is too distant with his emotions. He won't talk to me. He doesn't give me the love and affection that I need. The kids are not respectful. They won't gladly do the chores around the house. No one in this family will give me the love and respect that I need. Oh why did God give me such a burden?"

She complained that her family did not show her enough love, but so often the children felt that she pushed them away with her angry words. They, on the other hand, were constantly on guard and though they were often careful of their words around her, it was not unusual for one child or another to snap back at her, adding to the stress in the house.

When she was happy her true nature showed through. She was generous with her money, time and love. She knew right from wrong and guided her children as well as she could towards the right paths in life. She knew how tough the world could be and so she encouraged and helped her children as much as she was able. Through it all she struggled with the demon of depression that nearly brought her down and everyone else with her.

She did eventually reach a point where she could manage her depressive tendencies, but the stress on the family during her bad years was great. Depression truly makes victims of the whole family.

*M*argaret needed to work outside the home, not only for the money, but as a distraction from the troubles of everyday life. In time she was able to find another job, strangely enough, teaching once again in a one room school house. In September of 1974, she found a job teaching in a Hutterite colony near the town of Beiseker, just outside of Calgary. She was to teach grades one through eight.

She was again plunged headfirst into a culture completely different from her own. When she drove into the colony for the first time she saw long clapboard buildings all painted sky blue, fanned out on about an acre of colony land. No bushes, trees or flowers broke the monotony of grass, and paths led like rabbit runs to each house. A gravel road wound its way into the colony. She drove past signs reading "Eggs for Sale" and "Potatoes for Sale" and "Enter the colony at your own risk." In front of each house was a fenced lawn and to the side of each was an outhouse.

The church, which did double-duty as the schoolhouse, had windows all on one side. Each window had a blind, which was carefully pulled down on Sundays, and prayer time on weekdays, so that the people could keep their minds on hymns and prayers.

Margaret pulled into the colony and parked in front of the school and was met by a reception of four women clothed in dark long skirts, dark printed blouses and black jackets, with bonnets and shawls on their heads. Round, rosy faces beamed, plump arms extended with sleeves rolled to the elbows, they chorused "Welcome teacher! You are very welcome. Come in once. See the kids."

In a valley cut by the creek that winds through their land, the people lived communally in their little blue houses, surrounded by barns, which housed their animals. The rules that governed their way of life were strict and numerous. They were not allowed to smoke or watch television or listen to the radio. They were not allowed to play musical instruments. The singing of hymns was the only music allowed. They could not have their photographs taken or hang any sort of pictures on their walls. At the age of fifteen the children were compelled to quit school and start working as adults on the farm. At the age of eighteen they usually got married and at that time the men grew a beard, but no moustache. Margaret felt like she had stepped back in time. It was a world unto itself.

The leader of the colony was the preacher. He was authoritative and stern in his direction, and the people respected and obeyed him. He had the authority to punish any child on the colony and punishments were harsh, usually involving a leather strap on the hands or backside. The children endured without complaint.

The Hutterites made trips to Calgary from time to time to sell their eggs, potatoes and chickens, and the Shaws became regular customers. They knocked on the door once a month and Margaret bought huge bags of potatoes and other produce as well as tubs of freshly slaughtered chickens, semi-gutted, with heads and legs still attached, which she purchased for $2.00 per chicken.

The preacher would then sidle up to Margaret and quietly ask, "Mrs. Shaw, do you have a little bit of whiskey for me?" He would then settle into the sofa, glass in one hand, the other laying contentedly on his belly. His wife sat in a chair opposite him, and appeared quite uncomfortable in what must have been for her, a very strange environment. The preacher looked around the room and remarked to Margaret, "You have ten children. You are a good woman. My wife, she only has three children." He looked at his wife and sneered and she meekly lowered her eyes, and said nothing

In early January, 1975, deep snow blanketed the Hutterite colony. Margaret had been teaching at the colony for five months. While she directed the children in their lessons, Sammy, one of her former students, slogged through the snow outside, making his way to the cow barn. He stopped to watch the preacher repair a barbed wire fence with a pair of pliers.

Sammy was nearly fifteen and newly exempted from his school days. He was from that time on expected to take on adult responsibilities and work along side his parents. He was dressed in black tight pants, black jacket, black cowboy hat and a green plaid shirt as dictated by Hutterite tradition. His hands were blue from the cold and calloused but he didn't seem to mind. He kicked the snow with his black boots and looked up as a helicopter flew over the colony. "Do you think I'll ever ride in one of those?" He wiped his dripping nose with the back of his hand and waited for a reply.

The preacher took his time answering and regarded his cousin scornfully. Sammy was small for his age and not very bright. In his fifteen years he had absorbed many strappings from the preacher but Sammy forgave easily. "You'd better not ride no helicopter. Why do you talk such rubbish? Hutterites stay on the ground, not like Englishmen!"

The preacher could deny and hide most progress from his people, but he couldn't hide flying machines from their view. Even their loud nasal chanting at prayer time couldn't drown out loud jet liners and highway travel past their doors.

A highway divided their land and Sammy and others had to cross it to get to the cow barn. Sammy's mother and father were the Cow bosses. The business of the colony ran smoothly because everyone knew his job. There was a Field boss, Chicken boss, Garden boss and so on. Sammy's mother, Anne, directed the milking in the cow barn. Anne was dressed the same as all the other women in the colony. Her hair was tied in tight braids and then in a bun, and then neatly tucked under a kerchief. Her polka-dot dress was floor length and extremely modest. Like the men, she wore black shoes. She was not allowed to adorn her body with any sort of jewellery or makeup.

The cows waited patiently to be milked while a small puppy ran between their legs. Sammy gave a cow a shove and reached down to pick up the puppy.

"Sammy, Nipper, listen to me once! Mind! Be careful of that old cow. Don't pull her tail. You'll spill the milk, and put down that dog!" Sammy released the squirming dog and went to help his mother.

The steam rose from the flanks of the cows and the milk pails, as Sammy and his mother sent jets of the hot milk from the swollen udders of the cows. Anne's husky voice directed a stream of orders at her son in an odd German dialect, part English, and part German. "You are such a little Nipper, Sammy. I could just kiss you! But you are a bad boy sometimes...Where are you going now Sammy? Come back here! Get your work done!"

A noise had distracted Sammy. He always welcomed a distraction and he greeted the arrival of a flatbed truck with his usual enthusiasm. The puppy showed equal enthusiasm as it followed Sammy outside. The truck slowed down to cross the icy narrow bridge over the creek.

"Stay back you mutt, you'll get hurt," yelled Sammy.

"Come back Sammy," shouted Anne.

Sammy clambered aboard the slow moving flatbed pulled by the truck and sat on its edge. The truck had some trouble negotiating the bridge through the thick soft snow and it veered to the left and slid. The flatbed toppled off the bridge, and Sammy's slight body was thrown and landed on the frozen creek with a thump. He stood up, clutched his head with his hands and then pitched forward again into the snow.

"Sammy! Sammy!" yelled his mother, "What's the matter Nipper, are you hurt?"

Sammy didn't answer but his face was white and a trickle of blood ran from his mouth. His body was still and some Hutterite men, the truck driver and Anne knelt over him.

"Someone call an ambulance!" yelled the truck driver. Two black-clad men broke from the huddle over Sammy's body and made an ungainly, labouring dash through the deep snow for the preacher's house, which had one of two phones on the colony.

The highway roads were snow covered and driving them would be too slow and too dangerous. The quickest way to get Sammy to hospital in Calgary was by helicopter.

Anne cried and pleaded with those around her to save her son. Soon the whole colony was alerted and even the children from the school house and Margaret gathered around her and Sammy. The helicopter arrived and the inert form of a teenage boy was placed gently behind the pilot. Sammy's unconscious form was carried high in the darkening sky. Sadly, the trip was in vain. Sammy was dead on arrival at the hospital.

The next morning a black colony van was driven to Calgary to get Sammy's body from the hospital morgue. It was Hutterite tradition to wash and dress the bodies of their dead. This duty fell to the wife of the elder preacher, who combed his hair carefully and they laid him in the rough wooden coffin.

For three days they mourned him, and the children remarked that Sammy had a smile on his face but by the third day it was gone.

"He got his ride in a helicopter," one of the children told Margaret after the funeral.

Sammy's mother, tears streaming down her plump face remarked, "He was such a good boy. I'm so glad that he didn't have a radio in his pocket when he died."

Chapter Thirteen

Retirement

$\mathcal{M}$any people look forward to retirement. They imagine it to be a time of little responsibility. They think longingly of the time in which there will be no more worries about making a living. No more pulling that weary body out of bed at the sound of the alarm clock. The children have been launched into the world. Give up the big house and move to a condo. No more yard work, no more big house to clean. The only concerns would be where to travel to next and in what leisure activity to spend all that free time. Simply kick back and enjoy the fruits of your labours. This is a nice ideal but rarely is it a reality. The elderly are faced with increasing health problems, and grown children who land back on their parents' doorsteps because of their own financial burdens, or there are grandchildren who require babysitting. If one or more of the children is handicapped, the responsibility will never end.

Margaret was mostly free of the stresses of a big family, so her depressions lessened in intensity and frequency, making for a more relaxed retirement. The arrival of the grandchildren brought much contentment to Margaret and Albert and they were much relieved when none of the grandchildren showed signs of autism.

Albert looked forward to his retirement as a time to take university courses. He enjoyed studying Ancient Egypt and Mexico, and astronomy. He was also most interested in a course in buying and selling real estate. His dream was to sell the house and use the profits to buy or rent a small apartment, travel and study.

Margaret was less interested in selling the house. "Where would the children and grandchildren stay when they came to visit?"

Margaret was lying on the soft couch, hoping for some relief from her aching back when she felt a sudden urge to pee. She dared not wait too long to empty her bladder because she was becoming somewhat incontinent. Straining and wincing, she pulled herself up to a sitting position. Using the coffee table for support, she was able to stand. A sharp pain shot up her backbone as she straightened and she let out a small moan. Gritting her teeth, she hobbled to the bathroom. Stabbing pain gripped her spine with every step. In the bathroom she tightly held the handrails and slowly lowered herself on to the toilet. Afterwards, she made the same slow, painful journey back to the couch and prayed that the soothing effect of the painkillers would kick in soon. She lay down and breathed a sigh of relief. She closed her eyes and started to drift into peaceful slumber.

The doorbell rang. She grunted and heaved herself up again and tottered ungracefully to the stairway. Using the railing for support, she struggled down the steps to the front door. Thankfully, she didn't have to go down all twelve steps. The door opened and in popped her daughter Rita and three grandchildren.

"Hi Mom!" came the cheerful greeting.

"Hello dear, hi kids."

"Just a quick visit and I have to run. Would it be okay if the kids stayed here for an hour or two?"

"Of course they can."

"Grandma can we have ice-cream?"

"Yes, of course, help yourselves."

The children raced toward the deep-freezer which was always well stocked. They excitedly dug through the selection of frozen treats, each choose his favourite and tore off the paper wrapping, and carelessly dropped it to the floor. They licked their ice-cream contentedly while Margaret looked on. She watched her grandchildren devour rich, delicious chocolate ice-cream bars, vanilla drumsticks mixed with caramel and topped with nuts in a crunchy, sweet cone and bright orange flavoured cream sickles. She could resist no longer.

"How would one of you like to go and get your grandma an ice-cream?"

"Sure Grandma."

"How did the doctor's appointment go Mom? Did he have any suggestions as to why you're so tired all the time?"

She smacked her lips as the sweet, sumptuous ice-cream disappeared down her throat. "He says I have diabetes and he gave me a diet plan to follow. I also have to lose some weight. He also says I should try and get some exercise, but how can I do that if I can barely walk?"

"Oh, that's too bad. How about if I help you get started? I'll clear away everything in your cupboards that has a lot of sugar," Rita said as she walked towards the kitchen.

"No! No don't do that!" She thought quickly…"When people come to visit I want something nice to serve them."

And so Margaret continued with her sporadic diet, more or less following the rules set out by her doctor.

After years of having her hours filled with work or child care, she had a lot of difficulty finding a hobby. She tried her hand at needlepoint, sewing and knitting but did not pursue any of these hobbies to any great extent, then, she took some courses in Creative Writing and finally found an activity she really enjoyed. She began to write her memoirs.

*O*nce or twice a year, Albert and Margaret departed on a bus trip. They travelled across Canada, from the west coast to the east coast. They also travelled to many destinations in the United States and Mexico. It was an economical way to travel but not always relaxing.

They assembled in the entrance to a restaurant, some fast-food emporium in the city, to wait for the tour guide, or escorts as they were generally called. They were a group of fairly young to elderly people from farms, small towns and a few from the city, and all about to face the unknown. A few had travelled a fair bit, but most had not. Many hovered protectively over baggage and eyed each other with faint suspicion. The suspicion dissipated as the trip proceeded though.

The escort arrived wearing a bright red jacket with a badge and an officious expression on her face. She could have been anywhere from forty-five to sixty and she was not shy or about to take nonsense from anyone. Suddenly without individuality and much like young school children they looked to her for guidance and reassurance and seemed to need plenty of both.

"Have you got your luggage tagged? You were given tags from the tour company, remember? These must be in place now. One piece of luggage each and a carry-on bag for the bus. Now away we go!" Like an elementary school teacher she herded her charges onto the bus for an extended field trip.

She hurried them forward and everyone scrambled for the best seats. The polite or timid or slow travellers got the back seats and the last one on got the seat beside the toilet. It didn't matter that much, because they had three stops a day and had to move one seat forward or one seat back, depending on the side of the bus they were sitting on. Thus, each one had a chance to endure or enjoy as the case may be, for three hours at a time.

They were a regimented group. The tour company had to make a profit, and although they were good to the travellers, like a Victorian father was good to his children, their pleasure on the trip partly depended on their conduct. It also partly depended on their willingness to silently put up with a certain amount of inconvenience. With forty-four strangers living cheek to jowl in a thirty by five foot space for two or three weeks, it behoved them all to be patient. This tested the metal of their characters and before the trip was over there was a decided line drawn between the mature and the immature. All false fronts gave way to stark reality and real personalities emerged with all their human frailties.

They were introduced to the driver, who held their lives in his hands. They clapped loudly and the adventure began. They were asked to rise one by one, to introduce themselves. After a wobbly trip down the aisle, each took hold the microphone so everyone could hear. Then the beginnings of good fellowship took place. They were told to swap seats, one from each double seat with the one across the aisle to get to know each other. There seemed to be an urgency to break down reserve of one's fellow passenger by hook or by crook. For some reason, perhaps a case of nerves, this seemed to compel some folks to divulge particulars about themselves that they wouldn't tell a priest in a confessional. On the other hand, just get some old fellow who hadn't been off the farm in forty years and on his first trip and he'd probably reward your efforts with a blank stare and proceed with chewing his snuff. In due time, they were relieved of this agonizing duty to be fraternal, and returned to their seats hoping for a quick snooze or a look out the window.

This would never do, of course, and the escort reminded one and all that, "We are on a trip to enjoy ourselves. Let's tell some jokes or has anybody any good experiences to talk about?"

This was the moment all the closet comedians had been waiting for. Here was a captive audience for sure. No one could leave, except to go to the toilet and that only held one person at a time. There were some genuinely funny jokes, but most were not, but to be polite most people laughed anyway. Much guffawing went on and as the trip extended hour by hour the laughter increased until everything seemed funny. Either the passengers became more charitable to other's efforts, or a slight case of mass hysteria took place.

In numbed obedience, they filed on and off the bus, for coffee, lunch and bathroom breaks. They were told not to use the toilet on the bus too much. They stopped for observation of the scenery or points of interest and finally for bedtime. Motel accommodations were secured, and key in hand they paused, while the escort issued more orders concerning rules and punctuality for meals and at the bus in the morning. Visions of being left in some strange landscape caused them all to dread balky zippers in suitcases and clothes, and uncooperative bowels and bladders. The farmers were always the first on the bus in the morning due to habits of early rising. Everyone learned to rush and leave partly finished meals if they were unfortunate enough to be the last served. The last to arrive on the vehicle were clapped unmercifully by other self-righteous travellers, even though they were ten minutes earlier than the appointed time. It was a very hard world for the tardy on a bus trip.

Onward they went, pushing four or five hundred miles in a day, depending on the set destination. They had to arrive at the motel or dining room, at the minute expected or the conscientious bus driver and escort will be held accountable, and they, the travelling troupe, would pay the price. If they were naughty in not pushing their limbs ever faster, they deserved to be chastised. For those who were unlucky enough to get sick the price they paid was even higher. They were expected to push themselves as hard as anyone. A bus trip was no place for the weak.

There was always a comic or two on every trip who could cajole the escort into good humour on stressful occasions. The rest of the passengers warmed to him or her as a buffer between their temperamental keepers

Margaret and Albert on a bus trip.

and themselves. Escorts varied in lovability and the passengers did their best to endear themselves.

Sometimes little love affairs broke out among the younger people and provided amusing relief. Traffic between motel rooms was secretly observed and tittered about. Some folks took a trip to solve their marital problems and ended up appraising forty or so new souls of their unhappiness. Sometimes the bus passengers took sides, but why it mattered no one would ever know. In all likelihood they would never see each other again.

Sometimes, small things got Margaret and her fellow travellers down on those days of imposed intimacy with strangers. Strangers one day and confidante the next, they would to be annoyed that a nice man or lady hid for a time, some unredeemable character flaw or habit. Tolerance was as short lived as the time it took to get to know each other. They were outraged that their hopes and expectations were dashed. They formed small alliances with others and sneered quietly.

Farmers, who wore peaked hats night and day, were a huge annoyance to Margaret as their bits of grey hair escaped through the tiny air holes, or the high crown of the ill-fitting cap sat inches above a bald pate. Some older lady from a small town insisted on wearing a stiffly styled dark wig every day, and since there was never adequate time for preparing one's appearance, it was improperly fitted and revealed a shaved grey neck and heavy bangs at the front. Margaret's temptation to adjust it more attractively or simply snatch it off her head and throw it out the window became almost a compulsion. As time went on, the coughing, hoarse voices, forced laughter and trips to the toilet by the nicotine addicts who were not allowed to indulge their habit except in the bathroom, began to aggravate even the most insensitive. The excursions outside were more and more welcome.

There was much to see and learn on a trip as well as much to be endured. Some, such as Albert, pursued their growth in knowledge most arduously. They carried cameras and notebooks and fired endless questions at the tour guides. They spend their days climbing stairs to exhibits, walking with ankles swollen with oedema, and relentlessly pushed on the next new experience and sight. The optimistic stayed as optimistic as ever and the pessimistic remained as troublesome in their complaints as ever.

The trip came to an end and at the end was a party. They broke up in groups and put on skits. Surprising talent surfaced every time.

The bus trip was the poor man's answer to a thirst for seeing part of the world, those who are middle income poor, not poor enough to stay on the homestead all one's life, or rich enough to take charter flights to Europe or the Far East. There was no snob value in recounting a bus trip. It embraced its own type of pleasure.

*M*argaret and Albert could escape the stresses of life for a short time on their holidays, but they were compelled to face the same old difficulties on their return home. While Margaret and Albert's other children grew up, were educated, worked in their chosen fields, got married, and had children, Elizabeth and Christopher were the children who never grew up. They were and always will be dependent on their family and on society for their care. So Margaret and Albert, even in their advanced age, had to deal with issues involving those two handicapped people. Christopher was taken out of Michener Centre and was delivered into the hands of some people who wanted to operate a ranch and care for mentally handicapped men. However well intentioned they may have been, it was not a successful operation.

Christopher paced the yard aimlessly in front of the old house. He had just come from the barn and was agitated. He watched the other men who also wandered the yard in a similar fashion. One muttered to himself and the other mostly rocked from side to side, left foot, right foot, left foot...

Christopher was upset because of an incident that had just occurred.

"Come and milk the goat Christopher," the staff member had said to him.

"No," he answered blandly.

"Come on, don't be scared. Are you afraid?"

"No."

He was no longer afraid of the goats, but he didn't like their warm bodies, their strong smell and the feel of the udders in his hands. It was bad and he couldn't make them understand his feelings of revulsion. They pushed him to make him touch the goat and he had to bite his hands hard to make them stop. His hands were bleeding now and they hurt.

A car approached from down the road. He heard the crunching of the tires on the gravel road. He peeked through the bushes to see who it was. Mommy! Daddy! He smiled and ran to greet them but stopped short, about five feet away. That was close enough. If he got closer they would want to touch him and put their wet mouths on his face. He didn't like it when people touched him and invaded his space.

"How are you sweetheart?" said his mother.

"Fine," he answered softly, like a little boy. He loved his mom. She was always kind to him, and his daddy too. Daddy kept examining him. He peered at his eyes and at his hands.

"What happened to your hands Christopher?" Daddy asked.

Christopher didn't have the words to tell him what happened. His father's close inspection made him feel shy. He ran into the house, to his room, into his bed and under the covers. It was dark and quiet there. He had to wait for the apprehension to pass before he went outside again.

"Mr. and Mrs. Shaw are staying for lunch. Don't serve the leftover goat. Get out the beef, and find some fresh vegetables," he heard one staff member whisper to another.

Christopher was glad. He didn't like goat. It smelled funny.

His mom came into his room. "Come on Christopher, get up and visit with us," she said softly. "Why are you wearing those old jeans? Where are the new ones I bought you?" She searched his drawers and closet. "Albert, his new clothes are missing again. Someone is stealing his clothes."

Mom sounded mad. He didn't know how to answer her question. He looked down at his shirt and tried to avoid eye contact. There were so many pieces of lint. If he concentrated on the task of picking it off, he could take his mind off his mom's anger. He followed his mom out of the room and hid behind her. He didn't like one of the staff who was working today. He yelled a lot, and got in his face. One time he punched Christopher in the stomach and yesterday Christopher saw him burn someone with a cigarette.

"You look tired," Mom said to the man preparing the lunch. "Is your shift almost over?"

"Not for another eight hours. I'm working a twenty-four hour shift this weekend."

"Twenty-four hours! That's too much," Mom exclaimed.

Staff, clients and the visitors sat down to eat. No one had washed their hands.

Mom whispered to Dad when the staff momentarily left the room, "I'll be glad when we can find another place for Christopher to live. This house is dirty, and the meals are served at all hours. They don't seem to have any kind of schedule. What is happening to Christopher's clothes? I don't think this so-called ranch is a good placement for him."

"I would agree with you," said Dad.

"How is Christopher's sinus infection? Is he getting better?" Mom asked the staff when they returned.

"He's getting better," said the young man.

"I'm upset that it took so long for him to see a doctor. It wasn't until we threatened to pull him out of here that he got a doctor's appointment. Why is that?"

The man shrugged. "The boss said that they don't need to go to the doctor. They should just tough it out."

"That's awful. No one should have to tough it out," said Mom.

"I'm getting very tired of all the problems here. The funding is always in dispute. That is reason enough to find him another situation. He's been here eight years already. We'll find something closer to home, in Calgary," said Dad.

Christopher smiled. He could not follow all of the conversation but Dad said he would take him to Calgary. That made him happy. He liked Calgary.

$\mathcal{M}$argaret and Albert and other parents of handicapped people fought hard for their children to be taken out of the Red Deer institution and moved to group homes in their own communities. In 1984, Elizabeth was assessed for a group home in Calgary.

She was twenty-six years old and was home for the weekend. As part of her readjustment after twenty years in the mental institution, it was decided that she should spend more time with her parents. For people with autism though, change is always difficult and their reactions can be violent.

"Mommy! Take me back to Red Deer!" she shrieked, over and over.

She became more and more enraged. She bit her own arms and hands and slammed her head on the wall repeatedly. She tore at her clothing, shredding it with her bare hands. With her fingernails she scratched at her bare belly and chest, until it bled. She slapped and punched her own face. She then proceeded to punch, bite and scratch those around her. Three of Margaret's daughters and her husband struggled to control her. They held down her arms and legs as she raged on and on. This was one tantrum she could not be talked her out of. After thirty minutes the tantrum showed no signs of subsiding so Margaret phoned an ambulance.

Ten minutes later three men and a young woman charged up the stairs and into the living room.

"She's in the bedroom and she's pretty wild," Margaret ventured.

"What's the problem?" said one man.

"She's autistic."

No understanding greeted this remark.

Much screaming and cursing from Elizabeth elicited sympathetic sounds from the medics.

"Where does she live?" asked one man.

"Red Deer, up until recently, she's in a group home now in Calgary, for an assessment."

"Are you the surrogate mother, ma'am, the leader of this group home in Calgary?"

"No, I'm her natural mother and this is my home."

The young lady medic kneeled in front of Elizabeth and asked, "What do you want Elizabeth?"

"I want to go back to Red Deer you bitch, you bunch of bastards!" she roared.

Turning to Margaret the young woman asked, "Ma'am, has your daughter ever had a history of mental illness?"

Elizabeth and Christopher were eventually placed together in the care of an agency in a house in Calgary where they received twenty-four hour care. They became calmer and happier, and as a result, Margaret also became happier.

Margaret made a number of philosophical observations of life. In one observation she said, "I noticed that throughout a lifetime we go from innocence in extreme youth, to the adoption of a more sinful nature in our middle life, only to obtain innocence again in old age. The idea is not original of course, and not consistent in its manifestation. The appearance of innocence in old age could be caused by some degree of mental impairment in declining years. Declining, meaning that the number of years lived gets greater, while the number of years yet to live, gets smaller."

She came by the idea while observing groups of oldsters on bus trips. They enjoyed singsongs and corny jokes, or playing little games at birthday dinners. She commented, "Was this behaviour the onset of mild senility or simply the continuation of an innocent life, which was interrupted by the years where they had to be serious, and focused on jobs and child rearing?

I like to believe that we attain again our innocence so that we can descend gracefully and lightly to the end of life. I take solace in this light-hearted philosophy but I know for a fact that it is full of bunk."

When her hometown celebrated its hundredth birthday, Margaret went with her husband to the Munson homecoming. They stayed at the Rockhound Motel with Margaret's sister Bernie and her husband, her brothers George and Ed and their wives and her brother Bill. They had supper with 1200 people and got stuck in a traffic jam, in Munson!

As friends and enemies of fifty years ago converged at the reunion to reacquaint themselves, they resurfaced with basically the same faults and feelings. The same school girls who were catty and small-minded in their youth had not changed that much, Margaret discovered with some dismay.

"Did you notice that old lady Connor is the same old bitch, hasn't improved much with age, eh?"

"You're right, and did you see Patsy, that flirt, she stole everyone's boyfriend when we were young, and there she is, fluttering her eyelashes at that arthritic old codger."

"Did you notice how the Smith girls are still showing off with their clothes? Something new every few hours."

"When do old antagonisms die?" Margaret asked her sister.

Margaret took note of other's faults, but for the most part, kept her uncharitable thoughts to herself. She spied an old man across the room and thought, "Why don't you go comb your hair? It bothers me the way the long wisps, which you intended to comb over your baldhead are now hanging in mid air like a thin suspended waterfall. And you over there, your lips are all wet. Dry them with a Kleenex and don't let them hang slack. And you there, you long, thin, skeletal man, you have no muscles at all and you laugh too hard and send your body into such jerky spasms. Control yourself!"

Alas, the members of the human race, except for the truly innocent and pure at heart, struggle daily with their faults. We can only wish that we can endear ourselves to a few other people and hope that our Creator is forgiving.

On the first day of the reunion, a woman embraced Margaret and called her by name. The curtain of uncertainty parted. What a start it gave her! It was her old friend Mary. She used to think she was a ringer for Shirley Temple. She looked a little tired and sad now.

Another woman greeted her with, "Are you Margaret MacCallum's mother?"

"No, I am not my own mother," she thought, but she was struck by an odd thought. "Do we turn into replicas of our parents as we get older? Doesn't Gerry's son look just like his father did many years ago?"

Some of the girls who were flappers in the Roaring Twenties were there, looking a bit faded but lively still. She remembered going to concerts as a child and seeing them in shows.

The most popular girl in the town at that time was Grace. She was tall, skinny and outgoing. She and Margaret argued with each other over a dime when they were children. She was the envy of the quiet girls. She towered over Margaret but she was no longer skinny. Her bosom was huge like her mother's. She was a little worn looking with whiskers on her face, but she had a hearty laugh and presumably a happy life.

The wildest and most unrepentant girl in the town couldn't join them, as she was lying in a hospital bed, helpless after several crippling strokes. She was missed. She would have been a colourful addition to the greying throng if she had still been in good health.

The most arrogant girl-chaser had turned into a dapper little man with a white moustache. He kissed all the women that day, even Margaret, with whom he had never spoken a civil word in his life.

The least popular girl and the homeliest, as many uncharitably said, was having the best time of any of them. There she was, charging about like a ship in full sail, head erect, eyes ablaze with excitement, greeting all affectionately. She greeted everyone with hugs and kisses and with the stubby hair on her chin gave them all a gentle brush on the face. What a forgiving soul she was. She was an only child who married a local farmer, also an only child. When their parents died they inherited quite a fortune and retired to Victoria, B.C.

In Margaret's mind she saw the playground and the small village the way it was. She didn't need a photo album to remember their faces as children. There was Donny, who had so much trouble in school in every subject, now a school supervisor with a fat salary. She talked with poor Peggy who married a no-good bum. They had a large family and then he left her. She went on to live on welfare.

A girl named Nancy who married at eighteen to a boy she knew since she was fourteen came up to say hello. She was so stout and had so many huge warts on her face Margaret would never have known her for the round faced little girl of so many years ago.

Most of the people at the reunion had grown considerably wider and grey haired. Bernie's best friend Millie did not recognize her. Bernie and Margaret had both increased in girth considerably, considering they used to be built like reeds.

Millie squealed in disbelief when Margaret told her who she was looking at. "You're both so fat now!" she exclaimed with unsettling candour. She hadn't changed much, which was odd, Margaret thought, after so many years. Millie's mother had a habit of telling everyone that her family was of royal blood.

Anna was one of Margaret's best friends in her teenage years. She came to the town when she was seventeen after her father died on a farm east of out town. He suffered terribly from asthma and Anna had to learn how to administer the needles that would give him relief. Anna had one brother whom she loved but bullied a great deal. Their problems were so big in other ways that this facet of their relationship didn't matter much. She was one year older than Margaret. Anna's mother suffered from some serious mental disorder that made her simple minded. She walked sideways in a crab-like manner and was wrinkled and bewildered looking and even poorer than the proverbial church mouse.

Anna and Margaret managed some normal good times despite their limited circumstances. When the MacCallums finally got a radio in 1938 they spent evenings listening to Old Time Music, Fibber McGee and Molly, Big Sister and other rages of that day. Anna still lived there in that little town. She spent many years off and on in a mental institution where she was diagnosed as a paranoid schizophrenic. Before Margaret heard of such a condition she used to wonder why Anna was so hard to understand but this did not affect their affection for each other. She and her husband had two children who married and did quite well for themselves.

At mealtime, they stood while eating hotdogs and trying to balance a salad and coffee. Mustard leaked on Margaret's blouse, which she wiped ineffectually with a paper napkin. Oscar's son noticed her distress and hurried over with two chairs for her and Bernie. Margaret was surprised because he had always been so mean to them when they were kids.

"Do you know who we are?" Margaret asked.

"Of course I know who you are," he answered.

Across from Margaret was a man named Allen who welcomed her with such a big smile that his upper plate clattered down and out of his mouth. He caught it before it hit the ground. She felt embarrassed for him. He was such a nice man. He had never been known to do or say an unkind thing to anyone. One of Margaret's brothers had christened him "sweet pants" in an affectionate, teasing way.

The next afternoon there was a prayer service for members of all denominations, held in the schoolyard. They sat in two rows of benches in the sun.

Another man approached Margaret and asked her how she liked the service. She recognized him as Johnnie, who was such a bully when he was young. He had always viewed her Catholic faith with considerable disdain and used to hurl insults when he was a boy. Margaret once hurled a brick at him to stop an attack. She told him she thought the service was beautiful and it did seem to heal a few religious rifts. He beamed in appreciation and they shook hands in real friendship. Two years later the poor man died of cancer.

Also at the reunion was Martin, the one whose mother used to call him "Pet". He grew up to become quite the lady-killer. He was married five times and fathered several children. No woman, married or single was safe from him.

Murray, who became a farmer as soon as he finished high school, found a poor living on his inherited farm and turned instead to artwork, sculpting riders on horses and all kinds of cowboy art. He made a good living.

Nick the arm-pumper was there too, with his wife. He ran a successful car dealership in Calgary before he retired.

Another school mate of Margaret's was a big hulking girl named Mabel. She was not very popular with the boys and ended up marrying a man many years older than herself and he was a terrible boozer. She was strong and hefty and was able to heave him to bed when he came home drunk. He died some years ago. She had a couple of grown children.

The last day of the homecoming ended in an aerial display at the old baseball diamond. They watched the small plane climb to a speck in the sky and then it discharged four men in parachutes. The parachute display was meant to be dramatic and send everyone away in a blaze of glory, but Margaret found it a little disappointing.

Most of the people who lived in the town left after growing up. Some found love, success and wealth. Other's dreams and expectations were dashed. Time worked its havoc on all of them. Their hair was white, their faces fallen and their figures were gone. The memories remained though. Hometown reunions have their good points but they can be disillusioning too. The past was presented in front of them for re-examination. Margaret wondered if it was really worth the effort to dredge up those old memories and relive the pain. "Perhaps it's better to let the past and present blend and just go on breathing as long as we can."

She felt a little sad though about it all coming to an end when it was time to go home. As they walked to their cars, they passed a small fenced-off area, which once was a garden. A few sickly plants and shrubs struggled to survive in the heavy soil that was good for crops but not so good for flowers, especially when water was scarce. A broken sign leaned against the fence, "This garden is dedicated to the memory of Mr. and Mrs. P.J. Tarr". It was a tribute to the postmasters, who lived there long ago. There were not many reminders of the past there, just a few old buildings, the grain elevator and the little garden, and it wasn't long after the reunion that they too were knocked over and destroyed. Then what was left to cradle the past, except for the people's stories and memories?

Chapter Fifteen

Old Age

$\mathcal{M}$argaret stared into the bathroom mirror. She was sixty-four years old, and was dismayed by the image staring back at her. She wrote in her memoir, "What happened to my youth? It fled so suddenly from me. I can't believe that heavy woman in the mirror is really me. Someone played a joke on me, and puffed out my abdomen and took away my ability to read without my glasses. My skin, which was once silky smooth, is lined and pouched with fat. I used to have big blue eyes that brought me compliments galore! Now they're mostly hidden under folds of skin. My hair was dark and shiny, now it's dull and dry. Worst of all, my husband had the nerve to say I snore, but I refuse to believe it. The inside of me says I'm young, but the outside tells the tale. I must not deceive myself; it does no good. It's better to accept my plight. Surely these old hooded eyes hold some answers, a little wisdom, and maybe a little truth. There must be some advantages to old age. It will be nice to get half-price bus passes and tickets to shows. I can collect the old age pension too, in a few months, but it seems little compensation, for all my aches and pains."

Margaret walked outside to her front yard to watch some workmen throw pieces of a fallen tree into the back of a truck. She strolled down the street to mail a letter and kept glancing behind her to see who was following, but it was only the rustle of the dry autumn leaves beneath her feet, "crunch, crunch", like walking on cornflakes. She folded her light jacket across her chest. It was not quite cold out, just the absence of the summer-kind of heat. The trees were colourful, dressed in gold, red, and brown. It was a gentle reminder that winter was coming. She didn't mind winter anymore since she didn't have to go out anywhere, unless she wanted to.

On the way back from the mailbox she stopped to chat to her next-door neighbour, who held a copy of the "Calgary Sun" newspaper under her arm. They talked about the horrors of getting really old and sick and the lack of compassionate medical care in the age of advanced technology and computers. In some ways they were better off in 1984, in some ways worse than fifty years ago. This subject was just one of many that they ruminated about, never getting very far or finding solutions, except for the matter of the tree.

Margaret and Albert grew a tree. It stood between their property and their neighbour's. They gloried in its spreading branches and stately height until a harsh wind plucked it brutally out of the ground and leaned it to the east. They both grew up on the bald prairie, so to them, a tree was a most marvellous thing. They hated the thought of losing their beautiful tree. In an attempt to save its life, Albert made a valiant attempt to brace it, to coax it in an upright position once more. The neighbour watched Albert with dismay. She had grown up where trees were plentiful and she couldn't understand their grief. She offered many pointed suggestions that they cut it down.

A good neighbour relationship is more important than a tree they decided, so down it came. The neighbour brought Margaret a potted plant, a peace offering, though there was no quarrel. She wondered about another smaller tree in the yard. "Will it get big like the other one?"

Margaret smiled, "Who knows? Maybe I'll get another potted plant in a few years."

Margaret crunched the dry leaves underfoot again on her way back to her house. The wind picked up and more leaves fluttered to the ground. She felt sorry for the trees. They looked scared and vulnerable without their leaves.

"The trees in the fall are made bare by the blistering wind, like our souls will be stripped of cover and pretence on Judgement Day," she thought.

Sometimes I think we live too long, beyond good looks and form,
Life leaches all the good parts out, and leaves us wan and worn.
Our hair turns grey, then thins, our heads look large,
Our necks grow thick, muscles weaken and backbones curl.
Much comfort lags, when stomachs sag, and flesh drips from upper arms.
How queer the fold that starts to roll, from ear to chest.
Beneath our old relaxing form, our spirit struggles on.
Youth is captive in this mound, refusing to give ground,
to aged appearance.

$\mathcal{T}$here was a flurry of activity at the airport as crowds of people bustled back and forth on their way to catch this flight or that. Her carry-on bag seemed heavier than it should as they walked through the concourse and Margaret was forced to slow her pace, feeling weary and short of breath. She and her sister Bernie boarded the plane for the short flight from Calgary to Victoria, B.C., where she leaned back in her seat and closed her eyes. She was completely drained of energy by the time they arrived at the hotel room, so she went immediately to her bed and collapsed. They were there to attend the funeral of their Aunt Vera, the youngest sister of Daisy.

"Let's just order room service Bernie. So this is what it feels like to be old. I sure can't travel the way I used to, but it's be expected I suppose. I am seventy."

When she got up the next morning, she was unexpectedly struck with what felt like severe heartburn She pressed both hands to her chest. Her breath came in gasps and pants. "Bernie, do you have any antacids?"

Bernie looked intently at her sister and handed over the package of Tums. "Here you go. You look awful Margaret. Maybe you shouldn't go to the funeral. Just stay here and relax."

"Oh no, I'll go. What will the family think if I don't show up?" So with dogged determination she put her own discomfort aside, put on her dress and brushed her hair and went to the lobby for breakfast. She moved the bacon and eggs around on her plate with her fork, too nauseous to eat. Every so often she would press her fist to her chest and wince. "I have never had heartburn like this before. I wonder what's the matter with me."

The pain in her chest continued during the church service with a pressure that left her gasping for breath. She tightly grasped the back of the pew in front of her and leaned her head on her outstretched arms. Sweat beaded on her forehead and under her arms. The priest's voice droned on and on as Margaret's pain became more and more intense. "What could this be? Maybe I'm having a heart attack," she thought. "I'll offer up the pain for my Aunt Vera." Margaret bit her lower lip and endured. She refused to consider the idea of going to the hospital and soldiered on through the rest of the funeral and then joined the family at the gravesite. It was there that her distress was finally noticed by relatives and she was whisked to the hospital where it was discovered that she had indeed had a heart attack. That was not the end her life. It was only a warning of future troubles.

My Aunt Vera was Irish
Her face was filled with lines.
Her brogue was tinged with British
Where she visited at times.
She phoned me once a month to talk
Recalling all the past
Of all my mother's family
She was the very last.
Last week her mood was pensive
As she pondered all the years.
Her brothers and her sisters gone,
Her parents and her peers.
"If I could have a vision
before I die," she said,
"I'd wish that all my dear ones
would gather round my bed.
I'd hold my arms to hug them,
And beg them please to stay,
Until I'd rendered recompense
For times long gone away.
The times I failed to cherish them,
To love them as I should.
I'd pour such warmth and affection,
I'd do everything I could.
We talked about the brevity
Of life and all its trials,
That blinds us to the beauty
Of folks just here a while.

*T*wo years had passed since her Aunt Vera's funeral. In that short amount of time Margaret watched her husband change from a vibrant and energetic intellectual into a forgetful, bent old man. She saw him amble slowly to the kitchen. His back was hunched, causing his white shirt to hang unevenly on his thin frame. His pants were cinched with a belt, but drooped nevertheless on his hips. Even his glasses seemed too big for him now, hanging as they were on the end of his nose. He was seventy-three years old. His hair that had mostly stayed its natural brown color until into his seventies had turned completely white within two years.

"Stand up straight Albert. You're all hunched over."

He stood straight for a moment, and then relaxed again to a bent position. He wandered from room to room in a distracted way.

"What's wrong Albert? Are you looking for something?"

"I can't find my car keys. We need to get the shopping done."

"It's not like you to misplace things. Where did you have them last?"

He hit his fist on the table. "I don't know! I don't remember!" he barked.

Margaret was taken aback by this small outburst. "It's alright. I have a set of keys." She handed the keys to her husband and they climbed into the Volkswagen Jetta for a ride to the grocery store.

He plodded behind Margaret as she piled groceries into the cart, as he normally did. "Would you help me reach that box of cereal, Albert? ... Albert?" She looked left and right, but didn't see him. She looked up and down the aisles until she finally found him in the produce department, examining some apples. "Albert, you should have told me you were coming over here. I had the worst time finding you." He smiled but looked unconcerned. "Come on now we should go home," she said.

Albert and Margaret

The groceries were placed in the car and Albert proceeded to drive home. In a neighbourhood where he had lived for thirty years, Albert became lost and disoriented. He looked left and right. His eyes were full of confusion and alarm. "Where is our turn? I don't recognize anything! Margaret! Which way do we go?"

"Just pull over dear," she said as calmly and gently as she could. "Let me drive."

He pulled the car to the side of the road, laid his head on the steering wheel and wept brokenheartedly. "I don't know where I am. I can't find my way home."

Margaret cried also, seeing the distress on her husband's face. It was the last time he drove a car.

In the past, salespeople who called on the phone or at the door were given the bum's rush by Albert. They couldn't say two sentences before Albert would politely, but firmly, send them on their way. Then, for the first time, at the age of seventy-three, Albert invited them into his house. He listened to their pitches and bought their products. Every piece of junk mail that arrived at the house was answered with cheques or credit card number enclosed. Packages arrived regularly at the door containing books he would never read, CD's he would never listen to, junk jewellery and gizmos and gadgets galore. With increased frequency and intensity, advertisements for contests arrived in the mail. "Respond within 5 days for a chance to win $1,000,000!" He did respond. Foreign lotteries had his VISA number on file. The situation was out of control and he could not be reasoned with. He and Margaret were thousands of dollars in debt.

Much to his dismay, his children took away his charge cards and his chequebook. He hated their interference. "I'm only trying to pay my bills," he said. The distressed expression on his face seemed pitiful to his children.

Albert became more easily agitated. "There is something terribly wrong with me," he confessed to his wife. His frustration was obvious. He paced the floor and became moody. He kept the temperature in the house at 80 degrees Fahrenheit and became angry if anyone touched the thermometer. At times, his mind was clear, but those times were becoming less frequent. He would tell the same stories over and over or ask the same question repeatedly.

A visit to the doctor confirmed the family's suspicions. He had dementia. The man who had taken such pride in his ability to recall details and explain complex ideas, the man with almost encyclopaedic knowledge of mathematics, history and geography was slowly losing his memory.

One night Margaret awoke at 2:00 a.m. to find Albert was not in bed. She found him in the living room, sitting in a chair, dressed in his suit. "What are you doing Albert?" she asked.

"I'm getting ready for church," he said. It was a Wednesday. In the kitchen, Margaret found every burner on the stove set to maximum, their burners glowing red-hot in the dark room. Apparently, he had attempted to make breakfast, but gave up.

He went for walks and got lost. Kind neighbours, storekeepers, and the police brought him home. Margaret had memories of Elizabeth's early escapades.

She struggled for as long as she could but decided she could no longer care for him at home. He was put in the care of the staff at a local nursing home and Margaret sold the house and took an apartment in a senior's building. It was a huge shock and adjustment for them both

Margaret set off on her first holiday without her husband. It was a cruise to the Caribbean and South America. It was supposed to be a relaxing adventure in the company of her friends and she really wanted to get away from it all. Instead, she found the trip to be very trying and difficult, and most of all, she missed Albert. "I keep wishing my husband were here. There are so many things I want to tell him about, and so many people I would have liked to introduce him to, but he was too ill to join me on the trip. He was never the same after his second open heart surgery. The doctor told me he suffered a stroke during the surgery and nearly died. It seems as though a part of him did die."

> *Life passes on from earnest hope and wonder in our youth,*
> *To quiet acceptance of inevitable truth,*
> *That often what happens to us is not our option.*
> *We can colour the fabric a little on the way,*
> *But the final answer is not ours to say.*
> *Our children come to see us, a joy fulfilled.*
> *We hold them to our hearts, their souls self-willed.*
> *Men and women so designed,*
> *To keep us much perplexed and more inclined,*
> *To introspection in old age.*

Dear Lord. My load is heavy.
I'm old and tired. Do I lack faith?
I'm only human and my endurance has limits.
Are my prayers too shallow?
You know I don't want to wallow in self-pity
Please have mercy on me.
I need to feel your support and warmth.
I'm only flesh and blood and my spirit is hiding.
I have tried for many years, seventy plus three, to do your will.
I am discouraged.
Life's few delights and pleasures were soon buried by
pain and disappointment.
I feel so much self-doubt and self-loathing.
I failed many times to solve life's many complexities.
Do I feel my conscience stir?
I've spent a lifetime searching out the nature of my nature.
Self-absorbed I trod the maze of a life I never understood.
I try to look back with honesty, avoiding vanity and
smallness of mind.
What do you think of me God, of my inconsistencies and weaknesses?
No answers for my writhing mind, contorted with indecision.
When will I feel relief? When will I feel peace?
I call on you Lord, to be my support.

In the winter of 1996, after eight months in the nursing home, Alzheimer's disease had stolen not only Albert's memory but also his ability to speak and the ability to control his bladder and bowels. He could not feed, dress or bathe himself and even laboured to breathe.

They found him sitting silently in a chair in the hallway, staring straight ahead. He didn't greet or appear to recognize his wife and daughter, and showed no emotion when they sat with him at lunch time.

Madelaine spoon-fed him his meal. "Would you like some more, Dad?" He nodded in response. "More?" He nodded again. The blank expression on his face showed no enjoyment of the food or awareness of the people present and with every spoonful, Albert's mouth became more and more full. Apparently, he was chewing his food but forgetting to swallow, and consequently, began to cough and choke. He coughed up most of what he had been fed. Margaret stepped in with a napkin and tenderly wiped his face and clothing. Her mouth was sad but her eyes glistened with affection for him.

At last, when it was time to leave Margaret rose and put on her coat, then bent to kiss his cheek.

"Don't go," Albert said.

Margaret and Madelaine were astounded. These were the first words he had spoken in many days. Margaret sat back in the chair as if pulled down by a magnet. Despite her exhaustion, she took off her coat and held her husband's hand. Margaret stayed by her husband's side until late in the evening and in the morning she returned and stayed with him all day. By suppertime, exhaustion had overtaken them both so she kissed him goodbye and went home.

That night, she was awoken from her sleep by a phone call from the nursing home, "We're very sorry to tell you Mrs. Shaw, but your husband passed away about half an hour ago." She rose from her bed, her whole body shaking, reached for the phone again and called her brother George.

Trembling and teary eyed she entered his room at the nursing home. Albert stared with unseeing eyes at the ceiling and his mouth hung open. His chest no longer laboured for breath. Five hours after kissing her husband goodbye she was again by his side. She sat beside him on his bed and put her hand over his eyes to close them, then laid her head on his chest and cried. The memories of their forty-six years together came flooding back to her. She remembered the pains, sorrows and joys they shared and remembered their marriage as one of partnership and devotion.

*W*idowhood was difficult for Margaret, but over time she adjusted to life without Albert. Unfortunately, like many elderly people, she felt lost and without purpose. What bothered her most of all was the boredom. She stared, disinterested, at the television and wished she was healthy enough to go shopping. "I should give one of the girls a call and see if they'll take me out to get a few more blouses. Now that I finally have money to spend I can't get out to the stores much. How is an old lady like me supposed to spend her time? I wish that someone would come to visit. All I have for company is the television. I sure miss Albert."

Her strength and health were diminishing year by year. She had been in and out of the hospital many times, mostly due to heart problems.

She did her best to remain independent, and sometimes, when weather permitted, she went out with her walker and picked up the few groceries she needed. "I hate to bother you when I know you're so busy with your own families," she told her kids.

Year by year she became feebler, so she decided to move into a senior's lodge. It meant giving up more independence but she knew she had to be sensible. She was eighty-two years old and at a point where she needed more care. She looked around her small room. It was only big enough to hold her single bed, a soft rocking chair, a bookshelf, television and nightstand. She thought longingly about her house, and wished she was still living there.

She was frustrated with all her health problems. Her walking was unsteady and she had trouble negotiating the hallways of the lodge to go for meals. Her feet were so swollen that some days she could hardly walk at all. She could only take a shower with assistance and was, "...so bloody tired all the time. My back still gives me a lot of grief and I'm still pretty weak from my heart attacks and angioplasty operations. I'm also suffering from angina now and then, and take medication for that, not to mention medicine for my back pain and blood pressure, pills to reduce cholesterol, and throat medication and medicine for my stomach and bowels, as well as pills to help me sleep. In all, it's thirty or so pills a day. It's a terrible amount of pills. Sometimes I wonder if the medicine is doing me more harm than good."

She sat back in her rocking chair and sipped her water. She was always thirsty these days, probably a side effect of some medicine or another. She wondered idly to herself, "Let me think now, how long have I been living here? Must be a year already, if I'm not mistaken. Anyway, I'd better get up to the bathroom." She pulled herself up and took hold of her walker. She looked down at her ankles which were horribly swollen and puffy, and that made it pretty hard to walk. "I wonder if I'll be able to get my shoes on my feet to get down to supper tonight." She hobbled to the washroom and looked in the bathroom mirror. "Look at the way my flesh drips off my bones," she said to herself. She lifted her hands to her cheeks and pulled back the skin, hoping to grasp an image of her former self. "Oh, what's the use? I'm old and that's all there is to it." She did her business on the pot and got up, too quickly, and before she could stop herself she fell facedown on the hard bathroom floor. Her head throbbed with pain and blood gushed from the open wound. She struggled to get to her feet but it was impossible.

"Help!" she called as loudly as she could. No one could hear her. Slowly and agonizingly she crawled towards the alarm button. Her eyes rolled back in her head and she nearly lost consciousness. "Stay alert," she willed herself. "Keep going." Inch by inch she made her way across the floor, leaving a trail of blood from the terrible gash on her head. Finally, the alarm was within arm's length. She reached up and pulled the cord.

She was taken to hospital and what followed would prove to be yet another distressful time in her life. The head wound was easily treated but her doctor recognized Margaret was taking an excessive amount of pain killing medication, such as morphine and oxycodone, so much in fact, that it had become an addiction.

When Madelaine arrived at the hospital she was shocked to see her mother restrained in a high-backed chair with a tray attached. Margaret was unable to get up because the screws for removing the tray were too far for her arms to reach. She rolled her head from side to side as she pushed hopelessly against the tray. Her eyes were wide with misery and fear. Madelaine wondered at the cruelty of the heartless nurses. "Why wasn't she in her bed?"

A nurse explained that Margaret was apt to fall and hurt herself, so for her own safety they had to restrain her. Margaret later described it as "a cruel medieval torture device." The chair felt tortuous because her drug withdrawal filled her with a panicky sensation, an uncontrollable urge to move, and the chair prevented movement.

"Oh Madelaine," she moaned upon seeing her daughter. "Please get me out of this thing." Madelaine walked with her mother back to her room and eased her into her bed.

"Oh my God, oh..." Margaret moaned as her arms and legs trembled. She writhed in her bed and arched her back. "God help me. I need to get up. Help me get up."

"Okay mom, take my arm." She helped her mother to her feet.

"I need to walk. It's like snakes crawling under my skin. I'm alive with nerves. Oh, what shall I do? Tell them I need some medicine. I can't stand it."

Madelaine walked her mother around the room. "Ok mom. I'll go talk to them."

"I need to lie down now. I'm so tired." Madelaine helped her aged mother back to her bed. Margaret rolled from side to side. Her arms and legs trembled. Tears streamed from her eyes. "Help me, I need to get up," she said again. "Oh dear God, I can't stand it." She was crazy with nerves in coming down from the drugs and was out of control with an insane desire to keep moving. She wanted to jump and run, stretch, and scream and shout, a reaction of a body that was crying for more of the drugs. Her need for the painkillers was becoming more and more urgent and that need was denied. The effect on the body was an ache worse than hunger, worse than thirst. The mind could not will the body to relax. Her heart raced and she perspired excessively. A nurse eventually administered a small intravenous dose of morphine to Margaret. When the drug entered Margaret's blood stream, her eyes rolled back in her head and her body immediately relaxed. She experienced a bit of calm between her bouts of misery, and at least for a time she could get some sleep. In the days that followed she would feel little peace. She suffered severe pain in her back and legs, muscle cramps and spasms, hot and cold flashes and insomnia.

"It was worse than giving birth to a baby," she later explained. "I would rather have had physical pain. At least that is something I can understand."

Margaret spent a month in hospital recovering from the injury to her head and the injury done to her mind and body from years of drug misuse. She said angrily, "Why hadn't my doctor realized sooner that the amount of drugs prescribed were excessive?" The fall was in a way a blessing in that her most grievous medical condition, an addiction to pain-killers, was brought to the attention of someone who could help her.

She moved from the senior's lodge to Father Lacombe Care Center. Madelaine entered the Nursing home followed closely behind by her children. She did not see that a lot had changed in the twenty-five years since she'd been there to visit her grandmother, Daisy. Today she was going to visit her own mother.

Here and there were elderly men and women slumped on couches or wheelchairs, some asleep, and some oblivious to their surroundings. A few waved to the newcomers, excited to see children.

"Yuk, this place smells funny," said the youngest child, holding his nose.

Margaret became physically more impaired as time went on and required increasing amounts of care. Her back stiffened up which relieved her of pain but made her very inflexible. As a result she lost her ability to walk unassisted. The lack of exercise compounded her disability. She even had to be helped on and off the toilet, which she felt was most undignified, since she always valued her independence.

Margaret had always been susceptible to bouts of uncontrolled giggling. It had been embarrassing in the past, but never before had it proved to be nearly fatal. Madelaine and Bernadette agreed to take her out for a day of shopping in her advanced years. The problem is that she was so feeble that she needed help with virtually every aspect of her life. She couldn't walk without assistance, nor could she wash or dress herself and she certainly couldn't step up into a minivan.

They pushed her in her wheelchair to the door of her daughter's van and then helped her to her feet. "Put your left leg up into the van," Madelaine said. She may as well have been asking her to do a back flip. She could not do it. Bernadette lifted her mother's leg and plunked it into the van.

"Now, hang onto this handle and pull yourself up," Bernadette said.

So while Margaret hung onto the handle of the car for dear life, her two daughters strained to heave her weight onto the seat. The three of them grunted, pulled and pushed, when suddenly Margaret was struck with the thought of how ridiculous they looked and started to laugh. Her whole body collapsed into a fit of giggles which left her weaker than she already was, and her whole weight fell into the arms of her daughter Madelaine, who held on with all her might, her arms clenched around her mother's chest.

"Get her out of the car. Get the wheelchair!"

"I can't. Her foot is stuck," said Bernadette.

"Stop laughing mom or I am going to drop you!"

Margaret pictured the three of them in a pile in the slushy snow, with one crushed daughter beneath her, and her other daughter on top to form the top layer of the sandwich, and she started laughing all the harder. Somehow they were able to push the wheelchair under her buttocks and she flopped into her chair. She glanced up at their faces, red from exertion, and continued to laugh uncontrollably.

> *A giggle is a laugh gone wrong, a slightly errant son,*
> *Of humour, who would love such a one?*
> *It bubbles, bursts and rumbles low. It dips and sways and curls.*
> *It fills the air with music, as its resonance unfurls.*
> *It catches fancies in its wake, and communicates its mirth.*
> *Grabs everyone infectiously, gives laughter all its worth.*
> *It captivates and fascinates, and gives in merriment.*
> *And to the sternest personality, some measure of content.*

*C*ataracts blurred Margaret's eyesight, despite two operations to remove them. It made it almost impossible to partake in her favourite pastime, which was reading. She was left alone for many hours or days at a time, unable to fill the remaining days of her life with meaningful activity. The television no longer interested her. She couldn't follow the programs. Eventually she forgot how to operate the remote control, so it didn't matter much anyway.

Old age is like a cruel tyrant who makes victims of all who dare to approach him. It takes away beauty, physical well being, and memories. Margaret remained alert and clear in her thinking until the latter part of 2006, and then confusion set in along with memory loss.

She picked up the telephone receiver and stared at the numbers, trying to recall her children's phone numbers. She used to have them all memorized, but not anymore. She couldn't control the shaking in her hands, a fairly recent addition to the list of troubles that affected her now that she was elderly. She repeatedly pressed series of numbers but was frustrated again and again by wrong numbers, out of service numbers or phones that just rang and rang. Tears welled in her eyes as she lay in her bed. She so badly needed to talk to one of her children. In desperation she tried again.

"Hello? Madelaine? Oh thank God I got a hold of you! I can't get my phone to work. I need you to phone somebody."

"Who?"

"Oh, just a minute now. I don't remember. Oh dear God, what is the matter with me? I knew a few minutes ago."

"Don't worry mom. It doesn't matter. You can just talk to me."

"I'm concerned about the boys. What will become of them?"

"They're grown men now mom. All of them are in their forties or fifties. They're in charge of their own lives."

"No, they couldn't be. My kids aren't that old."

"We are mom. We're all middle aged now."

"I can't believe it."

Margaret was long past her child rearing days, but this did not stop her from worrying about her children. She began to have more and more difficulty separating past from present and things that concerned, upset or frightened her many years ago came back to haunt her in her later years.

"Hi mom, how are you?"

"I'm not feeling well."

"That's too bad mom."

"I don't think I will ever teach again. I don't think I have the strength. How am I going to pay the bills?"

"You're retired now mom. You don't have to teach any more."

"Oh, that's right. I guess they wouldn't hire a woman my age would they?"

Margaret began to suffer again from depression, and would often call her children on the phone, despairing over her situation.

She sobbed into the phone, "Madelaine, you have to come and get me from this place."

"Why? What happened?"

"The kids are at home by themselves. I have to get home and look after them."

"What kids?"

"My kids of course. Who is going to make them their supper?"

"Your kids are all grown mom. We all have homes of our own now. We can look after ourselves."

"How can that be? I don't understand. I'm so worried about Elizabeth and Christopher. I want to get them out of Red Deer."

"They are out of Red Deer mom. They live in a house in Calgary now, remember?"

"They are? Are they okay?"

"Yes, they're doing well. They're happy now."

"That's good. Thank God. I sure miss your dad."

"I know mom. I miss him too."

"I haven't talked to him in such a long time. Why did he leave me without saying goodbye?"

"He would have if he could have. He had Alzheimer's, remember? He became very forgetful, and he wasn't able to talk towards the end of his life."

"Is your dad dead?"

"Well, yes mom. He died about ten years ago."

"He did? Oh. I forgot. I would like to go back to my house. I'm tired of this place. It's an institution. It's not my home."

"You sold your house mom. Somebody else lives there now."

"Really? I sold it? Do you mean the house with two colours?"

"Yes."

"Who lives there now?"

"I don't know."

"Well, I will have to move in with one of you kids. I don't like this place. Will you let me live with you? I can help you with the cooking and the cleaning."

"I don't think so mom. You need nursing care. You can't bathe yourself or even go to the washroom by yourself. I wouldn't be able to take care of you."

"I could sleep on your couch. I wouldn't get in your way."

"I couldn't take care of you mom."

"I can pay you, whatever it costs."

"I'm sorry mom."

My mother suffered terribly in her extraordinary life, and she did crack under the strain from time to time, but she was not defeated. She picked herself up, again and again, and simply carried on. In this way she taught me to be strong in the face of adversity. She also taught me to love with all my heart, to be independent, to have pride in my accomplishments, and to have faith in God above.

We are mostly unprepared for the hurt that awaits us in this life, much like the woman who faces the inescapable and inexplicable pain of childbirth. She has no choice but to push on and bear the pain for a greater good. We also continue nevertheless on our paths in life, plodding onwards to new and sometimes painful experiences. We can only pray that God will give us the strength to endure.

When the end of our lives draws near we may look back and wonder what it all meant. If we are one of those who are blessed with a long life we might recall our many achievements, failings, joys and sorrows, but most often we are startled to discover that our lives went by too fast.

What do we value the most in our lives, our outward appearances, our money and possessions, our bodies, or our intellects? All of these are meaningless in the end. At our deaths we are again pushed like newborn babies into a new existence. The struggle is over and our responsibility ends. Our bodies become like burnt wood, used up, and turned to ash. What is not meaningless is the legacy we leave behind.

Madelaine, Margaret and Daisy.

Bibliography

Alberta Teachers Association. A Brief History of Public Education in Alberta.
http://www.teachers.ab.ca/Albertas+Education+System/History+of+Public+Education/
A+Brief+History+of+Public+Education+in+Alberta/The+Great+Depression.htm

A Little History
http://www.alittlehistory.com/ViH-bgin.htm

Calgary Bridgeland-Riverside Community History
http://www.calgaryarea.com/ne/bridgelandriverside/communitynews/history.htm

Government of Alberta. About Alberta; History.
http://www.gov.ab.ca/home

Government of Canada. Library and Archives Canada; Second World War
http://collections.ic.gc.ca/courage/canadasroleinwwii.html

Heritage Community Foundation Presents, Alberta Online Encyclopaedia.
Albertans: Who do They Think They Are?
http://www.abheritage.ca/albertans

Our Roots; Canada's Local Histories Online
http://www.ourroots.ca

Palmer, Howard and Palmer, Tamara Jeppson.
Peoples of Alberta: Portraits of Cultural Diversity.
Douglas & McIntyre Ltd. November 1985.

Potter Creek Secondary School. The Funkalicious Canadian History Page.
http://www.yesnet.yk.ca/schools/projects/canadianhistory/depression/depression.html

Slang terms of the Seventies.
http://www.inthe70s.com/generated/terms.shtml

University of Calgary. The Applied History Research Group. Multimedia History Tutorials
http://www.ucalgary.ca/applied_history/tutor/calgary/FRAME1895.html